How to Prepare for SAT II:

Physics

Sixth Edition

HERMAN GEWIRTZ
Bronx High School of Science, Bronx, NY
(Retired)

and

DAVID S. MARTIN
Jericho High School, Jericho, NY

BARRON'S

All inquiries should be addressed to:
Barron's Educational Series, Inc.
250 Wireless Boulevard
Hauppauge, New York 11788

Achievement test questions selected from *The
College Board Achievement Tests in Science,*
College Entrance Examinations Board (1983).
Reprinted by permission of Educational Testing
Service, the copyright owner of the test questions.

Permission to reprint the above material does
not constitute review or endorsement by
Educational Testing Service or the College
Board of this publication as a whole or of any
other testing information it may contain.

Achievement Test questions pages 3–5, #1–7

Library of Congress Catalog Card No. 93-33563

International Standard Book No. 0-8120-1705-6

Library of Congress Cataloging-in-Publication Data

Gewirtz, Herman.
    How to prepare for SAT II: physics / Herman Gewirtz, David S.
Martin. —6th ed.
        p.   cm.
    Rev. ed. of: CBAT physics, 5th ed. ©1989.
    Includes index.
    ISBN 0-8120-1705-6 : $11.95
    1. Physics—Examinations, questions, etc. 2. Universities and
colleges—United States—Entrance requirements. 3. Universities and
colleges—United States—Examinations. I. Martin, David S., 1941– .
II. Barron's Educational Series, inc. III. Gewirtz, Herman.
CBAT physics, 5th ed. IV. Title.
QC32.G45   1994
530'.076—dc20   93-33563
                                                              CIP

PRINTED IN THE UNITED STATES OF AMERICA
4567   100   98765432

Contents

Introduction

Although the chief purpose of this book is to help you prepare for SAT II: Subject Test in Physics, it should be very useful also in preparing for any examination in physics.

PRELIMINARY

Before we discuss examinations, you should make sure that you have a copy of each of the College Board pamphlets *Taking The SAT II: Subject Tests* and the *Admissions Testing Program*. If you don't have them, you should be able to obtain them from your high school advisor or the guidance office. If not, write to

> College Board SAT Program
> P.O. Box 6200
> Princeton, N.J. 08541-6200

In the first pamphlet start reading the material at the beginning, such as Planning to Take the Tests, How to Register, How to Prepare for the Tests, and The Day Before the Tests.

Then turn to the section on the Physics Achievement Test, which describes the test and includes sample questions and answers. Because the instructions for the test may have changed, be sure to read them carefully. This will save you time on the actual test.

HOW THIS BOOK IS ORGANIZED

This Introduction gives you an overview of the subject matter and structure of the examination, of the type of questions used, and of the best way to prepare for the examination, as well as instructions on how to take the tests in the back of the book as preparation for the actual SAT II.

The Introduction also includes, with permission from the Educational Testing Service, seven questions that illustrate the different types of questions you will encounter and that have actually been used on examinations. The answers and explanations are also given so that you can get an idea of how well you are prepared.

The various chapters that follow the Introduction provide a brief review of subject matter that may be useful to you. Each chapter ends with relevant multiple-choice questions and answers with explanations. The last chapter includes four practice tests for diagnosing your problems and evaluating your progress, a table of Values of Trigonometric Functions, and a Summary of Formulas. Appendix I contains Physics Reference Tables; Appendix II lists Densities of Some Substances, and gives International Atomic Masses. The Index will help you locate specific topics in the book.

THE EXAMINATION CONTENTS

The College Board does not publish copies of former examinations each year and the scope of the examinations is not restricted by any given syllabus. The examinations are made up each year by a group of experts who are guided by a knowledge of what is commonly taught throughout the country. You will, therefore, be well prepared for the test if you know and understand what is taught in a good secondary school course in physics and if you get a little practice in the types of questions used. It is the aim of this book to help you in both areas.

The questions on the examination are based on the large subject matter areas of mechanics; optics and waves; electricity and magnetism; heat, kinetic theory, and thermodynamics; and modern physics. Some of the questions ask for mere recall of knowledge. Other questions are designed to see if you really understand concepts and principles, if you can reason quantitatively, and if you can apply scientific concepts and principles to familiar and unfamiliar situations. Some questions use more than one physical relationship. There are two basic types of questions; all questions are in the multiple-choice format, requiring you to choose the best answer from among the five choices given. The examinations at the end of this book reflect the subject-matter content and the question types you will encounter on the actual test.

HOW TO PREPARE FOR THE EXAMINATION

The best preparation results from regular study, reading, and review spread over a long period of time. This is done in connection with work in school and at home, assigned work, and voluntary study. This prolonged effort not only helps you remember the facts but also helps you get a better understanding of the concepts and principles. Study this book along with any other your teacher may want you to use for regular classwork and try to answer the questions at the end of each chapter before looking at the printed answers.

As mentioned above, the Examination is not restricted to any specific syllabus. However, an article published several years ago pointed out that the major programs have many topics in common. A good physics student from any course should be able to do well on the examination. Therefore, in order to be helpful to students with different course backgrounds, there is some material in this book which probably has not been covered in your course, and, possibly, will be of little importance on the examination you will take. This may be true of much of the information in Chapter 13 and of some of the discussion of Simple Machines in Chapter 3. For example, if you prepared for the New York State Regents Examination in Physics, you had nothing on the efficiency of simple machines. Don't spend time on this topic now. Your first objective in reviewing should be to know well what you were expected to know for your course, and then see how well you can answer questions related to that subject matter.

When you do well on one of the practice tests, try to learn some unfamiliar subject matter. Review all of this material, and then try another of the examinations at the end of this book. Review further any weak subject areas thus discovered and try additional examinations.

To aid in the final review, some items are italicized or printed in bold type. This should help locate some of the more important facts, formulas, and definitions. In memorizing such items, it is most helpful to study them and then try to write them down from memory. For example, after you have studied the Numerical Relationships on page 7, you should cover the page and write down the ten facts that are listed. Next, compare your version with the book. Repeat, if necessary, until you know all the facts correctly and completely.

HOW TO TAKE THE TESTS

The examinations at the end of this book are not copies of former tests, but practice with them should be valuable to you. However, be sure to read the instructions given with your test. Note the amount of time allotted and recognize that you may not be able to answer all questions in the available time.

The questions are not of equal difficulty, but each question usually gets the same credit. Do not waste time on questions that seem difficult or time consuming. Go back to them at the end of the test, if you have time. (As was pointed out above, some of the questions may be intended primarily for a different type of course.) Time can often be saved in numerical examples by making approximate calculations. Don't worry if you can't answer all the questions. Probably no one taking the test can and this is not needed for a perfect score. Should you guess? If you know anything about the subject matter of the question and can eliminate some of the choices, it is advisable to guess. A completely random guess, however, may cause you to lose a fraction of a point for an incorrect answer.

Pay attention to units. By doing so, you can catch many mistakes. Most problems in this book are in (metric) SI units, which are explained more fully in Chapter 1. The SAT II physics test is phasing in the SI units. Questions in other unit systems are still asked, however, particularly in questions dealing with common dimensions.

When taking the practice tests in this book, do not stop at the end of 1 hour. Follow the above advice and eventually try to answer all the questions. Practice keeping track of time without wasting it.

Each of the practice tests includes 75 questions. Some of the questions were deliberately made rather difficult to challenge you. On the actual examinations the questions are carefully evaluated, and individual performance is compared with group performance before a score is given.

Also *note* whether the **directions** on your test are the same as those used on the practice tests in this book. *When you take the test, be sure to read the instructions given with your test.*

SAMPLE QUESTIONS

These questions are reprinted with permission of the Educational Testing Service, which prepares the SAT II Subject Tests. You should try each question to familiarize yourself with the question format. Answers and Explanations follow.

Here is some helpful information:
1. All questions provide five choices, designated as (A)–(E). Many questions come in sets and are based on the same information.
2. Some questions call for interpretation of graphs.
3. Sometimes there are several questions on the same topic.
4. In some questions four choices are correct, and you are asked to select the exception. These questions will contain a word in capital letters (NOT, EXCEPT).
5. Sometimes the answer choices are given first; then the questions follow.
6. In some questions with more than one correct answer, you are asked to select a combination of statements that provide the best answer. On the actual test the individual statements will probably be designated by Roman numerals I, II, III.
7. It is advisable to consider all the lettered choices before you select your answer.

Part A

Directions: Each set of lettered choices below refers to the numbered questions immediately following it. Select the one lettered choice that best answers each question. A choice may be used once, more than once, or not at all in each set.

Questions 1–2 relate to a flat object lying on a frictionless table. Two forces, 1 and 2, are separately applied to the object as shown below. The line of action of each force is shown by a dashed line.

Top View

(A) 1 only
(B) 2 only
(C) Neither
(D) Both, but 1 will be greater than 2
(E) Both, but 2 will be greater than 1

1. If the object is free to rotate about a fixed axis through point *A*, which force will produce a rotation?
2. If the object is not fixed and point *A* is the object's center, which force will produce purely translational motion?

Part B

Directions: Each of the questions or incomplete statements below is followed by five suggested answers or completions. Select the one that is best in each case.

3. Two metal spheres of equal radius are each charged and mounted on insulated stands. Sphere 1 has a charge of +20 nanocoulombs; sphere 2 has a charge of –4 nanocoulomb. The two spheres are touched together and then separated. The charge on sphere 2 will now be
   (A)   0
   (B) +4 nC
   (C) +8 nC
   (D) +16 nC
   (E) +20 nC

4. An object of mass 5 kilograms has a momentum of 20 kilogram•meters per second. Its speed is most nearly
   (A)   0.25 m/s
   (B)   0.4 m/s
   (C)   4   m/s
   (D)   10   m/s
   (E) 100   m/s

5. As a child wearing wool pants slides down a plastic slide, gravitational potential energy may be converted to which of the following?
   I.   Thermal energy
   II. Kinetic energy
   III. Electrostatic energy
   (A) I only
   (B) II only
   (C) I and III only
   (D) II and III only
   (E) I, II and III

Question 6 relates to the figure below that represents a photograph of a wave propagating along a string.

If the frequency of the wave is 80 hertz, the speed of the wave is
   (A) 640 cm/s
   (B) 320 cm/s
   (C) 20 cm/s
   (D) 10 cm/s
   (E)   0.1 cm/s

7. A curved wave front could result from all of the following EXCEPT
   (A) a disturbance emanating from a point source
   (B) the passage of a plane wave through a very small opening
   (C) the reflection of a plane wave from a concave surface
   (D) the reflection of a plane wave from a convex surface
   (E) the reflection from a parabolic surface of the circular wave originating at the focus of the parabola

ANSWERS AND EXPLANATIONS

1. **(A)** Recall a lever balanced on a fulcrum. To rotate the lever clockwise or countercounterclockwise, a force (a hanging weight) is applied at some distance from the fulcrum. Here the line of action of force 2 goes through *A,* the fulcrum. Therefore it does not produce rotation. The line of action of force 1 does not go through the fulcrum, and therefore it will produce rotation, clockwise as viewed from above.

2. **(B)** Since *A* is the center of mass, and the object is free to move, force 2 will now produce translation; but, for the reason given in question 1, no rotation. Force 1 will now produce both rotation and translation.

3. **(C)** Since the two spheres are of equal size, they should end up with equal charges after they touch. The total charge is +20 nC – 4 nC = +16 nC. Since the spheres share the charge equally, each gets +8 nC.

4. **(C)** The momentum of an object is equal to the product of its mass and its velocity:
$$p = mv$$
$$20 \text{ kg} \cdot \text{m/s} = (5 \text{ kg})(v)$$
$$v = 4 \text{ m/s}$$

5. **(E)** At the top of the slide the child has stored some gravitational potential energy. As she moves down the slide some of the potential energy is converted to kinetic energy. The motion will also be against the friction between the pants and the slide and will produce heat or thermal energy at the expense of the kinetic energy. The rubbing between the two materials will also produce a transfer of electric charge from one to the other and thus produce electrostatic energy.

6. **(A)** The speed of a wave is equal to the product of its frequency and its wavelength. The wavelength is the distance between successive positive peaks: 8 cm.
$$v = f\lambda$$
$$= (80 \text{ Hz})(8 \text{ cm})$$
$$\lambda = 640 \text{ cm/s}$$

7. **(E)** You should recall that a point source produces circular wave fronts. Choice (B) should recall the diagram for diffraction by a small hole; a circular wave front is produced. Choices (C) and (D) should recall the diagrams for producing the location of the principal focus for the reflection from a concave and convex mirror; the parallel rays from the object represent the plane wave fronts from the object (see diagrams on p. 76). After reflection the rays converge or diverge, representing the spherical surfaces of the wave fronts. This leaves choice (E), which is correct. The reflection from a parabolic (or paraboloidal) surface of the circular (or spherical) wave originating at the focus of the parabola (or paraboloid) is straight—a plane in the case of the paraboloid.

If you had no difficulty in answering any of the seven questions correctly, you might try Practice Test 1 in the back of the book to identify any weakness before you review other subject matter.

GOOD LUCK!

1

Measurement and Forces

Do you know what is meant by significant figures? Can you combine and resolve forces? Do you understand what is meant by the moment of a force? Test your understanding by trying the following example:

A bar is pivoted at P and forces are applied as shown. Which force produces the greatest torque?

In this chapter we shall keep these and other questions in mind as we review forces, vectors, and basic ideas of measurement.

In physics, as in other sciences, a theory must agree with observation. In addition, a theory must lead to predictions which can be verified by experiment. Experimentation in physics usually involves careful measurement.

UNITS AND SYSTEMS OF MEASUREMENT

Powers of 10

$$10^0 = 1$$

$10^1 = 10$	$10^{-1} = 0.1$
$10^2 = 100$	$10^{-2} = 0.01$
$10^3 = 1000$	$10^{-3} = 0.001$
$10^6 = 1,000,000$	$10^{-6} = 0.000001$
$3 \times 10^4 = 30,000$	$3 \times 10^{-4} = 0.0003$

Prefixes

tera- (T)—10^{12}; one terahertz = one trillion cycles per second
giga- (G)—10^9; one gigahertz = one billion cycles per second
mega- (M)—10^6; one megawatt = one million watts
kilo- (k)—10^3; one kilometer = one thousand meters

centi- (c)—10^{-2}; one centimeter = 0.01 meter
milli- (m)—10^{-3}; one millimeter = 0.001 meter
micro- (μ)—10^{-6}; one microampere = 0.000001 ampere
nano- (n)—10^{-9}; one nanosecond = 0.000000001 second

Systems of Measurement

In 1960, a worldwide conference adopted the *Système International d'Unités* (SI). In America, it is referred to as the International System of Units. In familiar usage, it is called the metric system. In technical usage, it is usually referred to as SI. This standard has undergone, and will continue to undergo, subtle changes. The basic SI units of length, time, and mass are the meter (m), kilogram (kg), and second (s) respectively.

A metric system with units smaller that those in SI is sometimes used. The three basic units of the CGS system are the centimeter (cm), gram (g), and second (s). America is still living with English systems that use the foot (ft) and second (sec) as basic units. One English system uses forces in pounds (lb) as basic, and defines the slug as that mass which produces a weight of 32 pounds at sea level.

Like the SAT II test in physics, this book will use SI units primarily. Kilograms will be used *only* for mass, despite the street usage in metric countries where they are used as units of weight. Some problems will be given in the English system.

Some Numerical Relationships

1 meter (m) $\doteq$ 39.37 in.*   1 kg weighs 2.2 lb.
1 meter = 100 cm   1 ft^3 of water weighs 62.5 lb.
1 inch (in.) = 2.54 cm   A 1-lb weight has a mass of 454 grams (g).
1 liter (L) = 1000 cm^3 1 m^3 of water has a mass of 10^3 kg.
1 cm^3 = 10^{-6} m^3 1 cm^3 of water has a mass of 1 g.

Dimensional Analysis

A powerful tool for increasing understanding *and test scores* is called dimensional analysis. To utilize dimensional analysis, always carry units with numeric quantities, and treat them like algebraic quantities: If a room is 9 ft by 12 ft, it will require 9 ft × 12 ft = 108 ft^2 of flooring.

To convert units, always use numerators and denominators that are equivalent, so you are "multiplying physically by one," and thus making no changes in the quantity:

$$18 \text{ inches} \times \frac{1 \text{ ft}}{12 \text{ inches}} = 1.5 \text{ ft}$$

These examples no doubt seem trivial, yet how many times have you multiplied by a conversion factor when you should have divided, or *vice versa*? If you use dimensional analysis, such a mistake will lead to a nonsense result, requiring you to go back and invert your conversion fraction. Practice with simple problems in the early chapters. Dimensional analysis is far more important when you get to more complex units. In some cases, it becomes possible to solve problems you don't even understand, based only on their units!

Significant Figures and Standard Notation

We can count exactly but we cannot measure exactly. If twenty students count carefully the number of baseballs in a box, we have the right to expect the same answer from each of the students. If they say 45 baseballs, we don't think, maybe it's 45¼ baseballs. However, if we ask the same twenty students to measure very carefully the height of the box, we can expect different answers such as 62.3 cm, 62.4 cm, and 62.5 cm. Each of these answers has three significant figures, but the last digit is doubtful. If, as far as we can tell, the last digit should be zero, we write the zero down and thus

---

*The equal sign with a dot over it ($\doteq$) stands for "is approximately equal to." Another symbol used is $\approx$.

indicate the accuracy with which we tried to measure. In "62.0 cm" the zero is significant and we have three significant figures. In "0.0230 cm" we still have only three significant figures, the first two zeros being used only to indicate the location of the decimal point. In the *standard form* the same number would be written as 2.30×10^{-2} cm. This notation consists of two factors, one of which is an integral power of ten and the other has one digit (which is not a zero) in front of the decimal point. It is especially useful when dealing with large or small numbers. The *order of magnitude* of a quantity is its approximation to the nearest power of ten. The order of magnitude of 2.30×10^{-2} cm is 10^{-2} cm; one order of magnitude larger is 10^{-1} cm.

VECTORS AND FORCES

We shall now consider two important vector quantities, displacement and force. A *vector quantity* is completely specified by giving its magnitude and direction. Vector quantities can be added the way displacements are added. How do we add displacements?

Displacement is a change of position. Suppose we walk 30 meters to the east. We have now given the magnitude, 30 meters, and a direction, to the east. This is conveniently represented graphically by a *vector,* an arrow drawn to a suitable scale in the correct direction as shown below.

The vector *AB* represents the displacement of 30 meters to the east. If this displacement is now followed by a displacement of 40 meters to the north, the new displacement is represented by using the same scale for *BD:*

The net result of these two changes is that our change of position is from *A* to *D*, and the vector *AD* gives the resultant displacement. We can get the magnitude of the resultant, 50 meters, by applying the scale to vector *AD* or by using our knowledge of the right triangle (to be reviewed later).

A *force* is a push or pull. It is a *vector quantity*-i.e., to specify it we must give its *magnitude* (number and unit) and its direction. Example: 5 pounds acting westward. Another vector quantity is velocity. A *scalar* quantity is one that is fully specified by giving its magnitude, e.g., mass or speed. The *weight** of an object is a force: on the earth, it is essentially the pull of the earth on the object; its direction is "down." A more complete discussion of weight will be found in Chapter 2. Some *units* of force are the pound, dyne, and newton. The weight of one kilogram is approximately 9.8 newtons (N). In the diagram a three-pound force is represented to the right. A scale is arbitrarily selected and indicated. A certain length is used to represent 1 lb, and three of these lengths are laid off on a horizontal line to represent 3 lb. An arrowhead indicates the direction.

3-lb Force
to the Right

Scale

1 lb

Concurrent Forces

Concurrent forces are two or more forces acting simultaneously on the same point of an object. We are often concerned with getting the combined effect of these forces. The *resultant* of two or more forces is a single force which produces the same effect as these forces (and can therefore be used to replace them). For example, if a 4-lb force and a 3-lb force act in the same direction their resultant is a 7-lb force in the same direction; if they act in opposite directions (at an angle of 180°), their resultant is the difference between the two forces, a 1-pound force in the direction of the 4-lb force.

*The *weight* equals the product of the object's mass and the acceleration due to gravity: $w = mg$ if the buoyancy of the air is negligible.

PARALLELOGRAM OF FORCES When the angle between two forces is other than 0° or 180°, we usually get the resultant by a graphical method. Each force is represented by a vector drawn in the given direction from the same point and using the same scale for both as shown in the diagram. Using these two vectors as sides, the parallelogram is completed. The diagonal drawn from the common point of the two given forces is the resultant vector and will indicate both magnitude and direction of the resultant force. To get the magnitude of the resultant (R), we see how many of the scale lengths fit into it. In the diagram this is indicated as about 6½, and since each of these lengths represents one pound, the magnitude of the resultant is about 6½ lb. If the two given forces are perpendicular to each other, the Pythagorean theorem may be used: The square of the hypotenuse is equal to the sum of the squares of the other two sides (see diagram). To find the resultant of three

Forces of 3 lb and 4 lb at ∠ 50°

Scale
1 lb

Forces of 3 lb and 4 lb at ∠ 90°

$R^2 = 3^2 + 4^2$
$R = 5$ lb

concurrent forces we apply a similar procedure: first replace any two forces by their resultant and then combine this resultant with the third force to get the final resultant.

The *equilibrant* force is the force opposite and equal to the resultant force. If an object is in equilibrium under the action of several forces, any force may be considered the equilibrant of the other forces. (For *equilibrium* see p. 19.)

RESOLUTION OF FORCES A single force may be replaced by two or more other forces—its *components*. Usually we use two components at right angles to each other. For example, if, as shown, a box is pulled along the horizontal ground by means of a rope making an angle of 30° with the horizontal, the 10-N force applied to the end of the rope is equivalent to a horizontal force of 8.7 N and a vertical force of 5.0 N. We get the value of these component forces by constructing a rectangle as shown in the figure.

Vertical Component

Horizontal Component

Scale
1 N

P 30°

1. First we draw the three direction lines starting from the common point *P:* horizontal, vertical, and at 30° to the horizontal. 2. Using an arbitrary scale, we measure off the known force: 10 N at 30° with the horizontal. 3. From the end of this known vector, *F*, we draw horizontal and vertical lines to complete the parallelogram. 4. The intersections of these two lines with the original vertical and horizontal lines mark the ends of the two desired components; we put arrowheads at these ends. 5. We measure the length of each component vector and use the scale to translate the lengths to units of force. The 10-N force is shown crossed out because we are replacing it by its components.

You must know and understand the graphical solution. If you already know a little trigonometry, it may sometimes save you time to apply it instead of using the graphical solution. You may recall that, in a right triangle, the sine of the acute angle is equal to the ratio of the side opposite the angle to the hypotenuse.

$\sin \theta = a/c$
$\cos \theta = b/c$

For example, in the previous diagram, the rope pulls on the box at an angle of 30°.

$$\sin 30° = \frac{\text{vertical component of force } F}{\text{force } F}$$

$$\text{vertical component} = F \sin 30°$$
$$= (10 \text{ N})(0.5) = 5 \text{ N}$$
$$\text{horizontal component} = F \cos 30°$$
$$= (10 \text{ N})(0.866) = 8.7 \text{ N}$$

Illustration: The ends of a rope are tied to two points on a ceiling which are 6 ft apart. A 90-lb object is suspended from the middle of the rope; the middle of the rope is 4 ft from the ceiling. What is the pull in each half of the rope? First we make a scaled sketch of the situation; this helps to give us the angles of the rope. The pull in each part of the rope is in the direction of that part of the rope.

We are then ready to draw the vector diagram. Represent the proper angles without realistic details. To represent the *forces* properly we need a vector scale. Let ¼" equal 30 lb. The only force about which we know everything is the weight of the 90-lb object. We represent it by a ¾" line downward. The 90-lb weight is the equilibrant of the pull in the two halves of the rope. We then get the resultant (R) of these pulls by extending the equilibrant vector backward for the same length, ¾".

Next, we think of R as the diagonal of a parallelogram. From the head of R we draw two lines, each parallel to one of the lines representing the rope. The intersections of these lines mark the end of the vectors representing the pull in the ropes. To determine the magnitude of this pull, we measure the vectors. Since ¼ inch represents 30 lb, the pull in each half of the rope is 56 lb in the direction shown.

The successive steps in the method are summarized by the series of diagrams:

1. Sketch

2. Draw known lines and angles

3. Apply scale for known force(s)

4. From known equilibrant get resultant

5. Complete parallelogram

6. Measure vector: calculate F from scale for forces.

.47" = 56 lb

scale: ¼" = 30 lb

Parallel Forces

If two equal and opposite parallel forces (nonconcurrent) are applied to an object their resultant force is zero, but the object will rotate unless some other forces are properly applied. The *torque* or *moment of a force* is the effectiveness of a force in producing or tending to produce rotation. The magnitude of this

$$\boxed{\textbf{torque} = \textbf{force} \times \textbf{length of moment arm}}$$

The length of the moment arm is the perpendicular distance from the *fulcrum* or *pivot* (P) to the direction of the force. In the following diagram, the moment arm of the 2-lb force is 8 in. The moment arm of the 4-lb force can be found graphically and is approximately 3 in.

In general, the moment arm, and therefore the torque, are greatest when the force is perpendicular to the bar.

Here, we see that the 2-lb and 4-lb forces tend to produce counterclockwise rotation around the fulcrum or pivot at *P*. To balance these torques, clockwise moments must be applied. For equilibrium:

> **the sum of the clockwise moments = the sum of the counterclockwise moments**

Therefore, in the diagram, $F_1 \times 4'' = 2\,\text{lb} \times 8'' + 4\,\text{lb} \times 3'' = 28\,\text{lb-in.}$ $\qquad F_1 = 7\,\text{lb}$

Center of Gravity

Newton's *law of universal gravitation* states that two objects attract each other with a force that is proportional to the product of their masses and inversely proportional to the square of the distance between them. The earth's attraction for objects is known as *gravity*. This attraction of the earth for every portion of an object, therefore, consists of a set of practically parallel forces. The resultant of these parallel forces is the *weight* of the object. This resultant goes through a point known as the *center of gravity.* When talking about forces and moments of forces (torques) we can think of all the weight of the object as being concentrated at the center of gravity. If the fulcrum is placed just below the center of gravity, there will be no tendency for the object to rotate.

| Pos. 1 | Pos. 2 | Pos. 3 |

How can the center of gravity of an irregular object be determined? Consider the object depicted above. As in Pos. 1, first suspend the object so that it swings freely about point *A*. Repeat this process at least once by suspending the object from another point such as *B* (Pos. 2). The point where the vertical lines intersect is the center of gravity, *C*. Note that, if the object is in some position such as Pos. 3, with the pivot at *A*, the weight of the object acting at *C* produces a clockwise moment around *A* (equal to $W \times S$), which causes the object to swing to Pos. 1, where the length of the moment arm equals zero, i.e., the object comes to rest with its center of gravity directly below the point of suspension.

The stability of objects can be increased by building them with centers of gravity as low as possible. The stability of objects is also increased by providing them with as big a base as possible.

ANSWERING THE QUESTIONS Now let us consider briefly the questions asked concerning the first diagram at the beginning of the chapter. F_1 produces a moment greater than F_2 or F_3 because all three have the same magnitude, 4 newtons, but only F_1 is perpendicular to the bar. It therefore has the greatest moment arm of the three. Only a mental calculation is required to show that F_4 produces a larger torque than F_1: The torque due to F_1 is 4 N $\times$ 6 cm or 24 N-cm. The torque due to F_4 is 5 N $\times$ 5 cm or 25 N-cm.

Note that on these numerical questions much time can often be saved by making only approximate calculations.

Observe, in general, that the turning effect of a given force is greatest when it is applied at right

angles to the bar. (When the 4-N force is in a position such as F_2 or F_3, only a component of the 4-N force acts at right angles to the bar to produce a torque. The other component produces zero torque.)

QUESTIONS Chapter 1

Select the choice that best answers the question or completes the statement.

1. A length of 45 mm is equivalent to, approximately, **(A)** 1.8 in.   **(B)** 6.2 in.   **(C)** 11 in.   **(D)** 18 in. **(E)** 23 in.

2. A mass of 5 ounces is equivalent to, approximately,   **(A)** 11 g   **(B)** 50 g   **(C)** 90 g   **(D)** 120 g **(E)** 140 g

3. A length of 3.5 in. is equivalent to, approximately, **(A)** 2.5 cm   **(B)** 8.9 cm   **(C)** 11.4 cm **(D)** 13.9 cm   **(E)** 16.5 cm

4. An area of 2.5 square meters is equivalent to, approximately, **(A)** 100 in.^{2} **(B)** 140 in.^{2} **(C)** 180 in.^{2} **(D)** 220 in.^{2} **(E)** 3900 in.^{2}

5. The resultant of a 3-N and a 4-N force acting simultaneously on an object at right angles to each other is, in newtons, **(A)** 0   **(B)** 1   **(C)** 3.5   **(D)** 5   **(E)** 7

6. Two forces act together on an object. The magnitude of their resultant is least when the angle between the forces is **(A)** 0°   **(B)** 45°   **(C)** 60°   **(D)** 90°   **(E)** 180°

7. The resultant of a 5-lb and a 12-lb force acting simultaneously on an object in the same direction is, in pounds, **(A)** zero **(B)** 5 **(C)** 7 **(D)** 13 **(E)** 17

8. A uniform rod 30 in. long is pivoted at its center. A 40-lb weight is hung 5 in. from the left end. Where must a 50-lb weight be hung to maintain equilibrium? **(A)** 5 in. from right end **(B)** 6 in. from right end **(C)** 7 in. from right end **(D)** 8 in. from right end **(E)** 9 in. from right end.

9. A sled is pulled by means of a rope 0.6 m long; one end of the rope is attached to the sled and the other end is held 0.4 m above the level ground. If the force pulling the rope is 8 N, the horizontal component of the force (neglecting the height of the sled) is **(A)** 3 N **(B)** 4 N **(C)** 6 N **(D)** 8 N **(E)** 10 N

10. An object weighing 100 N is suspended from one end of horizontal rod X. The other end of the rod rests against a vertical wall. The weight of the rod is negligible. The system is kept in equilibrium by rope Y, one end of which is attached to the same end of the rod as the weight. The other end of the rope is attached to a point on the wall 30 cm above the other end of the rod. The rod is 40 cm long. The tension in rope Y is **(A)** 70 N **(B)** 90 N **(C)** 100 N **(D)** 130 N **(E)** 170 N

11. A meter stick weighing 0.8 N is supported by a pivot at the 40-cm mark. In order to maintain equilibrium a 1.0-N weight must be placed at the **(A)** 10-cm mark **(B)** 16-cm mark **(C)** 32-cm mark **(D)** 50-cm mark **(E)** 62-cm mark

EXPLANATIONS TO QUESTIONS Chapter 1

Answers

1. **(A)**	4. **(E)**	7. **(E)**	10. **(E)**
2. **(E)**	5. **(D)**	8. **(C)**	11. **(C)**
3. **(B)**	6. **(E)**	9. **(C)**	

Explanations

1. **(A)** We notice that the choices are not close in value. Therefore our calculation need not be very precise; we can thus save time. We recall that 1 meter = 39.37 inches. Therefore, 1000 mm ≑ 40 inches, 10 mm ≑ 0.40 inch; 45 mm ≑ 1.8 inches.

2. **(E)** We recall that 1 pound = 16 ounces = 454 g. Therefore, $5 \text{ ounces} \times \dfrac{(454 \text{ g})}{(16 \text{ ounces})} = 140$ g.

3. **(B)** We recall that 1 in. = 2.54 cm. Therefore, $3.5 \text{ in.} \times \dfrac{(2.54 \text{ cm})}{(1 \text{ in.})} = 8.9$ cm. Again, the choices are not close in value; it would have been enough to note that the answer is between 3×2.54 and 4×2.54; i.e., between 7.6 and 10. This would give (B) as the answer.

4. **(E)** 1 m = 39.37 in. ≈ 40 in. 1 m² ≈ 40 in. × 40 in. = 1600 in². Therefore $2.5 \text{ m}^2 \times \dfrac{(1600 \text{ in}^2)}{(1 \text{ m}^2)} = 4000$ in². The only answer close to this is (E).

5. **(D)** We can draw the two forces to *scale*, letting ⅛ in. = 1 N. If we complete the parallelogram and draw the diagonal, we notice that the resultant is 5 N. You should also recognize the *3-4-5-right triangle;* the resultant forms the hypotenuse of a right triangle whose arms are, respectively, 3 and 4. Therefore the hypotenuse is 5.

6. **(E)** When two vectors act in opposite directions (an angle of 180°), their resultant is the difference between the two vectors. When two vectors act in the same direction (an angle of 0°), their resultant is the sum of the two vectors. As the angle between the two vectors increases from 0° to 180°, their resultant decreases from the sum to the difference of the two vectors; to get the actual value for any of these angles, we may use a parallelogram.

7. **(E)** When two forces act in the same direction, the resultant of the two forces is their sum. If you said 13, you were too hasty. You should recognize the *5-12-13 right triangle,* but the two given forces were not at right angles to each other. Always read the question carefully.

8. **(C)** Make a simple, neat diagram putting in the given information. For equilibrium, clockwise moments = counterclockwise moments.

$$\text{moment} = \text{force} \times \text{moment arm}$$
$$50x = 40 \times 10$$
$$x = 8'' \text{ from fulcrum}$$

Ans: $(15 - 8)''$ or $7''$ from rt. end.

40 lb   50 lb

9. **(C)** You may make a scale drawing and obtain a graphical solution. You will probably save time by making a rough drawing, inserting the given values, and using a little algebra to obtain the solution. From the end of the vector representing the 8-N force we drop a perpendicular to obtain F, the horizontal component of the 8-N force. The two right triangles are similar. Therefore,
$\dfrac{F}{8 \text{ N}} = \dfrac{\text{base}}{0.6 \text{ m}}$. Length of base $= \sqrt{(\text{hypotenuse})^2 - (\text{height})^2} = \sqrt{0.36 - 0.16}$;

base $= \sqrt{0.20}$. $F = \dfrac{8}{0.6}\sqrt{0.20} = 5.95$ N. Choice (C) is closest. It is not necessary to take exact square roots. You note that the square root of 0.20 is between 0.4 and 0.5; using 0.45 is adequate.

10. **(E)** First we insert into the diagram the given information. Then we think of a method for solving the problem.

Method 1—Components
For equilibrium, the upward component of the rope's tension, S_Y, must equal the downward pull of 100 N. The diagram shows two right triangles—the force triangle and the dimension triangle, a 30-40-50-right triangle. These two triangles are similar; a pair of equal acute angles is marked (alternate interior angles). We then write the proportion for the two similar triangles:

$$\frac{S_Y}{100 \text{ N}} = \frac{50 \text{ cm}}{30 \text{ cm}}; \quad S_Y = \frac{5}{3} \times 100 \text{ N} = 167 \text{ N}$$

Method 2—Moments
This is more difficult. Take moments about K, the point where the rod touches the wall. The clockwise moment = 100 N × 40 cm. The counterclockwise moment is due to S_Y. Remember that the moment arm is the perpendicular distance from the fulcrum to the direction of the force. This distance is given by L', forming one side of the shaded right triangle. This triangle is similar to the 30-40-50 right triangle. The proportion from these two similar triangles is:

$$\frac{L'}{40 \text{ cm}} = \frac{30 \text{ cm}}{50 \text{ cm}}; \quad L' = 24 \text{ cm}$$

clockwise mom. = ccl mom.; $100 \times 40 = (S_Y \times L') = S_Y \times 24$; $S_Y = 167$ N .

NOTE: Method 2 is longer than Method 1, but it is the more general method. If the rope were not tied to the same point on which the other force(s) act, Method 1 could not be used.

If you know trigonometry, note that the tension's vertical component is $S_Y \sin\angle 1$, which equals $S_Y \times {}^3/_5$. Taking moments about K,

$$S_Y \times {}^3/_5 \times 40 = 100 \times 40$$
$$S_Y = 100 \times {}^5/_3 = 167 \text{ Nt}$$

11. **(C)** We must assume that the meter stick is uniform. Therefore, the 0.8-N weight of the stick may be considered acting at the center, the 50-cm mark. To produce equilibrium the 1.0-N weight must be placed on the other side of the fulcrum, a distance x cm away from the fulcrum. Counterclockwise mom. = clockwise mom. $1.0x = 0.8 \times 10$; $x = 8$ cm from the 40-cm mark. This is at the 32-cm mark.

2

Motion and Forces

 Object *A* moves with constant speed down the inclined plane. Object *B* on the table (not shown) moves with constant speed. Do you realize that the unbalanced force acting on *A* is zero but that an unbalanced force may be acting on *B*? If object *C* moves with decreasing velocity down the plane, what is the net force acting on *C*? In this chapter we shall consider some of the important types of motion and the forces producing them.

SPEED AND VELOCITY

When we speak about motion or rest, the earth is our *reference point* unless some other frame of reference is specifically indicated. For example, in the above paragraph, the plane and table are assumed to be stationary with respect to the earth, and the speed of *A* is constant with respect to the plane.

Speed is distance covered per unit time. *Velocity (v)* of an object is its speed in a given direction. Speed is a scalar quantity. Velocity is a vector quantity—it has magnitude and direction. The magnitude of the velocity is the object's speed. The velocity changes if either the speed or the direction of motion, or both, change. You can think of direction as being given by the points of a compass. You can then see readily that if an object is moving at constant speed around a horizontal circle its direction, and therefore its velocity, are constantly changing; at one instant the object may be moving towards the north and a little later it will be moving towards the south.

FOR ALL TYPES OF MOTION

$$\text{average speed} = \frac{\text{distance covered}}{\text{time required}}$$

If speed is given in miles per hour, it can be converted quickly to feet per second:

$$22 \frac{\text{ft}}{\text{sec}} = 15 \frac{\text{mi}}{\text{hr}}$$

$$\text{Example:} \quad 30 \frac{\cancel{\text{mi}}}{\cancel{\text{hr}}} \times \frac{22 \frac{\text{ft}}{\text{sec}}}{15 \frac{\cancel{\text{mi}}}{\cancel{\text{hr}}}} = 44 \frac{\text{ft}}{\text{sec}}$$

You may find the formula easier to remember in its multiplicative format:

> **distance covered = average speed × time**
>
> $$s = v_{av}t$$

DO NOT CONFUSE the letter *s* used to represent distance in a formula, with the letter *s* used to represent the unit "seconds" in a quantity. The usage will always be clear in context.

Air resistance or friction of the air tends to slow an object down. An object dropped from a balloon may actually stop accelerating and reach a constant downward speed known as its *terminal velocity.*

The motion of an object can sometimes be thought of as the result of a *combination of velocities.* For example, if you walk at 4 kilometers per hour from the last car of a train towards the front while the train is moving at 60 kilometers per hour, your velocity with respect to the earth is 64 km/h in the direction of motion. (Note that it was implied that the 4 km/h was with respect to the train.) If the two given velocities are not in the same direction, we can get the combined velocity by using combination of vectors as we did for forces on page 8. *Example:* A plane is moving east in still air at 200 km/h. A steady south wind starts blowing at 100 km/h. What will be the plane's velocity? The solution is shown in the following diagram. (Recall that a south wind blows from the south towards the north.)

The plane's velocity will be approx. 220 km/h in the direction shown by *R*. (It would be wasteful to work for a more accurate solution.)

ACCELERATED MOTION

Uniform motion is motion in which the velocity is constant. If the velocity changes the motion is said to be *accelerated. Acceleration (a)* is the rate of change of velocity. Because of the definition of velocity, acceleration may result from a change in direction as well as from a change in speed. Acceleration is a vector quantity.

> $$\text{acceleration} = \frac{\text{change in velocity}}{\text{time required for change}}$$
>
> $$a = \frac{v_f - v_i}{t} = \frac{\Delta v}{t}$$

Δv (delta *v*) = change in velocity. Recall that we may use an arrow over the letter or boldface type to remind us that it is a vector quantity.

The formula indicates that the magnitude of the acceleration is expressed as a unit of speed divided by a unit of time. Examples: 6 miles per hour per second, 4 ft per second per second, and 10 meters per second per second. To save space the last two examples would be written as 4 ft/sec^2 and 10 m/s^2. To emphasize the meaning of acceleration it is a good idea to read such expressions as "four feet per second every second" and "10 meters per second every second."

If an object slows down we sometimes say that the object is *decelerated.* Sometimes we also say that such an acceleration is negative. This usage is not recommended but should be interpreted to mean that the direction of the acceleration is opposite to the direction of the initial velocity.

Uniformly accelerated motion is motion with constant acceleration. If the object starts moving from rest, the initial velocity is zero, and the expression for its acceleration becomes $v_f = at$. If an object is allowed to *fall freely* near the surface of the earth (its initial velocity is zero and no forces other than gravity act on it during its fall), the acceleration of the object remains constant and is independent of the mass of the object. The letter g is used universally for this acceleration. The value of g varies slightly from point to point on the surface of the earth. Unless told to do otherwise, in the MKS system use $g = 9.8$ m/s^2; in the English system use $g = 32$ ft/sec^2.

If an object is projected into the air in some direction other than the vertical, air resistance being negligible, the path is a parabola. The motion can be thought of as a combination of two separate motions: a horizontal motion in which the velocity remains constant and has the value of the horizontal component of the velocity with which it is projected, and a vertical motion due to gravity. If the object is projected horizontally, the vertical motion is the same as in free fall. You should memorize the following formulas, but be sure you memorize at the same time the situations for which each formula applies.

Motion with constant acceleration (starting from rest)		
$v_{av} = v_f/2$		v_{av} = average speed
$v_f = at$	$(v_f = gt)$	v_f = final velocity
$s = \frac{1}{2} at^2$	$(s = \frac{1}{2}gt^2)$	a = acceleration
$v_f^2 = 2as$	$(v_f^2 = 2gs)$	t = elapsed time
		s = distance covered

Additional notes on use of above formulas: The formulas in parentheses are for freely falling objects near the surface of the earth; in this case the acceleration has a known value and, as mentioned before, we use the letter g to indicate this. (Air resistance is neglected.) The same formulas may be used *for objects not starting from rest* (initial velocity not zero) if the final velocity is zero. In that case let v_f stand for the initial velocity. *Example:* A ball is thrown vertically upward and rises to a height of 4.9 m. With what speed did the ball leave the hand? *Solution:* Let v_f represent this speed.

$$v_f^2 = 2\,gs$$
$$= 2 \times 9.8 \text{ m/s}^2 \times 4.9 \text{ m}$$
$$v_f = 9.8 \text{ m/s}$$

For objects thrown vertically upward, the time required to reach the maximum height is equal to the time required for the object to fall back to the starting level.

For linear motion with constant acceleration not starting from rest, the original four formulas become:

$$v_{av} = \frac{v_i + v_f}{2}$$
$$v_f = v_i + at$$
$$s = v_i t + \frac{1}{2}at^2$$
$$v_f^2 = v_i^2 + 2as$$

NEWTON'S FIRST LAW OF MOTION

Statement: If the net force acting on an object is zero, the velocity of the object does not change (that is, speed and direction of motion remain constant). The term *net force* means the same thing as resultant force or unbalanced force. Newton's first law is often stated in other ways: When a body is at rest or moving with constant speed in a straight line, the resultant of all the forces acting on the body is zero.

Of course, an object at rest and remaining at rest is in equilibrium, but note that an object may be moving and still be in equilibrium. An object at rest tends to remain at rest; an object in motion tends to keep moving in a straight line unless acted on by an unbalanced force.

Illustration: Passengers in a car lurch forward when the driver applies the brakes. *Application*–In the diagram, a 200-lb object is suspended from a ceiling by means of a rope. The object is at rest; what are the forces acting on it? Since the object is at rest it is in equilibrium. Therefore Newton's first law applies and the resultant of all forces acting on it is zero.

(a)   (b)

The earth supplies a 200-lb force acting downward (gravity). An equal and opposite force must be applied to the object. This is done by the rope. This pull of the rope is referred to as the *tension* in the rope. The tension in this rope must be 200 lb. This is shown by the vector diagram, where the object is represented by the dot and the rope's upward pull by the vector *F*. Note that the tension of the rope also acts downward on the *ceiling*, but we are making no use of this because we are concerned with the forces acting on the *object*.

NOTE: It also follows from Newton's first law that, if an object is to remain at rest, any force acting on it in one direction must be balanced by an equal force on it in the opposite direction. For example, refer to the illustrative problem on page 9. Each half of the rope exerts a pull on the 90-lb object. This pull can be replaced by a horizontal component and a vertical component. The sum of the two vertical components must be 90 lb in order to balance the pull of the 90-lb object.

NEWTON'S SECOND LAW

STATEMENT 1 If the net force acting on an object is not zero, the object will be accelerated in the direction of the force; the acceleration will be proportional to the net force and inversely proportional to the mass of the object. *Example:* A push that is enough to give a 3000-lb car an acceleration of 4 ft/sec^2 will be able to give a 6000-lb truck an acceleration of 2 ft/sec^2. Twice as great a push is needed to give the car an acceleration of 8 ft/sec^2.

We can think of the net force as being used to overcome the inertia of the object. The greater the mass of the object, the greater is the force required to produce a given acceleration, or to "budge the object." This leads to a definition: *INERTIAL MASS*—the measure of an object's resistance to acceleration. The proportion between resultant force and acceleration can be represented as:

$$\frac{F_1}{F_2} = \frac{a_1}{a_2}$$

When the unbalanced force acting on the object is equal to the weight of the object, as in free fall, the acceleration is equal to *g*, the acceleration due to gravity. This leads to the useful proportion:

$$\frac{F}{w} = \frac{a}{g}$$

Note that the weight *w* and the resultant force *F* must be in the same units and the *g* and the acceleration *a* must be in the same units. *Example*: An automobile weights 8000 N. What unbalanced force will produce an acceleration of 2.0 m/s^2?

$$\frac{F}{8000\,N} = \frac{2.0\,m/s^2}{9.8\,m/s^2} \quad \therefore F = 1600\,N$$

Newton's law also leads to the equation

$$F = ma$$

where m is the mass of the object. Also, the weight of an object is equal to the product of its mass and the value of the acceleration due to gravity:

$$w = mg$$

There are some situations you have to watch. If you use Newton's second law, $F = ma$, different units must be used for force and mass, as indicated in the table below. If you use the relationship $F/w = a/g$, the same units are used for force and weight. Of course, if an object goes sufficiently far away from the earth, the gravitational pull of the earth on the object will become significantly less although the mass of the object remains constant. An orbiting astronaut is still attracted by the earth; his weightlessness is only apparent. (The definition of weight used in this book is the one used in most high school and college textbooks.) Also see the discussion on Newton's law of gravitation later in the chapter.

At this point some students may wish to review the material on proportional relationships and graphs presented in Chapter 15. For reference, the appropriate units are tabulated below; memorize the first row.

System	F & w	m	a	g	v
SI	newtons	kilograms	m/s^2	$9.8\ m/s^2$	m/s
CGS	dynes	grams	cm/s^2	$980\ cm/s^2$	cm/s
English	pounds	slugs	ft/sec^2	$32\ ft/sec^2$	ft/sec

Note: 1. The abbreviation for meter is m; the abbreviation for mile is mi.

2. $1\ lb \doteq 4.45\ N$; $1\ N \doteq 0.225\ lb$.

STATEMENT 2 Newton's second law is sometimes stated as: The rate of change of momentum is equal to the net force acting on the object.

MOMENTUM is defined as the product of mass and velocity. It is a vector quantity.

Example 1. A 500-g object is allowed to drop. After 2 seconds of free fall its speed will be (980×2) cm/s ($v = gt$). Its momentum will be $(500\ g)(980 \times 2)$ cm/s $= 980,000\ g \bullet cm/s$ downward. If we use MKS units: momentum $= (0.5\ kg)(9.8 \times 2)$ m/s $= 9.8\ kg \bullet m/s$ downward.

Example 2. An object moves along a straight line with a momentum of 5 units. If it slows down without change of direction so that its momentum is 3 units, its change of momentum is 2 units. However, if it had hit something and bounced back with a momentum in the opposite direction of 3 units, its change in momentum is 5 units — (—3 units) = 8 units in the new direction.

NOTE: At this point, you, like many others, may raise a difficult question: When you speak of a 50-lb object, do you mean that the object's mass is 50 lb or that the object's weight is 50 lb? We shall use the pound (lb) only as a unit of force. In that system the appropriate mass unit is the *slug*, but we won't use any mass unit with the English system. We shall use the metric *mass units* kilogram (kg) and gram (g), and the metric *force units* dyne and newton (N).

Example 1. How large a force is needed to give an acceleration of $9.8\ m/s^2$ to an object having a mass of 1 kilogram? $F = ma$; $F = (1\ kg)(9.8\ m/s^2) = 9.8$ newtons. You can now see why we said earlier that the weight of a 1-kilogram mass is 9.8 newtons. The weight of an object on earth is the earth's gravitational pull on it. When that pull is the only force acting on the object, the object is falling freely. The acceleration of a freely falling object, we know, is $9.8\ m/s^2$.

Example 2. How large a force is needed to give an acceleration of $3\ m/s^2$ to a 5-lb object?

We know that a 5-lb object falling freely has an acceleration of $g = 9.8\ m/s^2$ and that during its fall the net force acting on it is its weight. The 5-lb object has a weight of 5 lb.

$$\frac{F}{w} = \frac{a}{g}$$

$$\frac{F}{5\ lb} = \frac{3\ m/s^2}{9.8\ m/s^2}$$

$$F \doteq 1.5\ lb$$

Note that both accelerations must have the same units. Since we are given an acceleration of 3 m/s², we use $g = 9.8$ m/s². Likewise both units of force must have the same units. Since we are given that the object has a weight of 5 lb, the unit of the answer is the pound. Note also that we did not have to be concerned about the mass of the object.

IMPULSE AND CHANGE OF MOMENTUM

The *impulse* acting on an object is defined as the product of the net force acting on the object and the length of time that this force acts. The impulse acting on an object is equal to the change of momentum which it produces:

$$Ft = \text{change in momentum}$$

Example: If a 10-newton force acts on a 3-kilogram object for 2 seconds, the impulse acting on the object $= (10\text{ N}) (2\text{ s}) = 20$ N•s in the direction of the force. This is also the change in momentum of the object. (We can use the equivalent unit, a newton•second = a kilogram•meter/second.) What is the resulting change in the object's velocity?

$$\text{Change in momentum} = \text{mass} \times \text{change in velocity}$$
$$20\text{ kg•m/s} = (3\text{ kg}) (\text{change in velocity})$$
$$\Delta v = 6.7\text{ m/s (in the direction of the force)}$$

NEWTON'S THIRD LAW

When one object exerts a force on a second object, the second object exerts an equal and opposite force on the first object. (This is sometimes stated as: Action equals reaction.)

Note that two different objects are involved and that the two forces mentioned do not act on the same object. Therefore, they do not cancel each other.

Illustration: A rowboat stops at a pier and the boy in the boat steps toward the pier. The boat moves away from the pier and the boy falls into the water or barely makes the edge of the pier. Explanation: In order to move forward from rest the boy must have a force acting on him (Newton's second law); this force is supplied by the boat: When the boy pushes against the boat with his foot, the boat pushes against the boy's foot with an equal force (Newton's third law). Both the boat and the boy will move with respect to the spot where the boat had stopped, but the boy will probably have misjudged the needed push.

Measurement of the speed with which the boy and the boat start to move would show that the momentum of the boy equals the momentum of the boat, except for direction. The resultant of the two momenta is zero. This is an illustration of CONSERVATION OF MOMENTUM. When no external forces act on a system of objects, the total momentum of the system is unchanged. (This is true for collisions, explosions, etc. The objects in the system exert forces on each other, but these are internal forces. Also remember, momentum is a vector quantity.)

Newton's third law is also the principle underlying the operation of rockets and jet aircraft. As the hot gases are pushed out from the rear, they exert a forward push on the object from which they escape.

Example: In the diagram, block B is at rest on a horizontal, frictionless surface. It has a mass of 20 kg. Block A slides towards it with a velocity of 6.0 m/s. It has a mass of 10 kg. After block A hits block B they remain together.

Before the collision the momentum of block $A = (10\text{ kg}) (6.0\text{ m/s}) = 60$ kg•m/s. The momentum of block *B* is zero, since it is stationary. After the collision the momentum of the two blocks together still has to be the vector sum of the two blocks before the collision, or 60 kg•m/s. The combined mass is 30 kg. The blocks move off with a velocity of 2.0 m/s, since

$$\text{momentum} = \text{mass} \times \text{velocity}$$
$$60 \text{ kg•m/s} = (30 \text{ kg}) (v)$$
$$v = 2.0 \text{ m/s}$$

CENTRIPETAL FORCE

When an object moves around a circle, the object's velocity is constantly changing because its direction is constantly changing. Because the velocity is changing the object is accelerated. Note that this is true even if the *speed* of the object is constant. According to Newton's second law, this acceleration is produced by an unbalanced force. This is the *centripetal force:* the force acting on an object moving in a circle which keeps it moving in the circular path. The force is directed toward the center of the circle. The diagram represents a stone whirling at the end of a string. At the instant the object is at *A*, it is moving to the left; at *B* it is moving to the right. The centripetal force is always toward the center as shown by F_c. If the string should tear, the object would fly off tangent to the circle (because of inertia: Newton's first law); if this happens when the object is at *C*, the object flies off in the direction of *CD*.

Any centripetal force can be given by the square of the object's speed, divided by the radius of its circular path.

$$a_c = \frac{v^2}{r}$$

Since we know that F = ma, centripetal force must be given by the mass of an object times its centripetal acceleration, or

$$F_c = \frac{mv^2}{r}$$

There is no centrifugal force acting on the object moving in a circle. If the string pulls on the whirling stone, the stone reacts and pulls on the string. This equal and opposite force pulling on the *string* may be called a centrifugal force. The centripetal force on satellites is the gravitational force.

FRAME OF REFERENCE

To someone riding in a car which is moving at high speed around a curve, things seem different from the way they seem to someone standing at the side of the road. The rider will feel a push or force toward the outside of the curve, toward the right if he is facing forward.* We, who are watching from the outside, see the movement of the car merely as an illustration of Newton's first law of motion. The rider's inertia tends to keep him moving along a straight line and his unrestrained upper body will do this somewhat. (Seat belts and friction between him and the seat of the car provide the centripetal force to make him go around the curve.) For us, watching in the street or working in the laboratory, the reference for motion or rest is called an *inertial frame of reference*, a point or set of coordinates which is at rest or moves with uniform velocity, constant speed in a straight line. The laws of physics are the same in all inertial frames of reference. As stated on page 16, the earth is usually a satisfactory reference frame in spite of the rotation around its axis and revolution around the sun.

*In the diagram above.

GRAVITATIONAL FIELDS

Masses can affect other masses that are a great distance away. We say the earth is held to the sun "by gravity." Sometimes the distances involved are much smaller. A ball is pulled to the floor "by gravity." What is going on?

Objects having mass are subject to the gravitational fields of other masses. In fact, all objects having mass have their *own* gravitational fields. These fields can be thought of as a change in the space around the objects due to their mass. You can explore a gravitational field with a mass small enough so that it won't distort the field. If you release the test mass, it will be attracted to the mass whose field you are exploring. The force per unit mass will give the *magnitude* of the *gravitational field intensity* at the point of release, and the direction of the initial motion will complete the description of the gravitational field intensity vector. The continuous curves formed by such vectors are called *lines of force*.

Earth's Gravitational Field

The dashed lines represent *equipotential surfaces* (spheres in this case), along which an object's potential energy is constant. You may have noticed that there is a regular pattern: objects that are two earth radii away are subject to one-quarter the pull at the earth's surface, while objects that are three earth radii away are subject to only one-ninth the pull at the earth's surface. Note that lines of force are always perpendicular to equipotentials.

NEWTON'S LAW OF GRAVITATION

Indeed, Newton recognized that any two particles attract each other with a force which is proportional to the product of their masses, and inversely proportional to the square of the distance between them. The constant of proportionality (G) is called the Universal Gravitational Constant. DO

NOT CONFUSE the Universal Gravitational Constant (G) with local gravitational field intensity (g).

$$F_g = \frac{G \times mass_1 \times mass_2}{r^2}$$

Near earth's surface, small changes in distances ("heights") are miniscule compared to the distance to the center of the earth. Thus the gravitational field intensity vectors are essentially parallel and equal:

Gravitational Field at Sea Level

However, careful measurements can easily detect the differences in decimal place values of gravitational field intensity between sea level and mountain tops.

You may think it curious that the number 9.8 appeared again here. Let's look at some dimensional analysis:

$$\frac{Newtons}{kilogram} = \frac{kilograms \times \frac{(meters)}{(second^2)}}{kilogram} = \frac{m}{s^2}$$

Now you see—a freely falling object has an acceleration of 9.8 m/s² *because* it is acted upon by a gravitational field intensity of 9.8 N/kg! Also, you can now see that a better explanation of weight has nothing to do with an object falling: resulting from the presence of a gravitational field, weight is equal to mass times the strength of that gravitational field.

weight = mass × gravitational field intensity

w = mg

The *weight* of an object is the net gravitational pull on it. For objects near the surface of the earth, the weight of the object is practically the earth's gravitational pull on it. The distance is measured from the center of gravity of the earth to the center of gravity of the object. If the earth's radius is taken as 4000 miles, an object weighing 20 lb on the surface of the earth will weigh only 5 lb at a distance of 4000 mi from the earth, because the distance from the center of the earth has been doubled. Of course, the mass of the object is not changed.

Either acceleration due to gravity *or* gravitational field intensity may define g. Context determines which is more appropriate, but either yields the correct answer.

ANSWERING THE QUESTIONS Now let us return to the problem at the beginning of the chapter. Object *A* is moving down the plane with constant speed. Since *A's* speed and direction are not changing, its acceleration is zero. Therefore, according to Newton's first and second laws no unbalanced force can be acting on *A*. On the other hand, nothing was said about *B's* direction of motion. For example, *B* might be moving in a circular path. Then an unbalanced force (the centripetal force) would have to act on it. If *B* were moving in a straight line, then no unbalanced force could act on it. Since *C* is decelerating, an unbalanced force must be acting on it with a direction opposite to the direction of motion. This could be the force of friction.

QUESTIONS Chapter 2

Select the choice that best answers the question or completes the sentence.

1. The speed of an object at the end of 4 successive seconds is 20, 25, 30, and 35 mi/hr, respectively. The acceleration of this object is **(A)** 5 ft per sec^2 **(B)** 5 mi per hr per sec **(C)** 5 mi per hr^2 **(D)** 5 mi per sec^2 **(E)** 20 mi per hr per sec

2. A bomb is dropped from an airplane moving horizontally with a speed of 200 km/h. If the air resistance is negligible, the bomb will reach the ground in 5 s when the altitude of the plane is approximately **(A)** 50 m **(B)** 75 m **(C)** 125 m **(D)** 250 m **(E)** 300 m

3. While an arrow is being shot from a bow it is accelerated over a distance of 2 ft. At the end of this acceleration it leaves the bow with a speed of 200 ft/sec. The average acceleration imparted to the arrow is **(A)** 200 ft/sec^2 **(B)** 400 ft/sec^2 **(C)** 500 ft/sec^2 **(D)** 1000 ft/sec^2 **(E)** 10,000 ft/sec^2

4. An object whose mass is 100 g starts from rest and moves with constant acceleration of 20 cm/s^2. At the end of 8 s its momentum is, in g•cm/s, **(A)** 500 **(B)** 8000 **(C)** 16,000 **(D)** 33,000 **(E)** 64,000

5. A rock is dropped from a high bridge. At the end of 3 seconds of free fall the speed of the rock is, in cm/s, **(A)** 30 **(B)** 100 **(C)** 500 **(D)** 1000 **(E)** 3000

6. A person standing in an elevator which goes up with constant upward acceleration exerts a push on the floor of the elevator whose value **(A)** is always equal to his weight **(B)** is always greater than his weight **(C)** is always less than his weight **(D)** is greater than his weight only when his acceleration is greater than g (approx. 9.8 m/s^2) **(E)** is greater than his weight only when his acceleration is less than g

7. Two small masses, when 10 cm apart, attract each other with a force of F newtons. When 5 cm apart, these masses will attract each other with a force, in newtons, of **(A)** $F/2$ **(B)** $F/4$ **(C)** $2F$ **(D)** $4F$ **(E)** $5F$

8. When a certain object is 100 m above the surface of the earth, the earth's attraction for it is 10 N. In order for the earth's attraction for the same object to be only 5 N, the object must be taken to a distance from the surface of the earth of **(A)** 200 m **(B)** 400 m **(C)** 2600 km **(D)** 7300 km **(E)** 16,000 km

9. A car going around a certain curve at a speed of 25 km/h has a centripetal force acting on it of 100 N. If the speed of the car is doubled, the centripetal force **(A)** is quadrupled **(B)** is doubled **(C)** is multiplied by the $\sqrt{2}$ **(D)** is reduced to ½ of the original value **(E)** is reduced to ¼ of the original value

10. Two freely hanging weights, each having a mass of 60 g, are connected by a light thread which passes over a fixed pulley. The mass of the pulley and frictional losses are negligible. If a 10-g weight is now added to one of the weights, its downward acceleration, in cm/s^2, will be approximately **(A)** 32 **(B)** 80 **(C)** 160 **(D)** 320 **(E)** 980

11. A plane travels from point A for 1 hour towards the west at 400 km/h and then travels towards the north for 1 hour at 300 km/h, arriving at point B. A second plane, starting at A at the same time as the first plane and traveling towards B along a straight line, will arrive at B at the same time as the first plane if its speed is **(A)** 100 km/h **(B)** 250 km/h **(C)** 500 km/h **(D)** 700 km/h **(E)** 1200 km/h

12. A handball is tossed vertically upward with a velocity of 19.6 m/s. Approximately how high will it rise? **(A)** 15 m **(B)** 20 m **(C)** 25 m **(D)** 30 m **(E)** 60 m

EXPLANATIONS TO QUESTIONS Chapter 2

Answers

1. **(B)**		4. **(C)**		7. **(D)**		10. **(B)**
2. **(C)**		5. **(E)**		8. **(C)**		11. **(B)**
3. **(E)**		6. **(B)**		9. **(A)**		12. **(B)**

Explanations

1. **(B)** $\text{acceleration} = \dfrac{\text{change in velocity}}{\text{time in which change takes place}}$

$= 5 \text{ mi per hr/1 sec}$

$= 5 \text{ mi per hr/ sec}$

This means that each second the speed is changing 5 mi/hr.

2. **(C)** The horizontal velocity does not affect the vertical velocity. A suitable expression for free fall, since we know the time of falling and want to calculate the distance covered, is $s = \frac{1}{2}gt^2$; $s = \frac{1}{2} (9.8 \text{ m/s}^2)(5 \text{ s})^2 = 123$ m.

3. **(E)** The arrow is accelerated from rest. Its final speed is 200 ft/sec; it is accelerated over a known distance, 2 ft; $v^2 = 2\ as$; $(200 \text{ ft/sec})^2 = 2\ a\ (2 \text{ ft})$; $a = 40,000/4 = 10,000 \text{ ft/sec}^2$. The term *average acceleration* is used to take care of fluctuations; don't divide by 2.

4. **(C)** The momentum of an object = its mass $\times$ its velocity.
At the end of 8 sec, its velocity:

$v = at = 20 \text{ cm/s}^2 \times 8 \text{ s} = 160$ cm/s.

$\text{momentum} = mv = 100 \text{ g} \times 160 \text{ cm/s} = 16,000 \text{ g} \cdot \text{cm/s}$

5. **(E)** A simple problem! For a freely falling object, starting from rest, final velocity = acceleration $\times$ time; $v = gt = 980 \text{ cm/s}^2 \times 3 \text{ s} \doteq 3000$ cm/s. Notice that time can be saved by getting an approximate answer. Be careful about the value of g that you use.

6. **(B)** First apply Newton's third law: the man's push on the elevator is equal to the push of the elevator on the man. The push of the floor of the elevator must be enough to support his weight and in addition must accelerate him upward. Therefore, the push of the elevator on the man is greater than his weight by an amount necessary to give him acceleration $\left(F = W + W\dfrac{a}{g}\right)$.

7. **(D)** The gravitational force varies inversely as the square of the distance between the objects. When the distance is reduced to one-half of its previous value, the force is quadrupled.

8. **(C)** A little tricky. Let us get an approximate answer first. This should usually be sufficient for the test. First notice that the distance must be measured to the center of the earth; we'll take that distance as 4000 mi or 6400 km. If that distance were doubled, the earth's attraction would be one-fourth, or 2½ N. Therefore, 12,800 km from the center of the earth, or 6400 km from the surface of the earth, is too great. You may have a feeling that the first two choices are too low, leaving choice (C). The inverse square law tell us that

$$\frac{F_1}{F_2} = \frac{d_2^2}{d_1^2} = \frac{2}{1}$$

Therefore $d_2 = d_1 \sqrt{2} \doteq 6,400 \text{ km} \times 1.4 = 9000$ km from the center of the earth. The distance from the surface of the earth is $(9000 - 6400) \text{ km} \doteq 2600$ km.

9. **(A)** The centripetal force acting on an object is proportional to the square of its speed. If the speed of the car is doubled, the force acting on it is multiplied by four.

10. **(B)** This is an application of Newton's second law. The unbalanced force is provided by the 10-g weight. The masses that are accelerated are the 10-g weight and the two 60-g weights.

$$\frac{F}{w} = \frac{a}{g}; \quad \frac{10\,g}{130\,g} = \frac{a}{980 \text{ cm/s}^2}$$

$$a = 980 \times \frac{10}{130} = 77.7 \text{ cm/s}^2$$

11. **(B)** A little tricky. The total time required for the first plane is two hours. The distance to be covered by the second plane is 500 km (along the hypotenuse of a 3-4-5 right triangle. The arms of the right triangle are 300 and 400 km resp.).

$$\text{speed of second plane} = \frac{\text{distance covered}}{\text{time}} = \frac{500 \text{ km}}{2 \text{ h}} = 250 \text{ km/h}$$

Don't confuse this problem with a situation in which two velocities may be combined vectorially. For example, if the two velocities had acted on the plane at the same time, the resultant velocity would have been 500 km/h; but in this problem the two velocities acted consecutively and the total time was 2 hours.

12. **(B)** This is a problem in motion with constant acceleration equal to 9.8 m/s² downward, in which the object has an initial velocity (19.6 m/s), but its final velocity at the moment we are considering is zero. Since an object released from that height will hit the ground with a velocity of 19.6 m/s, we can use the appropriate formula for motion starting from rest and having a final velocity of 19.6 m/s:

$$v_1^2 = 2\,gs$$
$$(19.6 \text{ m/s})^2 = 2\,(9.8 \text{ m/s}^2)\,(s)$$
$$s = 19.6 \text{ m}$$

3

Work, Energy, Simple Machines

60 lb

A system of pulleys, arranged as shown, is used under ideal conditions to lift a weight of 60 lb at constant speed with an effort of F_E. What is the pull exerted on the ceiling? What is the pull in the rope at point A? If the 60-lb object is raised 4 ft in 2 sec, how far will point B move? How much work did Atlas do each day that he held up the earth? How much energy did he use?

WORK AND ENERGY

In physics we talk about work done on an object or work done by an object or by a force. When a force *moves* an object, the force does work on the object. If the 20-N force in the diagram moves the 50-N object 3 m, 60 joules of work was done on the object.

Work

Work is equal to the product of the force and the distance the object moves *in the direction of the force*. If the object moves in a direction other than the direction of the force we must take the

component of the force in the direction of motion of the object. For example, if a rope is used to pull a sled, the rope is flexible, and any force, F_1, that we exert on the upper end is to be thought of as a pull which is transmitted to the sled and acts in the direction of the rope. This usually results in moving the sled along the road, and to calculate the work done by F_1 on the sled we find the component F in the direction of motion and multiply it by the distance the sled moves while the force is applied.

$$\boxed{\text{work} = \text{force} \times \text{distance}}$$

The *units* of work are obtained by multiplying a unit of force by a unit of distance. In elementary courses the most common units are the *foot-pound* (ft-lb), the *joule* (newton-meter), and the *erg* (dyne-cm). The abbreviation for joule is J.

Energy

In elementary physics *energy* is defined as the ability to do work. If an object does work, it has less energy left. In mechanics, work is done on an object 1. to give it potential energy, 2. to give it kinetic energy, 3. to overcome friction, 4. to accomplish a combination of the above three. Energy used to overcome friction is converted to heat. *Units* of energy are the same as units of work.

POTENTIAL ENERGY is the energy possessed by an object because of its position or its condition. If we lift an object we change its position with respect to the center of the earth; we do work against the force of gravity. As a result the lifted object has a greater ability to do work. This increased ability to do work is the object's potential energy with respect to its original position. This can be illustrated by referring to the diagram. Boys A and B have lifted the object of weight *w* a vertical distance *h*. The object now can do work: if A lets go, the object may now be able to lift B thus doing work on B. If *w* = 200 lb and *h* = 15 ft, the object gained a potential energy of 3000 ft-lb.

$$\text{gravitational potential energy} = wh$$

where *w* is the weight of the object and *h* is the vertical height through which it has been lifted. Remember, the potential energy is with respect to the original position. The object has a greater potential energy with respect to a level lower than the one shown in the diagram.

If a spring is compressed or stretched it also gains potential energy. This potential energy is equal to the work which was done in compressing or stretching the spring if frictional losses are neglected and is equal to the work which the spring can now do.

KINETIC ENERGY is the energy possessed by an object because of its motion. Winds (moving air) can do more work than stationary air, as in turning windmills, lifting roofs, etc. The kinetic energy of an object is proportional to the square of its speed. If a car's speed is changed from 30 km/h to 60 km/h, the car's kinetic energy has become four times as high. A 6000-kg truck moving at 30 km/h has twice as much kinetic energy as a 3000-kg car moving with the same speed. Kinetic energy is proportional to the mass of the object.

$$\text{kinetic energy} = \tfrac{1}{2} mv^2$$

PRINCIPLE OF CONSERVATION OF ENERGY Energy cannot be created or destroyed but may be changed from one form into another. Mass can be considered a form of energy as a consequence of Einstein's theory of relativity. When mass is converted to forms of energy such as heat, the

$$\text{energy produced} = mc^2$$

where *m* is the mass converted and *c* is the speed of light. When *m* is expressed in grams and *c* in centimeters per second (3×10^{10} cm/s), the energy will be expressed in ergs. When *m* is expressed in kilograms and *c* in meters per second (3×10^8 m/s), the energy is expressed in joules (J).

In a swinging pendulum kinetic energy is changed to potential energy and potential energy back to kinetic. If A is the highest position reached by the pendulum, the energy is all potential (= *wh*). At B it is all kinetic; at C the energy is partly potential and partly kinetic, and at D, the highest point reached on the other side, the energy is all potential again. If the pendulum has 10 J of potential energy at A (with respect to its lowest position), then the kinetic energy at B is 10 J, provided energy losses due to friction are negligible. The height reached at D is the same as it was at A. (We'll just note in passing that the motion of the bob is *not* motion with *constant* acceleration.) Energy losses due to friction result in the production of heat.

FRICTION AND WORK *Friction* is a force which always opposes motion or a tendency for motion. For example, in the figure, imagine a block resting on a horizontal surface. If a one-pound pull is applied toward the left and the object doesn't move, a one-pound force must be acting toward the right on the block. If the pull is increased to 2 lb and the block doesn't move, the force to the right must have increased to 2 lb. In each case the force to the right is friction, acting between the block and the surface on which it rests. Once sliding has been produced the force of friction is practically independent of the speed with which the block moves. Friction is also practically independent of the area of contact (unless it is pointlike). Friction does depend on the nature of the surfaces in contact and on the force pushing the surfaces together (the so-called *normal force*). The coefficient of friction is used to describe the surfaces:

Friction

$$\text{coefficient of sliding friction} = \frac{\text{force of friction during motion}}{\text{normal force}}$$

Example: A 30-N object is dragged along a horizontal surface for a distance of 10 m. If the coefficient of friction is 0.2, what is the minimum amount of work that must be done? In this case, the normal force is the weight of 30 N. Therefore, during motion, friction is $0.2 \times 30\,\text{N} = 6\,\text{N}$. Therefore, a pull of 6 N will maintain motion at constant speed and the work against friction is $6\,\text{N} \times 10\,\text{m} = 60$ *joules.* A larger force could be used (requiring more work); this would result in accelerated motion.

$$\text{work against friction} = \text{friction} \times \text{distance object moves}$$

Friction during rolling motion is usually less than during sliding motion, if the normal force is the same. In reference tables, therefore, we may find coefficients of rolling friction as well as coefficients of sliding friction.

When an object moves through a fluid (gas or liquid), the force of friction acting on the object does depend on the speed with which it moves through the fluid. For example, as rain drops fall through the atmosphere the frictional force acting on the rain drop increases as its speed increases, until the friction equals the weight of the raindrop. Maximum velocity is then reached and is known as the *limiting* or *terminal velocity.*

INCLINED PLANE Sometimes an inclined plane is used to slide heavy objects up to a platform or other elevated area. This is represented by the diagram in which the height to which the object must be raised is indicated by *h* and the length of the plane by *L*. The weight of the object is *w*, but a smaller

effort, force *F*, is required if we apply this effort parallel to the plane. It is shown a few pages later, under Simple Machines, that the following proportion is true when friction is negligible:

$$\frac{F}{w} = \frac{h}{L}$$

Since *h* is less than *L*, the length of the plane, the *force F* needed to push the object up along the plane at constant velocity is less than the weight of the object. However, we do not save work. The distance *L* along which the object must be pushed is proportionately larger than *h*, the vertical distance we want to raise the object.

Suppose the object weighs 1000 N . What is the minimum effort needed to slide the object up along the plane?

We could make a scale drawing and get a graphical solution. We could also substitute in the above proportion since we have all the information needed. A third method is useful if we know the angle of the plane with the horizontal, but some of the other information is missing. We notice that the ratio h/L is equal to the sine of angle A:

$$\frac{\text{force parallel to plane}}{\text{weight}} = \sin A$$

$$\frac{F}{w} = \sin A$$

$$F = w \sin A$$

In this example angle A is 30° and the weight w is 1000 N . Therefore

$$F = (1000 \text{ N }) (0.5) = 500 \text{ N}$$

If we apply an effort of 500 newtons parallel to the plane we can get the 1000-newton object to the top of the plane.

Suppose we get the object near the top of the incline and let go. We know that the object is going to slide down the plane with increasing speed. Why? Gravity, the weight of the object, pulls vertically. We can think of a component of the weight acting parallel to the plane (and another one acting perpendicular to the plane), F_1.

This component must be equal and opposite to F, which we just showed is equal to $w \sin A$. The reason for this is Newton's first law of motion. Then F was the force we needed to slide the object up with constant velocity. The object therefore was in equilibrium. Thus F was opposed by the equal and opposite component of the weight.

Below is a diagram summarizing forces most often encountered in inclined plane problems. The object shown is in equilibrium, as all forces are balanced. With inclined planes, the perpendicular components of interest are not horizontal and vertical. Note also that the scale of the force vectors is independent of the inclined plane. (In the case shown, the weight vector drops below the horizontal line.)

w = weight of object = mg
F_1 = component of weight acting parallel to plane
F_2 = component of weight acting perpendicular to plane
−w = contact force of plane on object
F_3 = component of contact force perpendicular to plane
F_4 = component of contact force parallel to plane

Forces on an Object in Equilibrium on an Inclined Plane

ELASTICITY AND HOOKE'S LAW

Work is sometimes done by forces which do not remain constant. The most common such forces arise from *springs*. The stretch or compression of a spring is proportional to the applied force ($F = kx$). The constant of proportionality, k, is called the *spring constant*. It tells how much force is required to stretch a spring one unit length. For example, if a 1 N object suspended from a spring stretches it 3 cm, a 2 N object will stretch it 6 cm. Its spring constant $= \dfrac{1N}{3\,cm} = \dfrac{1}{3}\dfrac{N}{cm}$ or $k = 33\,\dfrac{N}{m}$, in SI units.

The work done in stretching or compressing a spring is proportional to the square of the elongation. This work is stored as elastic potential energy.

$$\text{elastic potential energy} = \frac{1}{2}kx^2$$

Power

Power is the rate of doing work.

$$\text{power} = \frac{\text{work}}{\text{time}}$$

in which we divide the work done by the time required to do the work. Since work is calculated by multiplying the force used (to do the work) by the distance the force moves,

$$\text{power} = \frac{\text{force} \times \text{distance}}{\text{time}}$$

Units for this chapter. Memorize the first row.

System	Work or Energy	Power
SI	N•m or joule	J/s or watt
CGS	dyne•cm or erg	erg/s
English	ft•lb	ft•lb/sec or horsepower*

* Units only: 1 hp = 550 ft•lb/sec = 746 watts

SIMPLE MACHINES *

Probably the most direct way of doing useful work on an object is to take hold of it and lift it. This is often difficult or inconvenient, and we turn to machines to help us. A *machine* is a device which will transfer a force from one point of application to another for some practical advantage. For example, we may want to lift a flag to the top of a pole. It is inconvenient to climb to the top of the pole each day and pull the flag up. Instead, we keep a pulley at the top of the pole and with the aid of a rope apply a downward force at A and produce an upward force on the flag at B. We have six *simple machines:* pulley, lever, wheel and axle, inclined plane, screw, and wedge. The force which we apply to the machine in order to do the work (such as at A in the above case) is known as the *effort*, F_E. The force which we have to overcome (such as the weight at B) is known as the *resistance*, F_R.

---

*Not taught in some courses. See Introduction.

Mechanical Advantage

The *actual mechanical advantage* (AMA) of a machine is the ratio of the resistance to the effort. If we want to lift a weight of 400 lb and need to exert an effort of only 100 lb, the AMA is 4.

$$\text{actual mechanical advantage} = \frac{\text{resistance}}{\text{actual effort}}$$
$$AMA = \frac{F_R}{F_E}$$

If we are interested in lifting an object, the *useful work* done with the machine, or the *work output,* or work accomplished, is equal to the weight of the object multiplied by the distance the object is lifted. In general,

$$\text{work output} = \text{resistance} \times \text{distance resistance moves}$$
$$\text{work output} = F_R s_R$$

In order to accomplish this work the effort must move a certain distance, s_E. The *work input* is the work done by the effort.

$$\text{work input} = \text{effort} \times \text{distance effort moves}$$
$$\text{work input} = F_E s_E$$

Under ideal conditions there is no useless work, such as work done in overcoming friction. Then,

$$\text{work output} = \text{work input}$$
$$\frac{F_R}{F_E} = \frac{s_E}{s_R} = IMA$$

where IMA is ideal mechanical advantage.

Note that for a given machine the ratio of the two distances is not affected by anything we do to change friction in the machine; it give us the ideal mechanical advantage even if there is friction. The ratio of the two forces is affected by friction, since for a given situation the required effort is decreased by decreasing friction. The ratio of the two forces gives us the actual mechanical advantage, but if friction is negligible, the actual mechanical advantage equals the ideal mechanical advantage.

Efficiency

With an actual machine some useless work must be done, such as work to overcome friction. The input work equals work output plus useless work. For a machine

$$\text{efficiency} = \frac{\text{work output}}{\text{work input}}$$

Sometimes these derived formulas are useful in problems with machines:

$$\text{efficiency} = \frac{AMA}{IMA}; \quad \text{efficiency} = \frac{\text{ideal effort}}{\text{actual effort}}$$

The Lever

When we use crowbars, bottle openers, or oars, we are using the simple machine known as the lever. A *lever* is a rigid bar free to turn about a fixed point known as the *fulcrum* or pivot. The things we said about the principle of moments (Chapter 1) apply to the lever. The oar can rotate around *P.* We pull on the oar handle at *A* and as a result a push is exerted on the water at *B* by the oar blade. We represent this schematically in the diagram. The fulcrum P is represented by a triangle; the pull we apply is the effort, F_E; the push *by the water* on the oar is our resistance, F_R. The moment arms are D_E and D_R, respectively. They are also called *lever arms*. From the principle of moments, $F_E D_E = F_R D_R$. From this we see that $\dfrac{F_R}{F_E} = \dfrac{D_E}{D_R}$, which gives us the mechanical advantage of the lever.

If the effort lever arm is greater than the resistance lever arm, the mechanical advantage is greater than one. In the case of the lever we often want a mechanical advantage of less than one. This, for example, is true in the above illustration of rowing a boat. The effort is greater than the resistance of the water, but as a result the handle at A moves a shorter distance than the blade does during each stroke, as indicated by the dotted lines in the diagram. This gives us a speed advantage when the ideal mechanical advantage is less than one. (The discussion of the boat is somewhat simplified, because in the actual boat the pivot moves with respect to the water.)

Notice, therefore, that the ideal mechanical advantage of a lever depends on where the fulcrum is located with respect to the points where the effort and resistance, respectively, are applied. The IMA may be less than one, greater than one, or equal to one. In the table below are shown three different arrangements of fulcrum (P), effort (F_E), and resistance (F_R). Look at the diagrams and, thinking in terms of the possible lengths of the lever arms, see if you can figure out the possible values of the IMA. Then compare your result with the table. It is not necessary to remember what class of lever each case represents.

LEVERS			
Class	Diagram	Characteristic	IMA
1st		P between F_E & F_R	$MA \gtreqless 1$
2nd		F_R between P & F_E	$MA > 1$
3rd		F_E between P & F_R	$MA < 1$

The Inclined Plane

When heavy objects have to be raised to a platform or put into a truck, it is often found to be convenient to slide these objects up along a board. An *inclined plane* is a flat surface one end of which is kept at a higher level than the other. F_E, the effort to pull or push the object up, is usually applied parallel to the plane. The input work, or work done by the effort, equals F_E times the length of the plane, L. The work output equals the weight of the object w times the height of the plane, h. Under ideal conditions the input work equals the output work, and, therefore,

$$\frac{\text{weight of object}}{\text{ideal effort}} = \frac{\text{length of plane}}{\text{height of plane}} = \text{IMA}$$

Under actual conditions friction opposes the motion. When the object is *moved up* the plane, the actual effort equals the ideal effort plus the force of friction. On the other hand, less force is required to keep the object from sliding down, and, when the object is allowed to *slide down* with constant speed, the effort applied up along the plane equals the ideal effort *minus* the force of friction.

(Occasionally the effort might be applied parallel to the base of the plane. Then the IMA equals the base of the plane divided by the height of the plane.)

Example: An inclined plane 13 m long and 5 m high is used to lift a 390-N object to a platform. The ideal MA is 13/5 or 2.6; the ideal effort parallel to the plane is 390 N $\times$ 5/13 or 150 N. Actually 200 N may be required; then the force of friction is 50 N. The AMA = weight/effort, or 390 N/200 N. Therefore the AMA = 1.95. The useful work = $w \times h$ = 390 N $\times$ 5 m = 1950 J. The input work = $F_E \times L$ = 200 N $\times$ 13 m = 2600 J. The efficiency equals

$$\frac{\text{output work}}{\text{input work}} = \frac{1950 \text{ J}}{2600 \text{ J}} = 0.75 \text{ or } 75\%$$

Note that efficiency also equals

$$\frac{\text{ideal effort}}{\text{actual effort}} = \frac{150 \text{ N}}{200 \text{ N}} = 0.75$$

The Pulley

Especially when heavy objects have to be lifted through a considerable distance, the pulley is a convenient simple machine for the job. The *pulley* is a wheel so mounted in a frame that it may turn readily around the axis through the center of the wheel. If the frame and wheel move through space as the pulley is used, we have a *movable pulley*. Otherwise we say we have a fixed pulley. The wheel is usually grooved to guide the string or rope which is used with it. The term *block and tackle* is used for the commercial assemblage of pulleys and rope.

The ideal mechanical advantage of pulleys can be figured out by determining the distance the effort has to move for every foot the resistance is moved. The IMA = s_E/s_R. For many common pulley arrangeemtns this ideal mechanical advantage can be determined visually by counting the number of rope segments supporting the movable puilley(s). Some typical pulley arrangements are shown below. You should be able to reproduce the diagrams quickly from memory and to determine their IMAs.

Single fixed — IMA = 1
Single movable — IMA = 2
Single fixed, single movable — IMA = 2
Two fixed, single movable — IMA = 3

Note that in these diagrams the rope segments are numbered to show how the ideal mechanical advantage can be determined visually from the diagram; the effort is applied to one end of the string while the other end of the string is attached to the weight to be lifted, to the pulley frame, or to a rigid support such as the ceiling. The weight to be lifted (*w*) represents the resistance if we neglect the weight of the movable pulleys and friction.

Example: A system of pulleys having an IMA of three is used to lift an object weighing 600 lb. The effort required is 300 lb. What is the efficiency? The ideal effort = (F_R/IMA) = (weight/IMA) = (600 lb/3) = 200 lb. The efficiency = (ideal effort/actual effort) = (200 lb)/(300 lb) = 2/3 or 66.7%.

QUESTIONS Chapter 3

Select the choice that best completes the sentence.

1. If the speed of an object is tripled, its kinetic energy is **(A)** 1/9   **(B)** 1/3   **(C)** 3   **(D)** 6   **(E)** 9 times its original speed.

For 2-4. A person having a mass of 60 kg exerts a horizontal force of 200 N in pushing a 90-kg object a distance of 6 meters along a horizontal floor. He does this at constant velocity in 3 seconds.

2. The weight of this person is approximately, in newtons, **(A)** 40   **(B)** 90   **(C)** 200   **(D)** 400 **(E)** 600

3. The work done by this person is, in joules, **(A)** 540   **(B)** 1080   **(C)** 1200   **(D)** 3600   **(E)** 5400

4. The force of friction is **(A)** exactly 60 N   **(B)** between 60 and 90 N   **(C)** exactly 90 N   **(D)** exactly 200 N   **(E)** greater than 200 N

For 5-6. The 1000-lb weight of a pile driver falls freely from rest; it drops 25 ft and strikes a steel beam and drives it 3 inches into the ground.

5. The kinetic energy of the weight of the pile driver just before it hits the beam is, in ft-lb, **(A)** 3000 **(B)** 25,000   **(C)** 75,000   **(D)** 200,000   **(E)** 800,000

6. The speed of the weight just before hitting the beam is, in ft/sec, approximately **(A)** 0.25   **(B)** 3 **(C)** 25   **(D)** 40   **(E)** 64

For 7-9. An inclined plane 5 m long has one end on the ground and the other end on a platform 3 m high. A man weighing 650 N wishes to push a 900-N object up this plane. The force of friction is 100 N.

7. The minimum force he must exert is, in N, approximately **(A)** 100   **(B)** 540   **(C)** 640   **(D)** 900 **(E)** 1000

8. In order to hold the object on the plane without letting it slide, the minimum force required is, in N, approximately **(A)** 0   **(B)** 100   **(C)** 440   **(D)** 540   **(E)** 640

9. The potential energy gained by the object when it is at the top of the plane is, in joules, **(A)** 100 **(B)** 324   **(C)** 2700   **(D)** 5400   **(E)** 9000

10. The power expended by the man in pushing the object to the top of the plane in 3 seconds is **(A)** 400 watts   **(B)** 800 watts   **(C)** 1070 watts   **(D)** 4500 watts   **(E)** 4500 joules

11. Within normal limits of use, if a 100-g object stretches a spring 3 cm, a 200-g object will stretch the spring, in cm, **(A)** $3 \times \sqrt{2}$ **(B)** 3×2 **(C)** 3^2 **(D)** 3×2^2 **(E)** $3^2 \times 2^2$

12. A uniform plank 1.0 m long weighs 50 N. The force needed to lift one end of the plank is, in N, **(A)** 10   **(B)** 12.5   **(C)** 25   **(D)** 50   **(E)** 100

For 13–16. The pulley arrangement shown is attached to a ceiling. A weight of 240 lb is to be lifted. The weight of the pulleys is negligible.

13. If frictional losses are negligible, the force *F* required to lift the weight at constant speed is **(A)** 48 lb   **(B)** 60 lb   **(C)** 80 lb   **(D)** 120 lb   **(E)** 240 lb

14. For the conditions in problem 13, the pull on the ceiling will be **(A)** 60 lb **(B)** 120 lb   **(C)** 240 lb   **(D)** 288 lb   **(E)** 300 lb

15. For the conditions in problem 13, the tension in the rope at *X* will be **(A)** 48 lb   **(B)** 60 lb   **(C)** 80 lb   **(D)** 120 lb   **(E)** 240 lb

16. If the actual force *F* is 180 lb, the efficiency of the system is **(A)** 25 **(B)** 35   **(C)** 50   **(D)** 75   **(E)** 90

EXPLANATIONS TO QUESTIONS Chapter 3

Answers

1. **(E)**	4. **(D)**	7. **(C)**	10. **(C)**	13. **(B)**	16. **(B)**
2. **(E)**	5. **(B)**	8. **(C)**	11. **(B)**	14. **(E)**	
3. **(C)**	6. **(D)**	9. **(C)**	12. **(C)**	15. **(B)**	

Explanations

1. **(E)** Kinetic energy $= \frac{1}{2} mv^2$. For a given object the kinetic energy is proportional to the square of its speed. When the speed is multiplied by 3, the kinetic energy is multiplied by 3^2, or 9.

2. **(E)** The weight of an object on earth is the gravitational pull of the earth on it and is equal to the product of the object's mass and the value of the acceleration of a freely falling object:

$$\text{weight} = mg$$
$$= (60 \text{ kg}) (9.8 \text{ m/s}^2)$$
$$= 600 \text{ N}$$

3. **(C)** Work done on an object is equal to the product of the force exerted on the object and the distance moved in the direction of the force:

$$\text{work} = \text{force} \times \text{distance}$$
$$= (200 \text{ N}) (6 \text{ m})$$
$$= 1200 \text{ joules}$$

4. **(D)** Since the force exerted is horizontal, none of it is used to overcome gravity. Also, since the velocity remains constant, none of the force (and work done) is used to give the object kinetic energy. Therefore all of the 200-N force used is required to overcome friction.

5. **(B)** The kinetic energy which the weight has just before it hits is equal to the potential energy it had at the top just before falling. The potential energy at the top = weight × height;

$$\text{pot. en.} = 1000 \text{ lb} \times 25 \text{ ft} = 25,000 \text{ ft-lb}.$$

6. **(D)** To calculate the speed of an object falling freely from rest if we know the distance of fall:

$$v^2 = 2gs = 2 \times 32 \text{ ft/sec}^2 \times 25 \text{ ft} = 64 \times 25 \text{ ft}^2/\text{sec}^2$$
$$v = (8 \times 5) \text{ ft/sec} = 40 \text{ ft/sec}$$

7. **(C)** The man has to overcome two forces: the force of friction and the component of the weight parallel to the plane.

$$\frac{\text{parallel component}}{\text{weight}} = \frac{\text{height of plane}}{\text{length of plane}}$$

$$\frac{\text{parallel component}}{900 \text{ N}} = \frac{3 \text{ m}}{5 \text{ m}}$$

and the parallel component = 540 N. Force required = 100 N + 540 N = 640 N.

8. **(C)** Friction will help in keeping the object from sliding down. The required force, therefore, is equal to the parallel component minus the force of friction = 540 N − 100 N = 440 N.

9. **(C)** Pot. energy = weight × height = 900 N × 3 m = 2700 joules.

10. **(C)** Power is the rate of doing work: Power = work/time. The work done by the man is equal to the product of the force required and the distance the object is moved in the direction of the force (which in this case is parallel to the plane).

$$\text{work} = \text{force} \times \text{distance}$$
$$= (640 \text{ N})(5 \text{ m})$$
$$= 3200 \text{ joules}$$

$$\text{power} = \frac{\text{work}}{\text{time}} = \frac{3200 \text{ joules}}{3 \text{ seconds}} = 1070 \text{ watts}$$

(Note that the work required is greater than the potential energy gained because work had to be done against friction as well as to raise the object against gravity.)

11. **(B)** According to Hooke's law, the distortion is proportional to the distorting force. Since the distorting force is doubled, the distortion is also doubled.

12. **(C)** The fulcrum is at one end, at the left in the diagram. The center of gravity of a uniform plank is in the middle; the weight of 50 N acts downward 0.5 m from either end. Counterclockwise moment = clockwise moment; $10F = 50\ N \times 0.5\ m$; $F = 25\ N$.

13. **(B)** There are 4 strands supporting the movable pulleys; therefore the ideal mechanical advantage is 4.

$$\text{Then IMA} = \frac{\text{weight of object}}{\text{ideal effort}}, \text{ and ideal effort} = \frac{\text{weight of object}}{\text{IMA}}$$

$$= 240\ \text{lb}/4 = 60\ \text{lb}$$

14. **(E)** If the weight of the pulleys is negligible, there are two basic forces pulling on the ceiling; force F and the 240-lb object. Pull on ceiling = 60 lb + 240 lb = 300 lb.

15. **(B)** Each of the 4 strands supporting the movable pulleys supplies $1/4$ of the upward pull on the weight or $1/4$ of 240 lb. Another way to look at it is to think of the force F as transmitted throughout the rope and therefore being equal to the tension.

16. **(B)** $\text{Efficiency} = \dfrac{\text{ideal effort}}{\text{actual effort}} = \dfrac{60\ \text{lb}}{180\ \text{lb}} = 33\%$

Fluid Mechanics

A piece of iron is put into a beaker partly filled with mercury. To what depth will the iron sink? Oil is poured on top of the mercury. How does this affect the pressure on the iron? How does it change the depth of the iron in the mercury? To answer these questions we need to consider the behavior of fluids.

The term *fluid* refers to both gases and liquids. A *solid* has definite shape and volume. A *liquid* has definite volume but it takes the shape of its container; its top surface tends to be horizontal (also see *meniscus* on page 43). A *gas* has neither definite shape nor volume and expands to fill any container into which it is put. A cubic foot of concrete weighs more than a cubic foot of water. We say the concrete is denser than the water. The *density* of a substance is the mass of a unit volume.

$$\text{density} = \frac{\text{mass}}{\text{volume}}$$

A solid tends to sink in a liquid of lesser density and to float in one of greater density. The units for density consist of a unit of mass divided by a unit of volume, such as g/cm^3, kg/m^3. Instead of speaking about the density of a substance, it has been found more convenient to speak about its relative density, or density compared to a standard. This is its *specific gravity* (sp. gr.). The standard for solids and liquids is water. The density of water is usually taken as $1 \ g/cm^3$. For solids and liquids

$$\text{sp. gr.} = \frac{\text{density of substance}}{\text{density of water}}$$

$$\text{sp. gr.} = \frac{\text{weight of substance}}{\text{weight of equal volume of water}}$$

$$\text{sp. gr.} = \frac{\text{mass of substance}}{\text{mass of equal volume of water}}$$

The specific gravity of mercury is 13.6; this means that 1 cubic centimeter of mercury has a mass of 13.6 g and that 1 cubic foot of mercury weighs (13.6×62.5) lb.

LIQUID PRESSURE

Fluids push against the container in which they are placed. *Pressure* is the force per unit area.

$$p = \frac{F}{A}$$

The liquid inside a *beaker* exerts a force on the bottom of the beaker because of its weight, *mg*. Therefore, the liquid pressure in this case is equal to the weight of the liquid divided by the area of the bottom of the beaker. A little algebra leads to another relationship: the pressure due to a liquid is equal to the height of the liquid (*h*) times its density (*d*) and *g*. This is true not only on the bottom of the container but also on the sides at any depth of the liquid.

$$p = hdg$$

$$F = hdgA$$

By combining the above two expressions for *liquid pressure* we find that on a horizontal area in a liquid the force due to the liquid (*F*) is equal to the height of the liquid times its density times *g* times the area on which the liquid pushes. Notice that, if the three vessels shown are filled with the same liquid to the same depth, the liquid pressure on the bottom will be the same; if the bottom area is the same, the force on the bottom will be the same although the weights of liquid in the three vessels will be different. Liquid pressure is independent of the size or shape of the container; it depends only on the depth and density of the liquid. *Example:* A tank is filled with water to a depth of 3 m. The bottom of the tank has an area of 10 m². What is the water pressure on the bottom of the tank?

$$p = hdg = (3 \text{ m}) (10^3 \text{ kg/m}^3) (9.8 \text{ m/s}^2) = 2.9 \times 10^4 \text{ N/m}^2$$

What is the force exerted on the bottom of the tank?

$$F = pA = (2.9 \times 10^4 \text{ N/m}^2) (10 \text{ m}^2) = 2.9 \times 10^5 \text{ N}$$

The SI unit for pressure is the pascal (Pa).

$$1 \text{ Pa} = 1 \frac{\text{N}}{\text{m}^2}$$

THE ATMOSPHERE AND GASEOUS PRESSURE

Gases have weight but their densities are less than those of liquids and solids. Gases exert pressure. The atmosphere is a mixture of gases. At sea level the pressure due to the atmosphere is about 14.7 lb/in². The air therefore exerts a force of more than 100 lb on the palm of one's hand. Imagine a U-tube partly filled with mercury. The tube is open at the top on both sides. The mercury is at the same level in both sides since a given liquid will reach the same level in connected open containers. The air exerts the same pressure on the surface of the mercury in each arm. However, if air is pumped out of the right arm the greater pressure in the left arm pushes mercury around into the right arm until the pressure due to the excess mercury (= *hdg*) is equal to the difference in the air pressures in the two arms. If all the air were pumped out of the arm on the right, the difference in the levels of the mercury in the two arms (*h*) would become about 30 inches or 76 cm. This is the principle of the mercury barometer. A *mercury barometer* is made by filling with mercury a glass tube about one meter long.

The air must be removed from the mercury. The tube is then inverted so that the open end will be below the level of some more mercury in a reservoir. Some mercury will flow out of the tube until the height of the mercury column is about 76 cm—a height whose pressure is equal to the pressure of the atmosphere which supports it. The atmospheric pressure is not constant. Its variation is used to aid in weather forecasting. A rising pressure usually indicates the approach of fair weather.

Standard pressure is the pressure of a column of mercury 760 mm high. This is enough to support a column of water 34 ft or about 10 m high. The atmospheric pressure decreases with altitude. Near the surface of the earth the barometer reading drops about 0.1 inch for every rise in altitude of 90 ft. *Aneroid* barometers do not use any liquid. They are sealed, partially evacuated cans. The variation in atmospheric pressure causes the deflection of a needle across a calibrated scale. Such barometers can be used conveniently as *altimeters* to measure altitude.

We can calculate the *standard atmospheric pressure*, that is, the pressure due to a column of mercury 76.0 cm high.

$$p = hdg$$
$$= (76.0 \text{ cm})(13.6 \text{ g/cm}^3)(980 \text{ cm/s}^2) = 10.1 \times 10^5 \text{ dynes/cm}^2 = 10.1 \text{ N/cm}^2 = 1.01 \times 10^5 \text{ Pa}$$

PASCAL'S PRINCIPLE

$$p = \frac{f}{a} = \frac{F}{A} = p$$

$$F = W$$

Pressure applied to a confined fluid is transmitted through the liquid without loss and acts perpendicularly on the surface of the container. For example, consider the hydraulic press shown. A small force (*f*) is applied to the piston of small area (*a*). This produces a pressure (*p*) on the enclosed fluid and this same pressure is transmitted by the fluid to act on the underside of the large piston, whose area is *A*. The resulting force ($F = pA$) is larger than *f* and is able to support the large weight *W*.

The hydraulic press can be thought of as a machine with *f* representing the effort and *F* the resistance (equal to the weight). The mechanical advantage is the ratio of resistance to effort. Therefore,

$$\text{IMA} = \frac{F}{f} = \frac{A}{a} = \frac{(\text{diameter of large piston})^2}{(\text{diameter of small piston})^2}$$

Example: The areas of the pistons of a hydraulic press are 50 in.² and 2 in.², respectively. If a force of 3 lb is applied to the small piston, how large a weight can be supported by the large piston?

$$\frac{F}{f} = \frac{A}{a} \quad \text{or} \quad \frac{F}{3 \text{ lb}} = \frac{50 \text{ in.}^2}{2 \text{ in.}^2} \quad \text{or} \quad F = 75 \text{ lb} = W$$

ARCHIMEDES' PRINCIPLE

The apparent loss in weight of an object immersed in a fluid equals the weight of the displaced fluid. When an object is placed in a fluid, some of the fluid is pushed out of the way—that is, some of

the fluid is displaced. This is so because no two objects can occupy the same space at the same time (impenetrability of matter). In the case of an object that is fully *submerged*, like object *A*, the *volume* of fluid displaced equals the volume of the object. A stone held in water appears lighter than when held in air. The apparent loss in *weight* equals the weight of the displaced fluid (Archimedes). (Remember: in air, $w = mg$; see p. 20.)

Assume that in the above diagram object *A* is submerged in water and that object *B* floats in the water. The pull that object *A* exerts on the spring is less than if *A* were in air. We can think of the water as exerting an upward push on the object. This upward push of a fluid on an object immersed in it is the buoyant force of the fluid or its *buoyancy*. The apparent loss in weight equals the buoyancy.

Example: Object *A* weighs (50 grams) (*g*) in air and (30 grams) (*g*) in water. Since the apparent loss in weight is 20 (grams) (*g*), the weight of the displaced water also is (20 grams) (*g*). Since the density of water is 1 g/cm³, the volume of water displaced is 20 cm³. Therefore the volume of object *A* is 20 cm³.

If an object, like *B, floats* in water, it appears to weigh nothing. The *weight* of the displaced fluid equals the weight of the object in vacuum. (If the fluid is a liquid, instead of using the object's weight in vacuum we use the object's weight in air.) Notice that the *volume* of the displaced liquid is less than the volume of the object.

Archimedes' principle can be applied to finding the specific gravity of solids and liquids. The specific gravity of a solid or a liquid equals its weight divided by the weight of an equal volume of water. A solid submerged in water displaces a volume of water equal to the volume of the solid; the weight of this equal volume of water is equal to the apparent loss in weight of the solid. Therefore, for a *solid that sinks in water*

$$\text{sp. gr.} = \frac{\textbf{weight in air}}{\textbf{apparent loss of weight in water}}$$

The specific gravity of a liquid can be found by using a solid that sinks in the unknown liquid as well as in water. The solid must be insoluble in both. The object displaces the same volume in water as in the unknown liquid. The solid's apparent loss of weight in water equals the weight of the displaced water; the solid's apparent loss of weight in the unknown liquid equals the weight of the same volume of the liquid. Therefore, for a *liquid,*

$$\text{sp. gr.} = \frac{\textbf{apparent loss in weight of solid in liquid}}{\textbf{apparent loss in weight of solid in water}}$$

The specific gravity of liquids can also be found by using a *hydrometer*. It floats higher in denser liquids and has a scale on it that gives specific gravity directly. Another instrument for measuring specific gravity of liquids is the pycnometer or bottle of known volume. (A *hygrometer* is used for measuring relative humidity of the atmosphere.)

The apparent loss in weight due to the buoyant effect of gases can usually be neglected. However, the rising of balloons depends on this. The lifting force of the gas in a balloon is equal to the weight of the air displaced by the balloon minus the weight of the gas in the gas bags.

Now let us consider the question asked at the beginning of the chapter. The iron (sp. gr. about 7.6) will float in the mercury (sp. gr. about 13.6). Therefore the iron will sink until the weight of the mercury it displaces equals its own weight. (Also, the volume of the displaced mercury equals the volume of the iron which is below the level of the mercury. If the iron has the shape of a rectangular solid, such as a cube, this volume equals the area of the base times the depth.)

When oil is poured on top of the mercury, the iron rises somewhat out of the mercury as shown in the diagram on the right. The reason for this is that the oil (sp. gr. usually less than one) floats on top of the mercury and pushes down on it. According to Pascal's Principle this push is transmitted in all directions and therefore results in an upward push on the underside of the iron. Note that this is true even when enough oil is poured in to cover the iron. The iron will rise until the buoyant force due to the displaced oil plus the buoyant force due to the displaced mercury equal the weight of the iron.

SURFACE TENSION AND CAPILLARY ACTION

Steel ships can float because they are filled with air. Yet it is possible to "float" a flat sheet of metal. If we gently place a double-edge razor blade on top of some water so that the flat surface of the blade is in contact with the surface of the water, we notice that the blade "floats" in spite of the high density of steel. Careful examination shows that this is *not* an example of buoyancy. The blade does not actually penetrate the surface of the water. The surface of the water acts as though it were a thin elastic membrane; this phenomenon is referred to as surface tension.

Surface tension is explained by noting that a molecule at the surface has neighbors different from a molecule in the body of the liquid. The latter is surrounded by molecules of its own kind, which attract it equally in all directions. The molecule at the surface of the water is not attracted by any water molecules above it (attraction by molecules in the air is negligible); it is attracted by molecules below and to the side of it. This leads to an unbalanced force tending to pull the molecule down. This contracting force on the surface of the liquid tends to keep the molecules together, thus opposing penetration.

If water is poured out of a beaker, the inside of the beaker remains wet even if we try to shake the excess out of the beaker. This indicates that the molecules of water are attracted by the molecules in glass. The force of attraction between molecules of different substances is called *adhesion*. *Cohesion* is the force of attraction between molecules of the same substance. Cohesion in solids is often quite great—it is very difficult to pull steel apart. Since water wets glass we deduce that the adhesion between water and glass is greater than cohesion of water.

Water

Mercury

If we examine the surface of the water in a glass, we find that it is not perfectly flat. We may notice that at the edges the water is slightly curved upward. If we use mercury instead of water we notice that the edges are slightly curved downward. The slight lifting of the water at the edges is due to the fact that the adhesion between water and glass is greater than the cohesion of the water. In the case of the mercury the cohesion is greater than the adhesion.

If we insert tubes of small diameter into the liquids, we notice that the level of the liquid inside the tube is different from the level outside. If the liquid wets the tube, the liquid rises in it; otherwise the liquid is depressed in it. *The smaller the diameter of the tube, the greater is the rise* (or depression) *of the liquid in it.* This phenomenon is known as *capillary action.* (Capiliary means hair-like; tubes of small diameter are known as capillary tubes.) Capillary action is not fully explained. Adhesion, cohesion, and surface tension must play a part. The curved surface of a liquid column is called *meniscus.*

BERNOULLI'S PRINCIPLE

If the speed of a fluid is increased, its pressure is decreased. This principle is made use of in the design of airplane wings to give the plane lift. The wing is designed so that the air will move faster over the top of the wing than across the bottom. As a result, the air pressure on top of the wing is less than on the bottom, with the consequence that the upward push of the air on the wing is greater than the downward push. (In applying the principle, it usually helps to think of *sidewise* pressure as decreased when the speed of the fluid is increased.)

Remember the following:

$1 m^3 = 10^6 cm^3$

mass of 1 cm^3 of water = 1 g

density of water = 1 g/cm^3 = 10^3kg/m^3

mass of 1 m^3 of water = 10^6 g = 10^3 kg

QUESTIONS Chapter 4

Select the choice that best completes the sentence.

1. Pressure exerted by a gas on the walls of its container is due to **(A)** adhesion between the gas molecules and the container **(B)** cohesion between the gas molecules and the container **(C)** collision between the gas molecules and the container **(D)** surface tension of the gas **(E)** gravitational pull on the gas

2. The term *Brownian movement* refers to **(A)** irregular motions of small particles suspended in a fluid **(B)** convection currents in a liquid or gas **(C)** convection currents in a gas but not in a liquid **(D)** the stretching of a body beyond its elastic limit **(E)** the sinking of mercury in capillary tubes

For 3–4. A rectangular piece of metal, whose dimensions are 5 cm × 20 cm × 30 cm, is submerged in a liquid. The sp. gr. of the metal is 7.0. The sp. gr. of the liquid is 2.0.

3. The mass of the block is **(A)** 3000 g **(B)** 3000 lb **(C)** 21,000 g **(D)** 21,000 lb **(E)** 210,000 lb

4. The apparent loss in weight of the block in the liquid is **(A)** 30 N **(B)** 60 N **(C)** 15 N **(D)** 21 N **(E)** 21,000 N

5. Two insoluble objects seem to lose the same weight when completely submerged in a liquid. The objects must have the same **(A)** weight in air **(B)** weight in the liquid **(C)** weight in water **(D)** density **(E)** volume

6. If an object weighs 90 N in air, 60 N in water, and 20 N in an unknown liquid in which it does not dissolve, the sp. gr. of the unknown liquid is **(A)** 1.3 **(B)** 1.5 **(C)** 2.3 **(D)** 3.0 **(E)** 4.5

7. The density of water is 10^3 kg/m^3. The water pressure on a submarine is 2.0×10^7 N/m^2. The depth of the submarine below the surface of the water, in meters, is approximately **(A)** 200 **(B)** 1000 **(C)** 2000 **(D)** 8000 **(E)** 11,000

8. The force exerted by the fluid in a hydraulic press on the piston is 2000 N. If the area of the piston is 10 cm^2, the fluid pressure on the piston is, in N/cm^2, **(A)** 20 **(B)** 200 **(C)** 2000 **(D)** 20,000 **(E)** 200,000

9. The column of mercury in a mercury barometer is 76 cm high on a certain day when the barometer is vertical. If the barometer is tilted a few degrees, the vertical height of the mercury column, *h*, is **(A)** still 76 cm **(B)** 76 cm minus the angle **(C)** 76 cm minus a function of the angle **(D)** 76 cm plus the angle **(E)** 76 cm plus a function of the angle

10. If water rises 4 cm in a long, thin tube because of capillary action, then, under corresponding conditions of use, the rise (in the tube) of a liquid whose density is 2 g/cm^3 will be **(A)** 1 cm **(B)** 2 cm **(C)** 8 cm **(D)** 16 cm **(E)** unpredictable with the given information

11. A container has a small hole in the bottom. Air can go through this hole, but water cannot. This can be best explained by the statement that **(A)** water contains hydrogen atoms, air does not **(B)** water molecules are larger than molecules in the air **(C)** water molecules are smaller than molecules in the air **(D)** water is more viscous than air **(E)** surface tension of the water prevents it from escaping

12. The two thin tubes which show most correctly the behavior of water are **(A)** 1 and 2 **(B)** 2 and 3 **(C)** 3 and 4 **(D)** 4 and 5 **(E)** 1 and 4

EXPLANATIONS TO QUESTIONS Chapter 4

Answers

1. **(C)**	4. **(B)**	7. **(E)**	10. **(E)**
2. **(A)**	5. **(E)**	8. **(B)**	11. **(E)**
3. **(C)**	6. **(C)**	9. **(A)**	12. **(A)**

Explanations

1. **(C)** According to the kinetic theory, the molecules of a gas collide with the walls of the container. Each collision exerts a push on the container. The effect of so many collisions is to produce a rather constant force. This force, divided by the area of the container on which it acts, produces the pressure of the gas.

2. **(A)** As described in the chapter, Brownian movement refers to the erratic movement of small particles suspended in a fluid. The movement results from the collision with the unseen but constantly moving molecules of the fluid.

3. **(C)** A simple exercise! Since density = mass/volume, the mass = density × volume. The volume of the block = length × width × height = $(5 \times 20 \times 30)$ cm^3 = 3000 cm^3. Since the sp. gr. of the metal is 7.0, its density is 7.0 g/cm^3. Therefore, mass = 7.0 g/cm^3 × 3000 cm^3 = 21,000 g. Its weight = $(21 \text{ kg})(9.8 \text{ m/s}^2) \doteq 210$ N.

4. **(B)** Apparent loss in weight = wt. of displaced fluid. Volume of displaced fluid = vol. of submerged block = 3000 cm^3.
Wt of 3000 cm^3 of water = $mg = (3 \text{ kg})(9.8 \text{ m/s}^2) \doteq 30$ N
Wt of displaced fluid = sp. gr. × wt of equal vol. of water = 2.0(30N) = 60 N

5. **(E)** Archimedes' principle: The apparent loss in weight is equal to the weight of the displaced fluid. Both displace equal weights of the same fluid; therefore, both displace equal volumes of the same fluid. But the volume each displaces is equal to the volume of the object. Therefore, both objects must have the same volume.

6. **(C)** sp. gr. of liquid

$$= \frac{\text{apparent loss of weight in liquid}}{\text{apparent loss of weight in water}} = \frac{90 \text{ N} - 20 \text{ N}}{90 \text{ N} - 60 \text{ N}}$$

$$= \frac{70 \text{ N}}{30 \text{ N}} = 2.3$$

7. **(E)** pressure = depth × density × acceleration due to gravity (g)

$$\text{depth} = \frac{p}{dg} = \frac{2.0 \times 10^7 \text{N/m}^2}{(10^3 \text{kg/m}^3)(9.8 \text{ m/s}^2)} \doteq 2000 \text{ m}$$

8. **(B)** $p = F/A = (2000 \text{ N})/(10 \text{ cm}^2) = 200$ N/cm^2

9. **(A)** Recall Pascal's vases? The liquid pressure depends on the vertical depth below the surface; this must remain unchanged to balance the pressure due to the atmosphere.

10. **(E)** Not enough information is supplied. As stated in the chapter, the rise or fall also depends on the surface tension of the liquid. We are not told how the surface tension of the new liquid compares with that of water. Instead of rising, the level in the new liquid may actually fall.

11. **(E)** This is a famous demonstration of surface tension. If the water is poured in carefully, the surface of the water at the hole acts like a stretched membrane and does not let the water escape.

12. **(A)** Water wets glass; therefore the water should rise in the capillary tube. This rules out tubes 4 and 5. The narrower the tube, the higher the liquid should rise. This fits tubes 1 and 2, not tubes 2 and 3. (It also fits tubes 1 and 3, but that was not a choice.)

5

Heat, Temperature, Thermal Expansion

A brass washer with a hole-diameter of one inch is transferred from ice water to boiling water. What happens to the size of the hole? What happens to the energy content of the washer? Discussion of these questions requires an understanding of heat and its effects.

THE KINETIC THEORY

The kinetic theory of matter states that all matter is composed of molecules that are relatively far apart and exert force on each other only when they collide. These molecules move freely and quickly between collisions. The pressure of a gas on its container is due to the collisions of the gas molecules with the walls of the container. The molecules of liquids are quite close to each other, but can move past each other readily. When a fluid is "still," its molecules are still vibrating. This is indicated by Brownian movements in which large particles are seen to move because of bombardment by invisible molecules. In solids the molecules are much closer together. There are considerable bonding forces between the molecules, and little freedom of motion. The molecules of the solids vibrate and therefore possess kinetic energy.

TEMPERATURE AND HEAT

One way of defining *temperature* is to say it is the degree of hotness or coldness of an object. If we think in terms of the *kinetic theory* we get another definition. The molecules of a substance are in constant random motion. If we heat a gas, its molecules move faster; that is, when the temperature of a gas goes up, the average speed of its molecules goes up. When the speed of motion of the molecule goes up, its kinetic energy goes up. The molecules in a substance are not all moving with the same speed and therefore do not all have the same kinetic energy. We can speak of the average kinetic energy of these molecules. When we heat a gas, the average kinetic energy of its molecules goes up. This leads to thinking of *temperature* as a measure of the average kinetic energy per molecule of the substance. If we take a cupful of water from a bathtub full of water, the *average* kinetic energy per molecule, and therefore the temperature, are the same in the tub as in the cup.

If we have two different gases at the same temperature, perhaps a mixture of oxygen and hydrogen at 0°C, the average kinetic energy of the oxygen molecules is the same as that of the hydrogen molecules. However, on the average, the oxygen molecules will move more slowly than the hydrogen molecules because the oxygen molecule has the greater mass. (Remember, $E_k = \frac{1}{2} mv^2$.)

We have seen that the molecules of a substance have kinetic energy. In the ideal gases to be described on page 49, we assume that this is kinetic energy of translation only. This is accurate enough for monatomic gases like helium and diatomic gases like oxygen and nitrogen at moderate temperatures and pressures. In actual gases the molecules may also have kinetic energy of rotation. They may also have potential energy with respect to each other. For example, when a solid expands, work is done to pull the molecules away from each other against the cohesive force. Until recently *heat* was thought of as the sum total of the energy of its molecules. We now say that a substance has *internal energy* as a result of the kinetic and potential energy of its molecules. In Chapter 14 we shall see that some of the internal energy is also due to potential energy of the atoms. In crystalline solids much of the internal energy is due to the vibration of the nuclei of the atoms. At the present time the physicist's knowledge of internal energy is incomplete.

When a hot piece of copper is brought in contact with a cold piece, the hot piece gets colder and the cold piece gets hotter—both pieces end up at the same temperature. The hot piece lost some internal energy and the cold piece gained some. We define *heat* as the form of energy which flows between two bodies because they are at different temperatures. It is energy in transit.

THERMOMETERS

When an object is heated, many of its characteristics may change. For example, when a solid gets hotter there may be a change in its color, electrical resistance, dimensions. We may use these changes as means for measuring temperature. Many thermometers depend on the fact that substances tend to expand when heated.

Let us describe briefly the making and calibration of a mercury thermometer. A uniform, thick-walled capillary tube with a glass bulb at one end is partly filled with mercury. The bulb is heated; the mercury expands and fills the tube, driving out all the air. Then the top of the tube is sealed. The selection of temperature scales requires the choice of a reference point and of the size of a unit. In practice two reference points are usually used for the mercury thermometer. If we insert the bulb of a mercury thermometer in water and heat the water steadily, the mercury level in the thermometer keeps rising until the water starts boiling. As long as the water keeps boiling, the level of the mercury in the thermometer remains constant, no matter how vigorously the water is boiled. This is, therefore, a readily obtained reference point. As the water is cooled, the level of the mercury keeps dropping until ice starts forming; as the water is cooled still further more ice keeps forming, but the level of the mercury remains the same as long as both ice and water are present and are mixed. This is the second reference point and is known as the *ice point*—the temperature at which ice melts or water freezes. On the *Celsius* scale the ice point is marked 0°; on the *Fahrenheit* scale 32°.

The temperature at which water boils is affected significantly by variation in atmospheric pressure. Therefore in specifying the first reference point we emphasize the pressure to be used: the *standard pressure* is that which would be produced by a column of mercury 76 cm high. For short, we speak of a pressure of 76 cm of mercury, or 30 in. of mercury, or 760 mm of mercury, or of one (standard) atmosphere. The first reference point is known as the *steam point:* the temperature at which water under standard pressure boils. On the Celsius scale the steam point is marked 100°; on the Fahrenheit scale 212°.

Therefore, (212 – 32) Fahrenheit degrees equal (100 – 0) Celsius degrees: i.e., 180 F deg = 100C deg. (N.B. In this book 180 F deg means 180 Fahrenheit degrees; 180°F is an actual temperature: 180 degrees Fahrenheit.)

change of temperature in Fahrenheit degrees = ⁹⁄₅ change in Celsius degrees

For example, if the temperature goes up 20 C deg (from 30° to 50°), the corresponding change on the Fahrenheit scale will be ⁹⁄₅ × 20, or 26 F deg. What will the actual Fahrenheit temperature be? Fifty Celsius degrees correspond to (⁹⁄₅ × 50) Fahrenheit degrees, or 90 F deg. To get the actual Fahrenheit temperature we must add 32 F deg to the change of 90 F deg, or 122° F.

This indicates the formula:

$$F = \frac{9}{5} C + 32° \quad \text{or} \quad C = \frac{5}{9} (F - 32°)$$

for obtaining *actual temperatures.*

The *Kelvin scale* is used as an *absolute temperature* scale. This scale has no negative temperatures. *Absolute zero* $\overset{\bullet}{=}$ -273° C = 0 K. Therefore, 273 K = 0°C. Each kelvin unit on the Kelvin scale has the same size as each degree on the Celsius scale. We shall say more about absolute temperature when we describe the behavior of gases.

EXPANSION AND CONTRACTION

Solids

Most solids expand when heated and contract when cooled. The same lengths of different solids expand different amounts when heated through the same temperature change. For example, brass expands more than iron. This difference is made use of in thermostats, where a bimetallic strip is used. The bimetallic strip (sometimes known as a *compound bar*) may be made by welding or riveting together brass and iron strips. When heated the bimetallic strip bends with the brass forming

the outside of the curve. When the strip bends it can make or break an electric contact. In cooling the reverse happens; making a circuit can result in the operation of a heater.

When a solid is heated, it expands not only in length but also in width and thickness. Therefore, thermal expansion results in an increase in length, area, and volume. If a hollow solid, like a glass flask, is heated, the empty space increases in volume just as though it were made of the same material as the walls.

The *coefficient of linear expansion* tells what change in length takes place per unit length when the temperature of the solid goes up 1 degree. For example, the coefficient for brass is 1.9×10^{-5} per C deg. This means that for each Celsius degree rise in temperature: 1 cm will increase in length 1.9×10^{-5} cm; 1 ft will increase in length 1.9×10^{-5} ft; 1 yd will increase in length 1.9×10^{-5} yd. Since the temperature change indicated by the Fahrenheit degree is only $\frac{5}{9}$ as great as by the Celsius degree, the coefficients per Fahrenheit degree are $\frac{5}{9}$ as great as those per Celsius degree. For example, the coefficient for brass is $\frac{5}{9} \times 1.9 \times 10^{-5}$ per F deg. When a solid is cooled the corresponding contraction takes place and the same thermal coefficient can be used. When a rod or wire is heated

change in length = original length × coeff. of expansion × temp. change

Liquids

Most liquids expand when heated, contract when cooled. Different liquids expand different amounts when heated through the same temperature change. The coefficient of volume expansion tells what change in volume takes place per unit volume when the temperature goes up 1 degree. This difference is greater for most liquids than for solids. For example, when the mercury thermometer is heated, the mercury expands more than the glass bulb. Therefore the level of the mercury rises to compensate for the difference in volume expansion.

Water behaves peculiarly in this respect. As water is cooled from 100°C it contracts until its temperature reaches 4°C. If it is cooled further the water will expand; that is, water is densest at 4°C. Therefore, as a lake is cooled at the surface by the atmosphere, the bottom of the lake tends to reach and maintain a temperature of 4°C. If the surface freezes, the resulting ice stays at the top since the specific gravity of ice is only about 0.9 that of water. Water molecules form hydrogen bonds with each other. These are abundant in ice and decrease in relative abundance as the temperature of water goes up.

Gases

If the pressure on a gas is kept constant, heating the gas will result in an increase in its volume. For all gases the coefficient of volume expansion is nearly the same. For example, if we start with a gas at 0°C, for each Celsius degree rise in temperature the volume increases by $1/273$ of whatever volume the gas occupied at 0°C, provided the pressure of the gas is not allowed to change. If a gas occupying a volume of 273 cm³ at a pressure of 700 mm is heated from 0°C to 10°C, and the pressure is kept at 700 mm, the volume of the gas will become 273 cm³ + 273 $(10/273)$ cm³ or 283 cm³. This rule also operates when the gas is cooled, provided it is not cooled too much. For example, if the above gas is cooled to –10°C, its volume will become 263 cm³. *If gases continued to obey this rule even at very low temperatures, the gas would disappear at –273°C.* This suggests using –273°C as the zero temperature on a gas scale of temperatures. No gas behaves this way. Fortunately, other theory indicates that no temperature below approximately –273°C can exist. Therefore, this is taken as the zero temperature on the absolute scales. 0 K $\doteq$ –273°C. Each kelvin unit measures the same temperature change as each Celsius degree.

Actual gases become liquefied at least a few degrees above absolute zero. The kinetic theory states that the speed of motion of the molecules in a substance decreases as the substance's temperature decreases. This does not mean, however, that all motion within the atom ceases at absolute zero.

A more convenient way than the one above to calculate the volume of a gas as the result of a temperature change is to use *Charles' law:* If the pressure on a gas is kept constant, its volume is directly proportional to its *absolute* temperature.

$$\frac{V_1}{V_2} = \frac{T_1}{T_2} \quad \text{or} \quad \frac{V_1}{V_2} = \frac{C_1 + 273°}{C_2 + 273°}$$

where V_1 is the volume of the gas at absolute temperature T_1, or temperature C_1 in Celsius degrees. The volume may be expressed in any volume units; of course, both volumes must be in the same units.

Another important gas law is *Boyle's law:* If the temperature of a gas is kept constant, the volume of the gas varies inversely with its pressure ($V = k/p$):

$$p_1V_1 = p_2V_2$$

(Note that the pressure may be in any unit and that the volume may be in any unit, but both pressures must be in the same units and both volumes must be in the same units.) For example, if the pressure on a gas is doubled without changing its temperature, its volume is reduced to half of its original volume.

Boyle's law and Charles' law may be combined to give the general gas law:

$$\frac{p_1V_1}{T_1} = \frac{p_2V_2}{T_2}$$

Note: Gauges used to measure air pressure in automobile tires do not give the true pressure that is required for the previously stated gas laws. To get the true or absolute pressure we must add to this gauge pressure the pressure of the atmosphere, about 15 lb/in^2.

These gas laws can be derived on the basis of the kinetic theory of gases.

ANSWERING THE QUESTIONS Let's look at the questions at the beginning of the chapter. The temperature of the brass washer is raised from 0°C to 100°C. The hole increases in size just as a brass disk of the same size would. The coefficient of linear expansion for brass is 1.9×10^{-5} per C deg. Therefore the increase in the diameter = original length × coeff. of expansion × temp. change = 1 inch × 1.9×10^{-5} per C deg × 100 C deg = 1.9×10^{-3} in. or 0.0019 inch. Since the temperature of the brass goes up, the kinetic energy of the particles in it goes up. We can say that the internal energy of the brass washer goes up. In the next chapter we'll find out how large this increase is.

QUESTIONS Chapter 5

Select the choice that best answers the question or completes the sentence.

1. On the Fahrenheit scale a temperature of 50°C will be recorded as approximately **(A)** 4° **(B)** 10° **(C)** 40° **(D)** 105° **(E)** 120°

2. A temperature of 100°C is equivalent to a temperature on the Kelvin scale of **(A)** 0 K **(B)** 173 K **(C)** 212 K **(D)** 273 K **(E)** 373 K

3. A change in temperature of 20 C deg is equivalent to a change in temperature on the Fahrenheit scale of approx. **(A)** 0.9° **(B)** 11° **(C)** 6.7° **(D)** 36° **(E)** 68°

4. An aluminum rod having a diameter of one inch is heated from a temperature of 27°C to a temperature of 54°C. As a result the diameter of the rod **(A)** does not change **(B)** increases to something less than two inches **(C)** doubles **(D)** shrinks to ½ inch to compensate for the increase in length **(E)** shrinks, but remains larger than ½ inch.

5. If the volume of a gas is doubled without changing its temperature, the pressure of the gas is **(A)** reduced to ½ of the original value **(B)** reduced to ¼ of the original value **(C)** not changed **(D)** doubled **(E)** quadrupled

6. The volume of a given mass of gas is doubled without changing its temperature. As a result the density of the gas **(A)** is reduced to ¼ of the original value **(B)** is halved **(C)** remains unchanged **(D)** is doubled **(E)** is quadrupled

7. The volume of a given mass of gas will be doubled at atmospheric pressure if the temperature of the gas is changed from 150°C to **(A)** 300° C **(B)** 423°C **(C)** 573°C **(D)** 600°C **(E)** 743°C

8. All of the following express approximately the same pressure *except* **(A)** 1 atmosphere **(B)** 15 lb/in.^{2} **(C)** 15 lb/ft^2 **(D)** 30 in. of mercury **(E)** 760 mm of mercury

9. If 500 cm^3 of gas, having a pressure of 760 mm of mercury, is compressed into a volume of 300 cm^3, the temperature remaining constant, the pressure of the gas will be, in mm of mercury, approximately **(A)** 500 **(B)** 900 **(C)** 1100 **(D)** 1300 **(E)** 1500

10. How many cubic meters of air at atmospheric pressure of 10^5 Pa must be pumped into a 2m^3 tank containing air at atmospheric pressure in order to raise the absolute pressure to 8×10^5 Pa? Assume that the temperature remains constant. **(A)** 8 **(B)** 10 **(C)** 14 **(D)** 20 **(E)** 24

EXPLANATIONS TO QUESTIONS Chapter 5

Answers

1. **(E)**	4. **(B)**	7. **(C)**	9. **(D)**
2. **(E)**	5. **(A)**	8. **(C)**	10. **(C)**
3. **(D)**	6. **(B)**		

Explanations

1. **(E)** $°F = \frac{9}{5}C + 32° = \frac{9}{5} \times 50° + 32° = 122°$

2. **(E)** $T = °C + 273° = (100 + 273) \text{ K} = 373 \text{ K}$

3. **(D)** change in F deg $= \frac{9}{5}$ change in C deg $= \frac{9}{5} \times 20° = 36°$

4. **(B)** When a metal is heated, its dimensions increase in all directions. Therefore, the diameter of the rod will increase. However, the expansion per degree of temperature rise is a very small fraction of the original length (check value of coefficient of expansion). The increase will be to something considerably less than two inches.

5. **(A)** Boyle's law applies. The pressure of the gas varies inversely with its volume. Since the volume is doubled, the pressure must be reduced to one-half of its original value.

6. **(B)** Density = mass/volume. The mass of the gas does not change in the problem; the volume is doubled. Therefore the density must go down to one-half of its original value.

7. **(C)** Charles' law applies: At constant pressure, the volume of a gas is proportional to its absolute temperature. Therefore, to double the volume of the gas we must double the absolute temperature. The starting temperature: $T = °C + 273° = (150 + 273) \text{ K} = 423 \text{ K}$. The final absolute temperature is $2 \times 423 \text{ K} = 846 \text{ K}$. The final Celsius temperature is $(846 - 273)° = 573°$.

8. **(C)** You should know the equivalent values of atmospheric pressure.

9. **(D)** Boyle's law applies.

$$p_1 V_1 = p_2 V_2$$
$$p_1 (300 \text{ cm}^3) = 760 \text{ mm} \times 500 \text{ cm}^3$$
$$p_1 = \frac{760 \times 500}{300} \text{ mm} = 1270 \text{ mm}$$

10. **(C)** The total volume of air at atmospheric pressure is the volume to be added (V) plus the 2 m^3 already in the tank. Therefore

$$10^5 \text{ Pa } (V + 2m^3) = 8 \times 10^5 \text{ Pa } (2m^3)$$
$$V + 2m^3 = 16 \text{ m}^3$$
$$V = 14 \text{ m}^3$$

Measurement of Heat; Humidity

When we want to measure the amount of heat that is transferred from one object to another, the laboratory equipment used includes an instrument called a *calorimeter.* This should be a container that is well insulated from the outside; in a high school laboratory, styrofoam cups can be used with reasonable accuracy. As with other measurements, we must establish units.

MEASUREMENT OF HEAT

Internal energy, work, and heat being transferred are all measured in Joules. In order to raise the temperature of 1 kilogram of liquid water 1°C, 4.19 kilojoules of heat are needed. Prior to SI units, heat was sometimes measured in *calories.* The calorie is the amount of heat needed to raise the temperature of 1 gram of water 1 C deg. The *kilocalorie* is the amount of heat needed to raise the temperature of 1 kilogram of water 1 C deg. (This is the calorie used to describe the nutritional value of foods.) The *British thermal unit* (*Btu*) is the amount of heat needed to raise the temperature of 1 lb of water 1 F deg.

$$1 \text{ kcal} = 1000 \text{ cal}$$
$$1 \text{ kcal} = 4185 \text{ joules} = 4.185 \text{ kilojoules (kJ)}$$
$$1 \text{ cal} = 4.185 \text{ joules}$$
$$1 \text{ Btu} = 252 \text{ cals}$$

SPECIFIC HEAT CAPACITY

From the definition of the calorie we know that if the temperature of 1 g of water goes up from 10°C to 11°C, then one calorie was added to the water. However, we find that less heat is required to raise the temperature of 1 g of most other substances one Celsius degree. We often define the *specific heat capacity* (sp. ht.) of a substance as the amount of heat required to raise the temperature of 1 g of the substance 1 C deg; this number is the same as the number of Btu required to raise the temperature of 1 lb of the substance 1 F deg. From the above we can see that the specific heat of water is 1 cal/g•C deg, or 1 Btu/lb•F deg. The specific heat capacity of copper is 0.092 cal/g.C deg or 0.39 kJ/kg•C deg.

The specific heat capacity of a substance is often obtained in the laboratory by using the method of mixtures. For example, a 100 g block of iron is moved from boiling water (100°C) to a beaker containing 110 g of water at 18°C. Assume that this raises the temperature of the water in the beaker to 25°C. We can now calculate the specific heat of iron:

heat lost by hot object = heat gained by cold objects

52

Also, for any object that loses or gains heat *without changing phase*,

$$\text{heat lost (or gained)} = \text{mass} \times \text{sp. ht.} \times \text{temp. change}$$

Using SI units,

$$\text{heat lost by the iron} = 0.100 \text{ kg} \times \text{sp. ht.} \times (100°C - 25°C).$$

$$\text{heat gained by the water} = 0.110 \text{ kg} \times 4.19 \text{ kJ/kgC}° \times (25°C - 18°C).$$

If we assume that no other substances are involved in the heat exchange,

$$0.100 \text{ kg} \times \text{sp. ht.} \times 75°C = 0.110 \text{ kg} \times 4.19 \text{ kJ/kg} \cdot C° \times 7°C$$

$$\text{sp. ht.} = .43 \frac{\text{kJ}}{\text{kg} \cdot C^c}$$

Using calories,

$$\text{heat lost by the iron} = 100 \text{ g} \times \text{sp. ht.} \times (100°C - 25°C).$$

$$\text{heat gained by the water} = 110 \text{ g} \times 1 \text{ cal/g} \cdot C° \times (25°C - 18°C).$$

If we assume that no other substances are involved in the heat exchange,

$$100 \text{ g} \times \text{sp. ht.} \times 75°C = 110 \text{ g} \times 1 \text{ cal/g}°C \times 7°C$$

$$\text{sp. ht.} = .10 \frac{\text{cal}}{\text{g} \cdot C°}$$

Note that you may work these problems either in SI units or in calories. Exam questions will gradually be switched over to SI units. Roundoff errors in the last decimal place are common in conversion between systems.

CHANGE OF PHASE

Earlier we defined solid, liquid, and gas. These are three phases of matter. If we heat a solid, its temperature goes up until it starts melting. Further transfer of heat to the solid results in melting without a change of temperature. (Removing the same amount of heat from the liquid would then result in *fusion* without a change of temperature.) Continued heating after all the solid has melted again leads to a temperature change—this time of the liquid. In the above equation the specific heat capacity of the liquid must be used; this is usually different from the specific heat capacity of the solid. For example, the specific heat capacity of ice is 2.05 kJ/kg • C° or 0.5 kcal/kg • C°. Recall that for liquid water the values are 4.19 kJ/kg • C° or 1 kcal/kg • C°.

When a substance is changed from solid to liquid, or from liquid to gas, heat must be supplied to pull the molecules away from each other against cohesive forces. This represents an increase in potential rather than kinetic energy. Therefore the temperature remains the same. When the reverse change of phase takes place, e.g., solidification, this heat is released. For a given crystalline substance (metals, ice, etc.), melting and freezing occur at the same temperature, at constant pressure.

Cooling Curve for Water

Heat of Fusion

Heat of fusion of a substance is the amount of heat required to melt a unit mass of the substance without change of temperature. For ice this is 335 kJ/kg or 80 cal/g.

$$\text{heat required for melting} = \text{mass} \times H_F$$

where H_F is the heat of fusion of the substance.

When we defined the ice point in the previous chapter we made use of this fact that the temperature does not change while melting takes place. It was also indicated there that this temperature is practically independent of ordinary changes in atmospheric pressure. If the pressure on ice is twice ordinary atmospheric pressure, its melting point becomes $-0.0075°C$. However, in ice-skating a person's weight is supported by a small area—the area of the bottom of the blades. This results in a high pressure (F/A) on the ice—enough to melt it; when the skater passes, the water freezes again. *Regelation* is this melting under increased pressure and refreezing when the pressure is reduced. This happens with substances like ice which expand on freezing. On the other hand, a substance that contracts on solidifying has a higher melting point at higher pressures. A lower melting point also results from dissolving solids in liquids. That is why salt sprinkled on an icy sidewalk tends to melt the ice.

Vaporization

Vaporization is the process of changing a substance to a vapor. It includes evaporation, boiling, and sublimation.

EVAPORATION. As explained above, the molecules of a liquid are in constant motion. The speeds of the different molecules are different. Some of the fastest moving molecules at the surface can escape from the liquid in spite of gravity and the attractive force between molecules. The molecules that escape are relatively far apart from each other, as in a gas, and form the vapor of the liquid. Since the molecules with the greatest kinetic energy escaped, the average kinetic energy of the remaining molecules in the liquid decreased; that is, unless the liquid is heated, the liquid cools when evaporation takes place. Evaporation is a cooling process. It occurs at the surface of the liquid. The rate of evaporation can be increased by making it easier for the molecules to escape from the liquid: heat the liquid to give more molecules higher speeds; spread the liquid over a greater area; decrease the air pressure on top of the liquid; blow away the vapor-filled air above the liquid.

BOILING In evaporation the liquid is converted to vapor at the surface of the liquid. In boiling the liquid is converted to vapor within the body of the liquid. We observe the vapor in the form of bubbles. Another way to define boiling is in terms of pressure. The molecules of the vapor move around freely like the molecules of a gas and exert pressure. We can speak of the pressure of a vapor as we speak of the pressure of the atmosphere. *Boiling* occurs when the pressure of the vapor forming inside the liquid equals the external pressure on the liquid; this is usually atmospheric pressure. During boiling the temperature of the liquid doesn't change. The temperature at which this occurs is the *boiling point* of the liquid. Although the temperature of the liquid does not change during boiling, energy must be supplied for the vaporization (to do work against the cohesive force between molecules). *Heat of vaporization* (H_v) of a substance is the amount of heat needed to vaporize a unit mass of the substance without changing its temperature. For water at 100°C this is 2260 kJ/kg or 540 cal/g.

> **heat required for vaporization = mass $\times$ H_v**

When the pressure on a liquid is increased, its boiling point goes up; when the pressure on a liquid is decreased, its boiling point goes down. For example, at standard atmospheric pressure (760 mm) the boiling point of water is 100°C. In mountainous areas the atmospheric pressure is usually considerably below 760 mm and water boils at temperatures significantly below 100°C. Cooking at these lower temperatures proceeds rather slowly. To hasten the cooking, pressure cookers may be used; in these the pressure is allowed to build up by using special covers which do not let the vapor escape. The building up of the pressure raises the boiling point.

SUBLIMATION is the direct change from solid to vapor. For example, at ordinary room temperatures, solid carbon dioxide ("dry ice") changes directly to carbon dioxide gas. *Condensation* is the changing of a vapor to a liquid. This is accompanied by the release of the same amount of heat that would be required to vaporize the same quantity of the liquid. The term *condensation* is also used occasionally to refer to the reverse of sublimation; that is, it refers to the direct conversion of a vapor to a solid, as in the formation of frost on a cold night.

When there is a change of phase, the method of mixtures described above has to be modified:

> **heat gained (or lost) = mass $\times$ sp. ht. $\times$ temp. change**
> **+ mass melted $\times$ heat of fusion**
> **+ mass vaporized $\times$ heat of vaporization**

In this formula any term may be omitted that does not fit the situation. *For example,* to calculate the heat required to boil away completely 10 grams of water at 100°C if the starting temperature of the water is 60°C. we omit the second term since no melting is involved in the illustration. Heat gained = mass $\times$ sp. ht. $\times$ temp. change + mass vaporized $\times$ heat of vaporization = (10 $\times$ 1 $\times$ 40) cal + (10 $\times$ 540) cal = 5800 cal = 5.8 kcal $\overset{\bullet}{=}$ 24. kJ.

TABLE OF CONSTANTS FOR LIQUID WATER

System	sp. gr.	density	sp. ht.	H_f	H_v
SI	1	10^3 kg/m³*	4.19 kJ/kg • C°	335 kJ/kg	2260 kJ/kg
old metric	1	10^3 kg/m³*	1 kcal/kg • C°	80 kcal/kg	540 kcal/kg†
CGS	1	1 g/cm³	1 cal/g • C°	80 cal/g	540 cal/g†
English	1	62.5 lb/ft³	1 Btu/lb • F°	144 Btu/lb	972 Btu/lb

*This can also be expressed as 1 kg/liter.
†For other conversions, remember that 1 cal = 4.19 joules (J), 1 kcal = 4.19 $\times$ 10^3 J.

HUMIDITY

The atmosphere contains water vapor, but there is a limit to how much water can be evaporated into a given volume of air, just as there is a limit to how much sugar can be dissolved in one cupful of coffee. More sugar can be dissolved in hot coffee than in cold. A given volume of air can hold more water vapor at a higher temperature than at a lower temperature. The air is said to be *saturated* when it holds as much water vapor as it can at that temperature. At 20°C, 1 cubic meter of air can hold about 17 g of water vapor; at 30°C it can hold about 30 g. Usually the atmosphere is not saturated. *Relative humidity* (expressed in percent) is the ratio of the mass of water vapor actually present in a given volume of air to the mass which would be present in it if it were saturated. For example, if 1 cubic meter of air at 20°C contains 12 g of water vapor, the relative humidity is $\frac{12 \text{ g}}{17 \text{ g}} \times 100 = 71\%$.

Hygrometers are instruments for measuring relative humidity. Readings on wet and dry bulb thermometers can be compared with the aid of a chart from which one can then read off the relative humidity. The basic principle of this is that evaporation is a cooling process. The rate of evaporation from the wet-bulb thermometer will be high when the relative humidity is low, and therefore on such a day the wet-bulb thermometer will read considerably below the dry-bulb one. There is no simple formula for converting this temperature difference to relative humidity, and therefore a chart is used.

If unsaturated air is cooled, its relative humidity goes up. If the temperature of the air drops sufficiently, saturation is reached and excess moisture precipitates out. The *dew point* is the temperature to which the air must be cooled so that it will be saturated and condensation will just form.

QUESTIONS Chapter 6

Select the choice that best completes the statement.

1. One thousand calories of heat are added to 100 grams of water when its temperature is 40°C. The resulting temperature of the water is **(A)** 10°C   **(B)** 32°C   **(C)** 50°C   **(D)** 80°C   **(E)** 100°C

2. If 2 Btu of heat are added to 504 grams of water at 100°C and standard pressure, the temperature of the water will **(A)** not change   **(B)** rise 1 C°   **(C)** rise 1 F°   **(D)** rise 2 C°   **(E)** rise 2 F°

3. A boy has 240 grams of water at 50°C. The number of grams of ice at 0°C which he must add to the water to lower the water temperature to 0°C is **(A)** 35   **(B)** 150   **(C)** 12,000   **(D)** 50,000   **(E)** infinite

4. A certain alloy has a melting point of 1000°C. The specific heat of the solid is 0.3 cal/g•C°; its heat of fusion is 20 calories per gram. The number of calories required to change 10 grams of the solid from room temperature (20°C) to the liquid at 1000 C° is approximately **(A)** 240   **(B)** 440   **(C)** 3140   **(D)** 3740   **(E)** 29,600   (How many joules is that equal to?)

5. When 10 grams of steam at 100°C condense to form water at 0°C, the number of calories liberated is **(A)** 10   **(B)** 800   **(C)** 1000   **(D)** 5400   **(E)** 6400   (How many joules is that equal to?)

6. When one gram of atmospheric water vapor condenses in the air, it results in   **(A)** always cooling the surrounding air   **(B)** always heating the surrounding air   **(C)** always leaving the surrounding air temperature unchanged   **(D)** heating the surrounding air only if the change occurs below 100°F   **(E)** cooling the surrounding air only if the change occurs below 100°F

7. If the temperature of the atmosphere rises above the dew point,   **(A)** dew will form   **(B)** precipitation will take place   **(C)** the relative humidity will become 100%   **(D)** evaporation is likely to take place   **(E)** condensation will take place if nuclei such as dust are present

EXPLANATIONS TO QUESTIONS Chapter 6

Answers

1. **(C)**	3. **(B)**	5. **(E)**	6. **(B)**	7. **(D)**
2. **(A)**	4. **(C)**			

Explanations

1. **(C)** Heat gained = mass × sp. ht. × temp. change. 1000 cal = 100 g × 1 cal/g•C deg × temp. change. Temp. change = 10 C deg. Final temp. × (40 + 10)° C = 50°C.

2. **(A)** The given temperature of the water is its normal boiling point. Further addition of heat allows boiling to go on without a change in temperature, as long as the pressure remains the same. (Did you read the question too quickly?)

3. **(B)** Heat gained by ice = heat lost by water.

$$\text{Mass} \times H_F = \text{mass of water} \times \text{sp. ht.} \times \text{temp. change.}$$
$$\text{Mass}_i \times 80 \text{ cal/g} = 240 \text{ g} \times 1 \text{ cal/g} \cdot \text{C deg} \times 50 \text{ C deg}$$
$$\text{Mass}_i = 150 \text{ g}$$

4. **(C)** Heat required = heat to raise temp. of solid to melting point + heat to melt solid

$$\text{Heat required} = \text{mass} \times \text{sp. ht.} \times \text{temp. change} + \text{mass} \times H_F$$
$$= 10 \text{ g} \times 0.3 \text{ cal/g} \cdot \text{C deg} \times 980 \text{ C deg} + 10 \text{ g} \times 20 \text{ cal/g}$$
$$= 2940 \text{ cal} + 200 \text{ cal} = 3140 \text{ cal}$$

The number of joules = $(3140 \text{ cal} \times 4.19 \text{ J/cal}) = 13.2 \times 10^3$ J

5. **(E)** Heat liberated = heat given off by steam when condensing at 100°C + heat given off by water when cooling from 100°C to 0° C.

$$\text{Heat liberated} = \text{mass} \times H_v + \text{mass} \times \text{sp. ht.} \times \text{temp. change}$$
$$= 10 \text{ g} \times 540 \text{ cal/g} + 10 \text{ g} \times 1 \text{ cal/g} \cdot \text{C deg} \times 100 \text{ C deg}$$
$$= 5400 \text{ cal} + 1000 \text{ cal} = 6400 \text{ cal}$$

The number of kilojoules = $(6.4 \text{ kcal} \times 4.19 \times 10^3 \text{ J/kcal}) = 27. \text{ kJ} = 27{,}000$ J

6. **(B)** Heat is required to vaporize a liquid. Whenever the vapor condenses to a liquid, heat has to be given off again to the surroundings. In this case the heat is given off to the surrounding air and heats it.

7. **(D)** At the dew point the air is saturated with water vapor. When the temperature of the air goes up it can hold more water vapor; its relative humidity is less than 100%. If water is present, evaporation will take place.

Heat and Work; Heat Transfer

It was the English scientist James Prescott Joule who, probably more than anyone else, was responsible for our belief that heat is a form of energy. He created the device shown below. The masses are raised by turning the drum at the top. The container is filled with water. As the masses fall, they give up their potential energy to the water, which in turn exhibits a rise in average kinetic energy (temperature).

Joule's Apparatus

Since energy is the ability to do work, we should not be surprised that we can use hot objects to do work for us; we have already studied the reverse—when work is done with a machine, heat is produced since some energy is used to do work against friction. How much work can be done with 1 Btu of heat? How can a hot object be used to do work for us?

Imagine a gas in a cylinder with a movable piston. The molecules of the gas bombard the piston and produce a pressure on it. If we want to compress the gas, we must exert a force against the piston. We do work in compressing the gas. As we push the piston, we exert a force on the molecules of the gas thus giving them greater speed. The temperature of the gas goes up; if the cylinder is insulated, the work done in compressing the gas results in an equivalent increase in the internal energy of the gas. If the cylinder is not insulated, the temperature of the gas can be kept constant by letting this heat equivalent go instead to the material outside the cylinder. Mechanical energy can be converted completely to heat. How much heat is produced?

1 cal	= 4.19 joules (J)
1 kcal	= 4.19×10^3 J = 4.19 kJ
1 Btu	= 778 ft-lb = 1.1 kJ

If the gas in the cylinder is allowed to expand, the gas does work as it moves the piston. If the cylinder is insulated, as the gas expands its temperature goes down; the energy required for the work comes from the internal energy of the gas. If the cylinder is not insulated, the temperature of the gas can be kept constant. Then, as the gas expands, heat flows into it from outside the cylinder; this heat equals the work done by the gas in expanding.

Recall that an isothermal process is one in which the temperature remains constant. Boyle's law ($pV = k$) applies to a gas which expands or contracts while its temperature is kept constant. An *adiabatic* process is one in which no heat is allowed to enter or leave the system. This is true in the above process in which the cylinder is kept insulated. Boyle's law does not apply to an adiabatic process.

HEAT ENGINES

Heat engines are used to convert heat to mechanical energy. Gasoline and diesel engines are examples of heat engines. In these heat engines hot gases are allowed to expand; as they expand they do work. If the fuel is burned inside the cylinder of the engine itself, the engine is known as an *internal combustion engine;* this is true of the gasoline and diesel engines. If the fuel is burned in a separate chamber outside the engine proper, the engine is known as an *external combustion engine;* this is true of the steam engine and steam turbine. In these, the fuel, which may be coal, is burned in a separate furnace and is used to heat water in a boiler. The steam is then directed into the engine.

Gasoline Engine

The *gasoline engine* is an internal combustion engine commonly used in automobiles. These engines frequently have six or eight cylinders connected to the same flywheel by means of a common shaft. One of these cyclinders is shown. A complete cycle of operation consists of four strokes: Intake, compression, ignition or power, exhaust. The cylinder is

shown at the beginning of the intake stroke. The exhaust valve *E* is closed. Gasoline and air mixture enters through the open intake valve *I*, and the piston moves down. Then both valves are closed and the mixture is compressed as the piston moves up during the second stroke. At the proper instant, high voltage is applied to the spark plug *S*; the resulting spark ignites the mixture. This produces an explosion which provides the power for pushing the piston and turning the crankshaft, flywheel, and ultimately the wheels of the car. During the last stroke the piston is pushed up again; this time the intake valve is closed and the exhaust valve is open. The waste gases are pushed out and the cycle can start again. Notice that there are two complete up and down motions during each cycle. The *carburetor* provides the proper mixture of air and gasoline vapor, which is then burned in the cylinders. The engine is kept running between power strokes by the flywheel *F*. The whole process is usually started by briefly switching a battery to a starting motor.

Diesel Engine

The *diesel engine* is also an internal combustion engine. Neither carburetor nor spark plug is needed. The air in the cylinder is compressed so much that its temperature rises sufficiently to ignite the fuel, which is then sprayed in. The fuel is denser and cheaper than gasoline. The efficiency of a diesel engine (about 40%) is higher than that of a steam engine or gasoline engine.

Jet and Rocket Engines

Jet and rocket engines operate on the principle of Newton's third law. Gases escaping under pressure in one direction exert a push on the engine in the opposite direction. The jet engine takes from the atmosphere the oxygen needed for burning its fuel, while the rocket carries its oxygen as well as its own fuel.

THERMODYNAMICS

Thermodynamics is the branch of science which deals with the relationship between changes in energy, the flow of heat, and the performance of work. For example, in the previous section we mentioned heat engines. Let us consider one in more detail. Heat is provided to a cylinder with a movable piston as shown for the gasoline engine. The heated gas pushes the piston which then does useful work in turning the wheel, and the piston returns to the starting position. During the cycle some of the heat supplied also goes into increasing the internal energy of the system, such as increasing the kinetic energy of translation and rotation of the molecules of the cylinder, piston, and waste gases.

These ideas can be quantified for any isolated system. The *first law of thermodynamics* is a form of the law of conservation of energy: the heat supplied to a system is equal to the increase in internal energy of the system plus the work done by the system.

---

heat flow = change in internal energy + work done by system

$$Q = \Delta U + W$$

It is important to use signs correctly. *Heat flow* is *positive* when heat is transferred *to* the system. *Work* is *positive* when it is done *by* the system. Changes in internal energy will be accordingly positive or negative.

The *second law of thermodynamics* states that heat cannot flow from a cold object to a hot object unless external work is done. The second law of thermodynamics also gives rise to the concept of *entropy*. Entropy provides a quantitative way to measure the disorder of a system. For any complete process in an isolated system, the entropy either remains constant or increases. Entropy can only remain constant in reversible processes, so the entropy of the universe is increasing. For reversible processes,

entropy change = heat added/Kelvin temperature

METHODS OF HEAT TRANSFER

Sometimes we want heat to escape; sometimes we want to keep it from escaping. In the case of heat engines, such as the gasoline engine, only some of the heat can be used to do work. It is necessary to get rid of the excess heat or the engine would rapidly overheat. In the case of heating a home, we want the heat to get from the furnace to the apartment, but we may want to keep the heat from getting out of the apartment. The three methods of heat transfer are conduction, convection, and radiation.

Conduction

Conduction is the process of transferring heat through a medium which does not involve appreciable motion of the medium. For example, if we heat one end of a copper rod, the other end gets hot, too. The energy transfer in metallic conductors is chiefly by means of "free" electrons, but also involves bombardment of one molecule by the next. In general, metals are good conductors; good conductors of heat are also good conductors of electricity. Silver is the best metallic conductor of heat and electricity. Copper and aluminum are also very good.

Liquids and gases, as well as non-metallic solids, are poor conductors of heat. Poor conductors are known as *insulators*.

Convection

Convection is the process of transferring heat in a fluid which involves the motion of the heated portion to the cooler portion of the fluid. The heated portion expands, rises, and is replaced by cooler fluid, thus giving rise to so-called convection currents. This may be observed over a hot radiator: The heated air expands; since its density is different from that of the surrounding colder air it reflects some light and can be "seen" to move up. Radiators heat rooms chiefly by convection, and, therefore, are more effective when placed near the floor than when placed near the ceiling. Also note that when the heated fluid rises it mixes with the cooler fluid.

Radiation

Radiation is the process of transferring heat which can take place in a vacuum; it takes place by a wave motion similar to light. The wave is known as an *electromagnetic wave* and will be discussed further in a later chapter. The higher the temperature of an object, the greater the amount of heat it radiates. Black objects radiate more heat from each square centimeter of surface than light-colored objects at the same temperature.

The *vacuum bottle* (thermos bottle) is designed with the three methods of heat transfer in mind. The bottle is made of glass—a good insulator. The stopper is made of cork or plastic—also good insulators. This minimizes heat transfer by conduction. The space between the double walls is evacuated, minimizing heat transfer by convection. The inside surfaces (facing the vacuum) are silvered; shiny surfaces reflect electromagnetic waves. This minimizes heat transfer by radiation. As a result, hot liquids inside the bottle stay hot and cold liquids stay cold many hours.

Cork
Double walled glass bottle
Vacuum
Silvered surfaces

ENERGY SOURCES

For heating buildings and operating machines human beings have depended almost solely on fossil fuels such as coal and oil. Although new deposits keep being located and tapped, many people think that these fuels will be found inadequate in very few years. Waterfalls, of course, can be used in locations close enough to exploit economically this source of energy. Waterfalls and fossil fuels ultimately owe their energy to the sun. Energy keeps coming to the earth from the sun by radiation (about 2 calories per minute on each square centimeter in full sunlight). In some parts of the world large, curved mirrors are arranged to permit the use of this sunlight for cooking and heating. A tremendous amount of energy is available in the constant motion of the tides. However, it is believed that as the population grows and the standard of living goes up, all these sources of energy will prove inadequate. Some think the hope of the future lies in nuclear energy—energy released when certain changes take place in the nucleus of atoms. Scientists have already learned to obtain nuclear energy resulting from the splitting or fission of nuclei of heavy elements such as uranium. This is done in a controlled manner in the nuclear reactor (or atomic pile). Only relatively small quantities of such fissionable materials are available. Nuclear energy can also be obtained by the combining or fusion of the nuclei of light atoms, such as hydrogen. If this can be done in a controllable manner, a practically endless supply of energy will be available, because hydrogen, the necessary "fuel," is obtainable from the oceans in almost unlimited quantity. Nuclear energy will be discussed further in a later chapter. (Also see *solar cells*.) Some houses have roof-top installations with circulating fluids to absorb solar energy for producing hot water and heat.

QUESTIONS Chapter 7

Select the choice that best answers the question or completes the sentence.

1. Radiation is the chief method of energy transfer   **(A)** from the sun to an earth satellite   **(B)** from a gas flame to water in a teakettle   **(C)** from a soldering iron to metals being soldered   **(D)** from water to an ice cube floating in it   **(E)** from a mammal to the surrounding air

2. Of the processes below, the one in which practically all the heat transfer is by conduction is   **(A)** from the sun to an earth satellite   **(B)** from a gas flame to the top layer of water in a teakettle   **(C)** from a soldering iron to metals being soldered   **(D)** from the bottom of a glass of water to an ice cube floating in it   **(E)** from a mammal to the surrounding air

3. Two kilograms of water are heated by stirring. If this raises the temperature of the water from $15°C$ to $25°C$, how much work, in joules, was done to the water by the stirring? **(A)** 20,000   **(B)** 40,000   **(C)** 60,000   **(D)** 80,000   **(E)** 100,000

4. In a certain steam engine, the average pressure on the piston during a stroke is 50 lb/in.^{2} The length of each stroke is 12 in., the area of the piston is 120 in.^{2}, and the diameter of the flywheel is 5 ft. The amount of work done on the piston during each stroke is, in ft-lb, approximately   **(A)** 250   **(B)** 6000   **(C)** 30,000   **(D)** 72,000   **(E)** 96,000

5. The work done *to* a system is characterized as **(A)** positive   **(B)** negative   **(C)** either positive or negative   **(D)** indeterminate   **(E)** of no consequence

6. Which of the following can actually lower the internal energy ("cool") a room? **(A)** a fan   **(B)** a refrigerator with its door open   **(C)** a refrigerator with its door closed   **(D)** an air conditioner in the middle of a room   **(E)** an air conditioner partially exposed to the outside.

7. Thirty joules of heat flow into a system. The system in turn does 50 joules of work. The internal energy of the system has **(A)** increased by 80 joules   **(B)** decreased by 80 joules   **(C)** increased by 20 joules   **(D)** decreased by 20 joules   **(E)** remained constant

8. Dark, rough objects are generally good for **(A)** conduction   **(B)** radiation   **(C)** convection **(D)** reflection   **(E)** refraction

9. Dark plastic handles are often used on kitchen utensils because **(A)** the black material is a good radiator   **(B)** the plastic is a good insulator   **(C)** the plastic is a good conductor   **(D)** the plastic softens gradually with excessive heat   **(E)** the material is thermoplastic

10. A person seated in front of a fire in a fireplace receives heat chiefly by **(A)** convection of carbon dioxide   **(B)** convection of carbon monoxide   **(C)** convection of air   **(D)** conduction   **(E)** radiation

11. The unit which does not represent the same physical quantity as the others is the **(A)** British thermal unit   **(B)** calorie   **(C)** horsepower   **(D)** joule   **(E)** foot-pound

12. If friction is negligible, when a gas is compressed rapidly **(A)** its temperature remains the same   **(B)** its temperature goes down   **(C)** its temperature rises   **(D)** it is liquefied   **(E)** work is done by the gas

EXPLANATIONS TO QUESTIONS Chapter 7

Answers

1. **(A)**	3. **(D)**	5. **(B)**	7. **(D)**	9. **(B)**	11. **(C)**
2. **(C)**	4. **(B)**	6. **(E)**	8. **(B)**	10. **(E)**	12. **(C)**

Explanations

1. **(A)** The space between the sun and an earth satellite is an almost perfect vacuum. Conduction and convection cannot take place through a vacuum. Although some particles are shot out of the sun and thus carry kinetic energy with them to the satellite, this energy is small in comparison with the amount constantly carried away by electromagnetic waves—by radiation. (Also see answer to the next question.)

2. **(C)** The soldering iron is in good contact with the metal to be soldered and thus provides excellent opportunity for heat transfer by conduction. The tip of a soldering iron is often made of copper to provide for better heat conduction. Although a teakettle, if made of metal, provides for some heating of the top layer of water in the kettle by conduction along the kettle, the top layer is heated chiefly by convection: the bottom layer gets heated, rises towards the top where it mixes with the colder top and also pushes the top layer toward the bottom. Similar reasoning applies to choice (D). Mammals lose heat by the exhalation of warm air, evaporation of perspiration from the skin, convection, etc.

3. **(D)** 100% efficiency is implied.

work done = heat supplied = mass × sp. ht. × temp. change
$$= (2 \text{ kg})(4.19 \text{ kJ/kg} \bullet \text{C}°)(25° - 15°) = 80 \text{ kJ} = 80,000 \text{ J}.$$

4. **(B)** pressure = force/area; force = pA

work = force × distance = pressure × area × distance
$$\text{work} = 50 \text{ lb/in.}^2 \times 120 \text{ in.}^2 \times 1 \text{ ft} = 6000 \text{ ft-lb}$$

Note that the distance the piston moves has to be converted to feet in order to have the unit of work be ft-lb. Also note that the diameter of the flywheel is irrelevant.

5. **(B)** By convention, the work done *by* a system is positive. Therefore, the work done *to* a system is negative.

6. **(E)** To cool a room, heat must be *removed.* In fact, *all* of the other choices result in an increase in room temperature, as the electric energy used to run the devices is dissipated as heat.

7. **(D)** $Q = \Delta U + W$

$$+30J = \Delta U + 50J$$
$$\underline{-50J \qquad -50J}$$
$$-20J = \Delta U$$

8. **(B)** This question involves mere recall of a fact mentioned in the chapter which everyone is expected to know.

9. **(B)** Although the black material is a good radiator, this is irrelevant. The important part is that the plastic is a good insulator of heat. It is not desirable that the plastic soften. The term thermoplastic is not essential for elementary physics. It refers to the property of softening when heat is applied. Such a plastic is usually not desirable in handles of kitchen utensils; choice (E) is essentially the same as choice (D).

10. **(E)** Convection of any kind would lead to the rising of the heated gases, in this case up the chimney, not to the person. Very little conduction to the person can take place, since the intervening air is a poor conductor.

11. **(C)** All units are units of energy (heat or any other form) except horsepower, which is a unit of power.

12. **(C)** When a gas is compressed, work is done on the gas. This tends to heat the gas even if friction is absent. If the compression takes place rapidly, the heat produced can't escape completely and the temperature of the gas rises. Similarly, if a gas is allowed to expand rapidly its temperature goes down.

Wave Motion and Sound

What is the difference between ultrasonic and supersonic? What happens to the speed of sound under a bell jar from which the air is being exhausted? What happens to the loudness of sound when a second wave arrives at a point where before there was only one wave?

WAVE MOTION

Wave motion in a medium is a method of transferring energy through a medium by means of a distortion of the medium which travels away from the place where the distortion is produced. The medium itself moves only a little bit. For example, a pebble dropped into quiet water disturbs it. The water near the pebble does not move far, but a disturbance travels away from that spot. This disturbance is the wave. As a result some of the energy lost by the pebble is carried through the water by a wave, and a cork floating at some distance away can be lifted by the water; thus the cork gets some energy. We can set up a succession of waves in the water by pushing a finger rhythmically through the surface of the water. A vibrating tuning fork produces waves in air.

Waves can be classified in different ways. The wave produced by the pebble dropped into the water is a *pulse:* a single vibratory disturbance which travels away from the source of the disturbance through the medium. If we push our finger regularly and rapidly down and up through the surface of the water, we produce a periodic wave.

Periodic Motion

Periodic motion is motion which is repeated over and over again. The motion of a *pendulum* is periodic. As long as its arc of swing is small, the time required for a back-and-forth swing is constant. This time is called its period and is given by the formula $T = 2\pi\sqrt{L'/g}$, where L' is the length of the string from which the bob is suspended, and g is acceleration due to gravity.

The motion of the tuning fork prongs is periodic. As the prongs vibrate back and forth they push particles in the air; these push other particles, etc. When the prong moves to the right, particles are pushed to the right; when the prong moves to the left, the particles move back into the space left by the prong. As the prong moves back and forth, the particles of the medium move back and forth *with the same frequency* as the prong. The energy travels away from the vibrating source, but the particles of the medium vibrate back and forth past the same spot (their equilibrium position).

Longitudinal and Transverse Waves

Two basic waves are the longitudinal wave and the transverse wave. The wave produced in air by a vibrating tuning fork illustrates the former. A *longitudinal wave* is a wave in which the particles of the medium vibrate back and forth along the path which the wave travels. Sound waves are longitudinal waves.

A *transverse wave* in a medium is a wave in which the vibrations of the medium are at right angles to the direction in which the wave is traveling. A transverse wave is readily set up along a rope. Either a longitudinal or transverse wave can be readily sent along a helical spring. A water wave is approximately transverse. The propagation of light can be described as a transverse wave. Since light can travel through a vacuum, this raises an interesting question regarding what is vibrating. This will be discussed further under the heading of electromagnetic waves.

Simple longitudinal and simple transverse waves can be represented by a sine curve. Let us first consider the production of a transverse wave set up in a rope. Imagine the rope stretched hori-

zontally with a prong of a vibrating tuning fork attached to the left end of the rope so as to produce a transverse wave in it. When the prong moves up, the rope is pulled up and the upward disturbance starts to travel to the right. As the prong moves down, the rope is pulled down and a downward displacement moves along the rope, following the upward displacement. When the prong moves up again, it produces the second peak to follow peak 1.

The whole pattern or wave shown can be imagined moving to the right with a certain speed, the speed of the wave in the medium (the rope). If we keep our eye on some specific spot on the rope, we see that part of the rope going up and down, transverse, or at right angles to the direction of motion of the wave as a whole.

The *frequency of vibration of each part of the rope is the same as the frequency of vibration of the source (the tuning fork) and the same as the number of peaks or troughs produced per second. The amplitude* of the wave is the maximum displacement or distance moved by each part of the medium away from its average or equilibrium position. In the diagram *A* represents the amplitude of the wave, and λ is the *wavelength*—the distance between any two successive peaks, or the distance between any two successive corresponding parts of the wave, such as *X* and *Y*.

As we watch the wave moving past a given spot of the medium, we can see peak after peak moving past the spot. The time required for two successive peaks to pass the spot is known as the *period* of the wave. It is the time required for the wave to move a distance equal to one wavelength. It is the same as the period of vibration of the source.

Since, for motion with constant speed, distance = speed × time, the speed of the wave equals the wavelength divided by the period. The *frequency (f)* of the wave is the number of complete vibrations back and forth per second. Since the period is the time for one vibration,

$$T = \frac{1}{f}$$

Therefore, the speed of the wave equals the wavelength divided by one over the frequency. Instead of dividing, invert and multiply. The end result is the important relationship for a wave.

speed of a wave = frequency of wave × wavelength

$$v = f \times \lambda$$

The Greek letter *lambda* (λ) is frequently used for wavelength.

When something occurs over and over again, the term *cycle* is sometimes used to refer to the event which is repeated. We can speak of a wave having 100 vibrations per second or having 100 cycles per second. The metric and SI unit for frequency is the hertz (Hz). The term *wave* is sometimes used to refer to one cycle of the disturbance in the medium. In the sine curve shown above, the portion of the curve from X to Y would then be one wave.

Example: A wave having a frequency of 1000 cycles per second has a speed of 1200 meters per second in a certain solid. Calculate the period and the wavelength.

The period $T = (1/f) = (1/1000)$ second $= 0.001$ second

The wavelength $\lambda = (v/f) = (1200$ meters/second$)/(1000$ cycles/second$) = 1.2$ meters/cycle. Notice that, in the calculation of wavelength, *second* cancels. Often we also drop *cycle* from the answer and give the wavelength as 1.2 m.

The sine curve shown above can be used to represent a longitudinal wave as well as a transverse wave. This will be described under the discussion of sound. The above relationships and definitions apply to both types of waves. All waves also exhibit certain phenomena in common: reflection, refraction, interference, and diffraction. In addition, transverse waves exhibit the phenomenon of polarization. These phenomena will be described later.

SOUND

In physics, when we speak about sound, we usually mean the sound wave. Sound waves are longitudinal waves in gases, liquids, or solids. They are produced by vibrating objects. Sound cannot be transmitted through a vacuum. In order to describe the sound wave let us imagine the production of sound by means of a tuning fork vibrating in air. As the prong moves to the right, air is pushed to the right; since the air at the right is pushed closer together, a region of higher pressure is produced. This region of higher pressure is known as a *compression* or *condensation.* Because of the higher pressure, some air from the compression travels on to the right, thus producing another compression. In this way a compression travels away from the tuning fork. The speed with which it travels is the speed of the wave in air. In the meantime, because of its elasticity, the prong of the tuning fork starts moving back towards the left. As it does so air from the right rushes into the space left by the prong. The space from which the air rushes then becomes a region of lower pressure than normal. Regions of reduced pressure are known as *rarefactions.* Air at the right of the rarefaction is pushed towards the left, in turn producing a rarefaction further over to the right. Thus a rarefaction travels out to the right, following the compression. When the prong starts moving to the right again it starts another condensation, etc. The *longitudinal wave* is a succession of compressions and rarefactions, one complete vibration of the fork producing one compression and rarefaction.

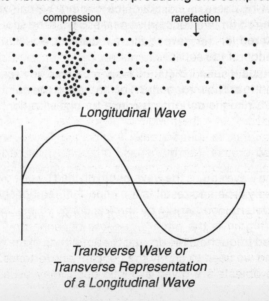

Longitudinal Wave

Transverse Wave or
Transverse Representation
of a Longitudinal Wave

If the wave hits another medium, such as a solid, compressions and rarefactions will be set up in the new medium. The frequency of the wave in the new medium will be the same as in air, but the speeds, and therefore the wavelengths, will be different.

If a sine curve is to be used to represent a longitudinal wave, the Y-axis may be used to represent the change in pressure of the medium as a result of the wave. A compression has an increase in pressure and can be represented as a positive number, while a rarefaction has a decrease in pressure, which would be represented by a negative number. The abscissa is used as for the transverse wave.

The abscissa may be the distance along the direction of wave travel. The curve then represents the change in pressure at a given moment plotted against distance along the medium. A crest then represents a compression, a trough a rarefaction. The wavelength is the distance between successive compressions or successive rarefactions. (It is interesting to note that a point of maximum pressure is also a point of zero displacement.)

A sine curve can also be drawn to represent the change in pressure at a *specific point* in the medium against *time.* The distance between successive compressions on such a graph would give the *period* of the wave as well as the period of vibration of a particle in the medium.

The *speed of sound* in air is approximately 1090 ft/sec or 331 m/s at 0°C. The speed goes up 0.6 m/s (2 ft/sec) for each Celsius degree that the temperature goes up. Don't get mixed up in memorizing this fact—note that the change in speed is given per Celsius degree in both systems of units. The speed of sound in air is independent of the atmospheric pressure. In general, sound travels faster in liquids and solids than in air.

Musical Sounds

Sounds produced by regular vibration of the air are musical. Irregular vibrations of the air are classified as unpleasant sounds or noise. This is often demonstrated with a *siren* consisting of a wheel with concentric sets of holes. The wheel rotates at constant speed around an axis perpendicular to the wheel and passing through its center. The holes in the two innermost circles are evenly spaced. When air is blown gently at either of these circles, a pleasant, musical sound is heard. The wheel blocks the air at a constant rate and the blasts of air going through the holes produce compressions at a constant rate. The holes in the outermost circle are irregularly spaced. When air is blown gently at this circle, air allowed through the holes produces successive compressions which follow each other at irregular intervals. What a person perceives is noise.

Siren

The *range in frequencies* of musical sounds is approximately 20-20,000 hertz or cycles per second. Some people can hear higher frequencies than others. Longitudinal waves whose frequencies are higher than those within the audible range are called *ultrasonic* frequencies. Ultrasonic frequencies are used in sonar for such purposes as submarine detection and depth finding. Ultrasonic frequencies are also being tried for sterilizing food since these frequencies kill some bacteria. Sound waves of all frequencies in the audible range travel at the same speed in the same medium. In the audible range, the higher the frequency of the sound the higher is the *pitch*. For example, in the above siren, the pitch produced with the middle circle of holes is higher than with the innermost circle. The term *supersonic* refers to speed greater than sound. An airplane traveling at supersonic speed is moving at a speed greater than the speed of sound in air at that temperature. *Mach 1* means a speed equal to that of sound; Mach 2 means a speed equal to twice that of sound, etc.

Musical sounds have three basic *characteristics:* pitch, loudness, and quality or timbre. As was indicated above, *pitch* is determined largely by the frequency of the wave reaching the ear. The higher the frequency the higher is the pitch. *Loudness* depends on the amplitude of the wave reaching the ear. For a given frequency, the greater the amplitude of the wave the louder the sound. To discuss quality of sound we need to clarify the concept of overtones. Sounds are produced by vibrating objects; if these objects are given a gentle push, they usually vibrate at one definite frequency producing a pure tone. This is the way a tuning fork is usually used. When objects vibrate freely after a force is momentarily applied, they are said to produce their *natural frequency*. Some objects, like strings and air columns, can vibrate naturally at more than one frequency at a time. The lowest frequency which an object can produce when vibrating freely is known as the object's *fundamental frequency;* other frequencies that the object can produce are known as its *overtones*. The *quality* of a sound depends on the number and relative amplitude of the overtones present in the wave reaching the ear.

When a wave reaches another medium, part of the wave is usually reflected. When a sound wave is reflected, a distinct *echo* is heard if the reflected sound wave reaches the ear at least 1/10 second after the sound traveling directly from the vibrating source to the ear. Echoes may be used to determine the distance of reflecting objects, as in sonar. The total distance traveled by the wave is equal to the speed of the wave in the medium multiplied by the time between the start of the sound and the arrival of the echo. If the reflected wave comes back along the same path as the incident wave, the distance to the reflecting surface, such as a wall, is one-half of the total distance.

Resonance and Interference

As was stated above, objects tend to vibrate at their natural frequency. A simple pendulum has a natural frequency. Recall that

$$period \text{ of a simple pendulum} = 2\pi\sqrt{length/acceleration\ due\ to\ gravity}$$

and *frequency equals one over the period:* $f = 1/T$. Similarly a swing has a natural frequency of vibration. If given a gentle push the swing will vibrate at this frequency without any other push. Because of friction the amplitude of vibration decreases gradually; to keep the swing going, it is necessary to supply only a little push to the swing at its natural frequency or at a submultiple of this frequency. The swing can be forced to vibrate or oscillate at many other frequencies. All one has to do is to hold on to the swing and push it at the desired frequency. Such vibration is known as *forced vibration*. For example, our eardrum can be forced to vibrate at any of a wide range of frequencies by the sound reaching the ear. We can think of a distant vibrating tuning fork forcing the eardrum to oscillate by means of a longitudinal wave from the fork to the ear.

Resonance

Resonance between two systems exists if vibration of one system results in vibration or oscillation of the second system, whose natural frequency is the same as that of the first. In the case of sound the two systems may be two tuning forks of the same frequency. We mount the two forks on suitable boxes at opposite ends of a table. We strike one tuning fork, let it vibrate for a while, and then put our hand on it to stop the vibration. We will then be able to hear the second fork. It resonated to the first one. What caused the second tuning fork to vibrate? Compressions starting from the first fork gave the second fork successive pushes at the right time to build up the amplitude of its oscillations. Thus energy was transferred from the first fork to the second fork by means of the wave. When resonance occurs with sound, the term *sympathetic vibration* is also used: the second fork is said to be in sympathetic vibration with the first one. Later we shall discuss cases of resonance which do not involve sound waves.

One can think of an *air column* in a tube as having a natural frequency. The natural frequency of an air column depends on its length. If a vibrating tuning fork is held over an air column of the right length, resonance will occur between the fork and the air column; if the length of the air column is varied, a loud sound will be heard at resonance. The length of the closed resonant air column is about one-fourth of the wavelength, as will be discussed later.

Interference

Interference occurs when two waves go through the same portion of the medium at the same time. If, at a given time and place, the two waves tend to make the medium vibrate in the same direction, we have *reinforcement* or constructive interference. For example, waves I and II combine to give wave III.

Note in the diagram that in waves I and II peaks coincide with peaks and troughs with troughs. Such waves are said to be in *phase*. They produce maximum reinforcement or *constructive interference*. Sometimes we speak about *points* in a given wave as being in phase. For example, which point is in phase with point *B*?

We can think of the diagram as representing a periodic wave moving to the right. The particles have been displaced from their equilibrium position represented by the horizontal line. Points on a wave which are a whole number of wavelengths apart are in phase; they are going through the same part of the vibration at the same time. Point *E* is two full wavelengths ahead of point *B*. They are in phase. Point *C* is about one-half of a wavelength ahead of point *B*. They are opposite in phase.

If two waves tend to make the medium vibrate in opposite directions, we have *destructive interference*. The two waves then tend to cancel each other. For example, waves IV and V together produce wave VI.

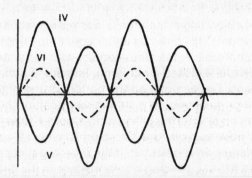

The peaks of one coincide with the troughs of the other. This is the condition for maximum destructive interference. Waves IV and V are said to be opposite in phase, or 180° apart, or 180° out of phase.

If two sounds reach the ear at the same time, interference takes place.

Beats are heard when two notes of slightly different frequencies reach the ear at the same time.

the number of beats = the difference between the two frequencies

A beat is an outburst of sound followed by comparative silence. Beats result from the interference of the two waves reaching the ear. When two compressions or two rarefactions combine, the eardrum vibrates with relatively large amplitude and a loud sound is heard. When a compression combines with a rarefaction, they tend to annul each other and relatively little sound is heard.

The resultant wave produced by two sources of slightly different frequencies sounded at the same time can be represented like this:

Notice that at *A* and *B* we have a relatively large amplitude corresponding to an outburst of sound and at *C* and *D* a rather small amplitude corresponding to comparative silence.

VIBRATING AIR COLUMNS

Some musical instruments, such as organ pipes, produce sound by means of vibrating air columns. We can set the air column into vibration by blowing across or into one end of the pipe.

Closed Pipes

A closed pipe has one end closed. The end we blow into is always considered open. As indicated before, one way to describe the vibrating air column is to say that it has natural frequencies of vibration. Its lowest frequency of vibration (fundamental) is one for which the wavelength equals approximately four times the length of the air column. *For example,* a closed air column which is one foot long produces a sound whose wavelength is 4 ft. If the speed of sound is 1100 ft/sec, the frequency of vibration = speed of sound divided by the wavelength, or 1100 ft/sec divided by 4 ft, which gives 275 vibrations per sec for the frequency (*f*). This is the fundamental frequency. The *overtones* which a closed air column can produce are odd multiples of the fundamental frequency (3*f*, 5*f*, 7*f*, etc.).

Another way to describe a vibrating air column is in terms of resonance. Imagine a narrow cylinder with some water at the bottom. This gives us an air column of length l_a. Since water is practically

incompressible, the air in contact with the water cannot move down. This is, therefore, a closed air column. Imagine a tuning fork vibrating above the air column. Concentrate on the bottom prong of the fork. Its rest or equilibrium position is shown at *r;* its highest position at *4;* its lowest position during vibration at *2*. As the prong moves from *4* towards *2*, a compression forms at *r* and travels down the air column; when it reaches the water surface the compression is reflected. If the reflected compression reaches the prong just when it is at *r*, sending a compression in the direction away from the tube, the fork's vibration will be reinforced. The result is resonance between the vibrating tuning fork and air column—a loud sound is heard if the right amount of water has been poured in. How long should this air column be? The time required for the prong to go from *4* to *2* is one-half of the period of vibration. During this time the wave travels a distance equal to one-half of a wavelength (λ). But in this experiment this distance traveled was up and down the air column. Therefore $2l_a = \lambda/2$; or

$$\lambda = 4l_a$$

That is, for a resonant closed air column, the wavelength of the fundamental is equal to four times the length of the air column, as was stated before. However, suppose with the same air column we use a tuning fork whose frequency is three times higher than the one we used before. Its prong will vibrate from *4* to *2* in one-third the time, but the speed of the wave is not changed. Therefore, during this time the wave will have traveled only one-third of the total back-and-forth distance, which is two-thirds of the length of the air column. By the time the wave is reflected by the water and comes back to the tuning fork the prong has gone back to *4* and has just reached *2* again. Again the reflected air wave reinforces the vibration of the tuning fork. Again the air column resonated to the tuning fork. This time the closed air column vibrated at three times its fundamental frequency and produced its first overtone.

Open Pipes

An *open pipe* is open at both ends; the air can move freely at both ends. When an open pipe is vibrating so as to produce its fundamental frequency, the length of the air column (l_a) is equal to one-half of the wavelength (λ) produced; or the wavelength is equal to twice the length of the air column.

$$\lambda = 2l_a$$

An open pipe can produce not only odd multiples of its fundamental frequency, but also even multiples. The first overtone is twice the fundamental frequency; the second overtone three times, etc. (2f, 3f, 4f, 5f, etc.).

VIBRATING STRINGS

If a string is fastened at both ends and plucked or bowed at some point in between, it will vibrate transversely. Some frequencies of vibration will be natural for the string and will persist. The *fundamental* frequency of the string is the lowest of these natural or free vibrations; for this frequency, the wavelength in the string is equal to twice the length of the string (l_s).

$$\lambda = 2l_s$$

Notice that this describes the wave in the *string*. The transverse vibration of the string sets up a longitudinal wave in the surrounding air: the sound wave. The frequency of the sound wave is the same as the frequency of vibration of the string; but since the speed of the wave in the string is different from the speed of the wave in the air, the wavelengths in the two media are different ($v = f\lambda$). The *overtones* which a string can produce are the odd and even multiples of the fundamental frequency (2f, 3f, 4f, 5f, etc.) Notice that in this respect a vibrating string is similar to a vibrating open air column.

Vibrating strings can also be described in terms of *standing waves* or stationary waves. When the string is plucked, the wave travels to both ends from which it is then reflected. These reflections can take place over and over again. As a result waves go in opposite directions through the string and interference takes place. At the ends, where the string is fastened, no vibration can take place. These places of no vibration are known as *nodes*. In between there may be one or more places where the waves reinforce each other completely. These places of maximum vibration are known as *antinodes*. When overtones are produced, there will also be one or more nodes along the length of the string. The distance between successive nodes is one-half a wavelength of the wave in the string. When a string produces its fundamental frequency, it is said to vibrate as a whole; when it produces overtones, it vibrates in parts.

Laws of Vibrating Strings

The fundamental frequency of vibration of a string depends on its length, its tension, and its mass per unit length. If one of these is varied at a time, the effect is as follows:
1. The frequency varies inversely as the length; i.e., making the string twice as long produces a frequency one-half as high.

2. The frequency varies directly as the square root of the tension; i.e., to double the frequency the force stretching the string must be quadrupled.

3. The frequency varies inversely as the square root of the mass per unit length.

DOPPLER EFFECT

If there is relative motion between the source of the wave and the observer, the frequency of vibrations received by the observer will be different from the frequency produced by the source. In the case of sound this will affect the pitch of the perceived sound, since pitch depends on the number of vibrations reaching the ear per second. When the source and observer approach each other, the pitch will be higher than if both were stationary; the pitch will be lower if source and observer are going further apart.

In the top diagram the source is stationary. The diagram shows compressions going to the right

and left away from the source at S. The compressions are equally spaced, and the pitch will be the same for the stationary observers at X and Y.

The bottom diagram shows the compressions going to the right and left as a result of motion of the source at constant speed from point 4 to 2. Compression 4' was produced when the source was at 4; compression 3' when the source was at 3, etc. Notice that the compressions are more closely spaced in the direction towards which the source is moving (towards the right in this case). Therefore the pitch for observer Y' will be higher than for observer X'. Notice that the wavelength changed as a result of the source's motion. It decreased in the direction of motion and increased in the opposite direction.

Decibel

The human ear responds to an extremely wide range of sound intensities. It has therefore become customary to express the level of sound intensity or sound power by the logarithm of the ratio comparing the intensity or power to that of an arbitrary sound. The bel was orginally used as the unit to express this level; the decibel is now used. The intensity or power is said to be a number of decibels (db) above (or below) the reference level as given by the expression:

$$\text{decibels} = 10 \log \frac{P_1}{P_2}$$

where P_2 is the power or intensity level of the reference and P_1 is the power or intensity of the sound being investigated. The reference level (zero db) is usually taken as the one that is barely audible. The sound level of ordinary speech is about 20 db. The same system is used to describe the output of electronic amplifiers.

9

Geometrical Optics: Reflection and Refraction

Why is it that images seen in plane mirrors seem smaller than the corresponding objects, although "the size of the image in a plane mirror is the same size as the object?" Why is it that we can take a photograph of our image in a plane mirror, although "the image is virtual and cannot be seen on a screen placed at the position of the image?" We need to understand reflection, refraction, the operation of lenses, and the eye to answer these and similar questions. Any phenomenon that can be described by thinking of light in a given medium as traveling in straight lines comes under the heading of geometrical optics. It is convenient to use the *ray* to represent the direction in which the light travels.

REFLECTION

When light hits a surface, usually some of the light is reflected. The *normal* for this light is the line drawn perpendicular to the surface at the point where the light ray touches the surface. The light that goes towards the surface is known as *incident* light and is represented by the incident ray. The angle of incidence (i) is the angle between the incident ray and its normal. The reflected light is represented by the reflected ray; the angle of reflection (r) is the angle between the reflected ray and its normal.

Normal   Normal

The *law of reflection* states that, when a wave is reflected, the angle of incidence equals the angle of reflection, and the incident ray, the normal, and the reflected ray lie in one plane. Notice that this applies not only to light but also to other waves and that this is true of smooth and rough surfaces.

If a surface is smooth and flat, we get *regular reflection*. Parallel incident rays are reflected as parallel rays. Most surfaces are rough to a degree. This is true even of this paper. From it we get

Diffuse Reflection

diffuse reflection: reflected light goes off in all directions even when the incident light is parallel. Non-luminous objects are visible because diffusely reflected light from their surfaces enters our eyes. A perfectly smooth reflecting surface cannot be seen. Luminous objects are seen because light they emit enters our eyes.

Image in Plane Mirror

A plane mirror is a perfectly flat mirror. The characteristics of an image produced by such a mirror can be determined by means of a *ray diagram:*

We can represent the object in some suitable way; often an arrow is used. We take two rays from the top of the object, point *A,* and draw the corresponding reflected rays, making the angle of reflection equal to the angle of incidence. The observer into whose eye these reflected rays go imagines them to come from some point behind the mirror: the point where the extensions of the reflected rays meet, point *A*. This is the image point corresponding to the top point on the object. The extensions of the reflected rays are shown dotted because the rays of light, and the image, are not actually behind the mirror. We do the same with the other end of the object. If we take a ray that is perpendicular to the surface, after reflection it will go right back along the same path. From the diagram we can determine the *characteristics* of an image in a plane mirror:

1. The image is the same size as the object.
2. The image is erect (if the object is erect).
3. The image is as far behind the mirror as the object is in front. (Every point is as far behind the mirror as the corresponding object point is in front.)
4. The image is *virtual.* This means that the image is formed by rays which do not actually pass through it; if a screen were placed at the position of the image, no image would be seen.
5. The image is laterally reversed. This can be thought of in terms of two people shaking hands: their arms extend diagonally between them. When a person holds his hand out to the mirror, the arm of his image comes out straight at him.

Image in Curved Mirrors

Spherical surfaces are commonly used as the reflecting surfaces of curved mirrors. A *convex* mirror is one whose reflecting surface is the outside of a spherical shell. A *concave* mirror is one whose reflecting surface is the inside of a spherical shell. The *center of curvature (C)* is the center of the spherical shell. The *principal axis* is the line through the center of curvature and the midpoint of the mirror. Incident rays parallel to the principal axis pass through a common point on the principal axis after reflection by a concave mirror. This point is the *principal focus (F)* of the mirror.

Concave Mirror   Convex Mirror

A convex mirror also has a principal focus. Incident rays parallel to the principal axis are reflected by a convex mirror so that the reflected rays seem to come from a common point on the principal axis. This principal focus is a virtual focus because the rays don't really meet there. The *focal length* (*f*) is the distance from the principal focus to the mirror. For a spherical mirror the focal length is equal to one-half of the radius of the spherical shell.

$$f = R/2$$

We need one more idea in order to draw ray diagrams of spherical mirrors: a radius is perpendicular to its circle and is the direction of the normal. Therefore a ray directed along the radius of the spherical shell is perpendicular to the spherical mirror. The angle of incidence is then equal to zero and so is the angle of reflection. Therefore a ray going through the center of curvature (*C*) of the mirror is reflected right back upon itself.

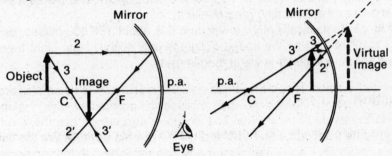

Images with Concave Mirrors

The technique for drawing the ray diagram follows: We try to find the points of the image that correspond to selected points of the object. We often use an arrow as the object, and if we place the arrow so that its tail touches the principal axis, we need to use rays only from the head of the arrow. The tail of the image will also touch the principal axis. We select two special rays from the head of the arrow; we already know their paths after reflection. Ray 2, parallel to the principal axis, after reflection, passes through the principal focus. Ray 3, whose direction passes through the center of curvature, is normal to the mirror and is reflected right back upon itself. The reflected rays, 2' and 3', intersect in the left diagram and produce a *real image* on a screen placed there.

In the diagram on the right the reflected rays don't meet and therefore do not produce a real image. However, a person into whose eye the reflected light goes will see an image behind the mirror, at the place where the extended reflected rays meet. This is a virtual image, as in the plane mirror. Rays extended behind the mirror are always drawn dotted. The virtual image is often shown dotted, too.

Any other ray starting from the head of the arrow, after reflection, will pass through the head of the image.

Notice that with the concave mirror we can get both real and virtual images. With the convex mirror we can get only virtual images. The procedure for the ray diagram is as above.

Images with Convex Mirrors

Notice that the center of curvature and the principal focus are on the inside of the spherical shell. The parallel ray is reflected so that it will seem to come from the principal focus. The ray directed towards the center of curvature is reflected right back upon itself. The rays originally starting from the same point on the object don't meet after reflection and therefore cannot produce a real image. The observer sees a virtual image behind the mirror. The virtual image formed with a convex mirror is smaller than the object; the virtual image formed with a concave mirror is larger than the object.

Careful analysis shows that spherical mirrors don't work precisely as described on the previous page. The difference is usually negligible. However, such aberrations can cause problems in astronomical telescopes using large mirrors. Instead of spherical mirrors they usually use parabolic mirrors, which are much more expensive.

REFRACTION

Refraction is the bending of a wave on going into a second medium. Refraction depends on the difference in speed of the wave in the two media. The medium in which the light travels more slowly is known as the optically denser medium or, for short, the *denser medium*. This should not be confused with mass density (ratio of mass to volume of a substance). The medium in which the light travels faster is known as the (optically) *rarer* medium.

The *speed of light* is fantastically high. In vacuum it is about 186,000 mi/sec, or about 3×10^{10} cm/s, or about 3×10^8 m/s. In air the speed of light is only slightly less. Light travels faster in air than in liquids and solids, and faster in water than in glass.

Law of Refraction

A ray of light passing obliquely into a denser medium is bent towards the normal; a ray of light

entering a rarer medium obliquely is bent away from the normal; a ray entering a second medium at right angles to the surface goes through without being bent or deviated. The angle formed by the refracted ray and its normal is known as the angle of refraction.

The *index of refraction* (*n*) of a substance is defined as the ratio of the sine of the angle of incidence in vacuum to the sine of the angle of refraction in the substance. For many puposes we can use air instead of vacuum.

$$n = \frac{\sin \theta_1}{\sin \theta_2}$$

The index of refraction is also equal to the ratio of the speed of light in vacuum to the speed in the substance:

$$n = \frac{\text{speed of light in vacuum (or air)}}{\text{speed of light in the substance}}$$

The index of refraction is usually given as a number greater than one. This becomes awkward when the light goes from the denser substance into air, as in the right of the preceding diagram, where the angle of incidence is in glass and is smaller than the angle of refraction formed as the ray comes out into the air. Therefore, once we understand the principles involved, it is desirable to leave out of the definition the phrases "angle of incidence" and "angle of refraction." To calculate the index of refraction we divide the sine of the angle in vacuum (or air) by the sine of the angle in the denser medium. In the first figure shown in this chapter, for example,

$$n = \frac{\sin \angle 3}{\sin \angle 2}$$

In the previous formulas for the index of refraction, vacuum is taken as the reference. These formulas give us the index of refraction with respect to vacuum, or the absolute index of refraction. If vacuum is not used, the relationship becomes:

$$\frac{n_2}{n_1} = \frac{\sin\theta_1}{\sin\theta_2}$$

Of course, this can be written as $n_1 \sin\theta_1 = n_2 \sin\theta_2$

If light goes through parallel surfaces of a transparent substance, such as a flat glass plate, the emerging ray is parallel to the entering ray, provided the two rays are in the same medium. If the two surfaces are not parallel, as in a triangular glass prism, the emerging ray is bent away considerably from its original direction. In drawing the ray diagram you should keep in mind the law of refraction.

The diagram assumes that light of a single wavelength (*monochromatic light*) is used.

Critical Angle and Total Reflection

Whenever light enters a second medium whose index of refraction is different from that of the first medium, some of the light is reflected. The greater the angle of incidence, the greater is the amount of reflection. This is called *partial reflection* and was deliberately omitted in the above diagrams on refraction. In some cases all of the light is reflected. Consider this diagram, in which rays are shown making different angles of incidence; notice that they are all directed from the denser medium towards the rarer one.

As we go from ray 2 to ray 3, etc., the angle (of incidence) in the denser medium keeps increasing, and therefore the angle (of refraction) in the rarer medium increases still more. For each ray the corresponding angle in the rarer medium is greater than the angle in the denser medium. As the angles of incidence increase, the refracted rays 2′, 3′, etc. lie closer and closer to the surface separating the two media. The *critical angle* is that angle of incidence in the optically denser medium for which the refracted ray makes an angle of 90° with the normal. *Total reflection* occurs when the angle of incidence in the optically denser medium is greater than the critical angle; then no light enters the rarer medium. Total reflection is made use of in prism binoculars and in curved transparent fibers and Lucite rods: the light stays inside the curved rod because of successive internal reflections. For all reflections the angle of incidence equals the angle of reflection. For a common variety of glass the critical angle is about 42°. In the triangular glass prism shown, total reflection can take place. The acute angles are 45° and the entering ray shown is perpendicular to the glass surface and therefore is not refracted. The angle of incidence on the hypotenuse is therefore 45°, which is greater than the critical angle, and therefore there is total reflection from the hypotenuse.

LENSES

A lens is a device shaped to converge or diverge a beam of light transmitted through it. Lenses described here are thin spherical lenses; one or both of their surfaces are spherical. If there is a nonspherical surface, it is plane. The material is transparent, usually glass. Unless stated otherwise in this description of lenses, the lens is surrounded by air. A *convex* lens is thicker in the middle than at the edges; it is also called a *converging* lens. A *concave* lens is thinner in the middle than at the edges; it is also called a *diverging* lens. The *principal axis* of a lens is the line connecting the centers of its spherical surfaces. A narrow bundle of rays parallel to the principal axis of a convex lens is refracted by the lens so that these rays, after refraction, pass through a common point on the principal axis known as the *principal focus* (F).

For the concave lens, rays originally parallel to the principal axis diverge after refraction and

seem to come from a common point on the principal axis known as the *principal focus*. It is a virtual focus (F). The extensions of the actual rays are shown dotted and are called *virtual rays*. For both lenses, the distance from the principal focus to the lens is the *focal length* (f) of the lens. The lenses are drawn quite thick, but remember that we are discussing thin lenses only, and therefore we may show the focal length as a distance to the center line of the lens.

Notice the similarity between lenses and curved spherical mirrors. The similarity will become even greater as we draw more ray diagrams for the lenses. Don't forget one important difference: lenses let light through and refract it; mirrors reflect light. Also, the focal length of a lens is not so simply related to the radius of curvature of its surfaces.

Images Formed by Lenses

The *convex lens* is similar to the concave mirror in that it can be used to form both real and virtual images. We can show this by means of ray diagrams.

In the diagram the formation of a real image is shown. This happens with the convex lens whenever the object is more than one focal length away from the lens. The procedure for making the ray diagram is as follows. Draw the lens and its principal axis. Then draw the center line of the lens and note the center of the lens (C) where the principal axis intersects the center line. Mark off a convenient length along the principal axis to represent the focal length; this gives the location of the principal focus (*F*) on both sides of the lens. A point twice as far is represented by 2*F*. We usually measure this distance from the center line; since the lens is thin we can think of the center line as representing the lens with the arcs merely drawn in to remind us of the type of lens with which we are working. Place the object at some appropriate distance from the lens, depending on the situation. In this case the object was placed at a distance between one and two focal lengths away from the lens. We draw two special rays from the head of the object; one ray, parallel to the principal axis, is drawn to the center line and from there is drawn straight through the principal focus, *F*. The second ray is drawn as a straight line through the center of the lens. Where the two rays meet, the head of the image is formed. We draw in the rest of the image. Note that although this diagram does not show the two refractions shown in the previous diagrams, the results are completely accurate for thin lenses (when thickness << diameter.)

It is also possible to get a virtual image with a convex lens. This happens when the object is less than one focal length away from the lens, as shown in the next ray diagram. Notice that the image is larger than the object and erect. A convex lens can be used as a magnifying glass.

A *concave lens* always produces a virtual image which is smaller than the object and erect (if object is erect). This is illustrated in the next ray diagram. Remember, except for aberrations which will be mentioned later, all rays which start from the head of the object will, after refraction by the

lens, pass through the same point of the image. This is shown by ray 3, drawn in after the rest of the diagram was drawn.

Numerical computations can be performed with the *lens equation.*

$$\frac{1}{\text{object distance}} + \frac{1}{\text{image distance}} = \frac{1}{\text{focal length}}$$

$$\frac{1}{p} + \frac{1}{q} = \frac{1}{f}$$

Rules

Rules in using lens equation: 1. Distances are measured from the lens; object distance is distance of object from lens, etc. 2. The object distance (*p*) is always positive. 3. The image distance (*q*) is positive for real images, negative for virtual images. 4. The focal length (*f*) is positive for convex lenses, negative for concave lenses.

The size (height) of the image can be calculated from this equation:

$$\frac{\text{size of image}}{\text{size of object}} = \frac{\text{image distance}}{\text{object distance}} = \text{magnification (m)}$$

The same equations apply to spherical mirrors, but what has been said in the rules about convex lenses applies to concave mirrors, and what has been said about concave lenses applies to convex mirrors.

Example: A convex lens whose focal length is 20 cm has an object placed 10 cm away from it. Describe the image.

$$\frac{1}{q} = \frac{1}{f} - \frac{1}{p}$$

$$= \frac{1}{20 \text{ cm}} - \frac{1}{10 \text{ cm}}$$

$$= -\frac{1}{20 \text{ cm}}$$

$$\therefore q = -20 \text{ cm}$$

$$m = \frac{q}{p} = \frac{-20 \text{ cm}}{10 \text{ cm}} = -2$$

The image distance is −20 cm. The minus sign means that it is a virtual image, on the same side of the lens as the object. The magnification is minus 2. This means that the virtual image is twice as large as the object.

Some of the characteristics of lenses and spherical mirrors are summarized in the following table.

OBJECT DISTANCE	IMAGE CHARACTERISTICS
Convex Lens (or Concave Mirror)	
greater than 2f	real, smaller, between f and 2f, inverted
2f	real, same size, 2f, inverted
between f and 2f	real, larger, greater than 2f, inverted
less than f	virtual, larger, q more than p, erect
Concave Lens (or Concave Mirror)	
any distance	virtual smaller, erect, q less than p

For example (referring to the first item in the table), when the distance of the object is more than two focal lengths away from the lens, the image is real, smaller than the object, between one and two focal lengths away from the lens, and inverted.

Note that, as the object gets closer to the lens, the image goes further away. An object "at infinity" will produce a point image a focal length away from the convex lens. A point source of light at the principal focus of a convex lens will produce light parallel to the principal axis after refraction by the lens.

Optical Instruments

The camera and eye have many points of similarity. The *camera* has a shutter to admit the light from the object at the right time. In the *eye* the eyelid corresponds to the shutter. In the camera the light then goes through an opening in a diaphragm, the aperture, through a convex lens (or combination of lenses) to the film with its surface sensitive to light. In the eye the light goes through the pupil, which is surrounded by the colored iris. The light then goes through a complicated lens system consisting of the "lens" and some liquids with curved surfaces. The light then falls on the retina where the image is formed. The image on the retina is real, inverted, reduced in size; appropriate electrical impulses are transmitted along the optic nerve to the brain. The image on the film of the camera is also real and inverted.

The refracting *astronomical telescope* and the *compound microscope* have some points of similarity. Both have convex lenses at opposite ends of a cylinder. The lens closer to the eye is known as the eyepiece; the other lens, closer to the object, is known as the objective. Keep in mind how these instruments are used. The telescope is used to look at very distant objects. Therefore the image produced by its objective lens is small in size and close to the principal focus of the objective. In order to make this image as large as possible, we examine it with the eyepiece, which is then used like a magnifying glass. The final image is virtual, if the telescope is used for visual examination.

$$\text{telescopic magnification} = \frac{\text{focal length of the objective}}{\text{focal length of the eyepiece}}$$

With the microscope we look at small things close by. Therefore, the object is placed at just a little more than one focal length away from the objective, to give an enlarged, real image to be examined by the eyepiece. This eyepiece is used like a magnifying glass, as in the telescope.

When we use a *projector*, we want an enlarged image on a screen. A convex lens will produce an enlarged, real image if the object is between one and two focal lengths from the lens. In a projector, the object (e.g., film) is a little more than one focal length away from a convex lens.

When a convex lens is used as a *magnifying glass*, the object is placed just a little less than a focal length away from the lens. The result is a virtual, erect, enlarged image.

With *nearsighted* people the image of objects at ordinary distances is brought to a focus too soon in the eye. Therefore, by the time the light gets to the retina, the light has diverged again, giving a blurred image on the retina. This is corrected by eyeglasses with concave lenses, which make the light converge more gradually. With *farsighted* people the image of objects at ordinary distances would be in focus beyond the retina. To make the image come to a focus sooner, eyeglasses with convex lenses are used.

A lens is sometimes described by an *f-number,* such as *f*/8. This means that the diameter of the lens (measured along the center line) is ⅛ of the focal length. In a camera this *f*-number would mean that the aperture has been adjusted to ⅛ of the focal length. This is related to the "speed of the lens." If the *f*-number is changed from *f*/8 to *f*/4, the diameter of the aperture is doubled. Therefore, the area of the opening is quadrupled and, if the illumination of the scene is constant, four times as much light goes through the lens, and only ¼ of the exposure time is required.

COLOR AND LIGHT

In describing refraction by means of a triangular glass prism we specified the use of monochromatic light. If so-called *white light,* such as light from an incandescent tungsten filament bulb, is used, we get a beautiful display of colors. *Dispersion* is the breaking up of light into its

component colors. Glass is a dispersive medium for light. That means that although the amount of refraction is primarily determined by the type of glass, the index of refraction has a slight—but significant—dependence on the frequency of the incident light.

Seven distinct colors may be detected if white light is used. If a glass prism is used, the order of the colors is, from the one bent the least to the one bent the most; red, orange, yellow, green, blue, indigo, violet. Some students like to remember this sequence by using the first letters to spell a name. The term *spectrum* is used in many different ways. Here we shall define the *spectrum* of visible light as the array of colors produced by dispersion; or, the range of waves capable of stimulating the sense of sight. This range of wavelengths is approximately 4×10^{-5} cm for the violet to 7×10^{-5} cm for the red. *Infrared* "light" has a greater wavelength than red; *ultraviolet* a shorter one than violet. Both are invisible to the human eye. Dispersion is produced by the prism because the violet light is slowed up more than the red light in the glass (or water); the other colors travel at intermediate speeds. In vacuum all electromagnetic waves travel at the same speed.

The *color of an opaque object* is determined by the color of the light it reflects. A red object reflects mostly red; it absorbs the rest. If an object reflects no light, it is said to be black. If a red object is exposed only to blue light, which it absorbs, the red object will appear black. If an object reflects all the light, it is said to be white. A white object exposed to red light, only, will appear red. The color of a transparent object is determined by the light it transmits.

Primary and Complementary Colors

If the above seven colors of light are recombined, white light is produced. However, it is possible to produce white light with fewer colors. *Complementary colors* are two colors of light whose combined effect on the eye is that of white light. They are: red and blue-green; yellow and blue-violet; green and magenta (purple). With the proper choice of three colors, known as the *primary colors*, it is possible to reproduce nearly all colors. The three primary colors of light are red, green, and blue-violet. If we mix two primary colors, we get the complementary color of the third. For example, if we mix red and green light we get yellow, which is the complement of blue-violet, the third primary color. Don't confuse this with the mixing of *paints*. Paints, like other opaque objects, absorb light and are seen by the color of the light they reflect. If we mix two paints, each paint subtracts the color of light it absorbs, and the color of the mixture is the color of light neither absorbs. Color obtained by the mixing of *lights* is known as an additive process.

Chromatic Abberration

Even a perfectly made thin lens doesn't function exactly as described above, if white light is used. The operation of a lens depends on refraction. We saw that refraction of white light by the triangular prism resulted in dispersion. The different colors in white light are brought to a focus at different points by the lens. The focal length of a lens depends on the color of the light used, just as the index of refraction of a substance depends on the color of light used. The result is that images produced by lenses have a slight color fringe, and photographs with such lenses may be slightly fuzzy. This phenomenon is known as *chromatic aberration*. It can be minimized ("corrected") by using a suitable combination of lenses known as an *achromat*.

Types of Spectra

When white light was used with the triangular prism, a *continuous spectrum* was produced: there was no gap as we went from on extreme, the red, to the other extreme, the violet. A continuous spectrum may be obtained from a glowing solid or liquid, or a glowing gas under high pressure. A *spectroscope* is an instrument used to examine the spectrum of light from any source. The light to be examined goes through a narrow rectangular slit before it reaches the prism which disperses the light. A telescope is then usually used to look at this dispersed light. A *bright-line spectrum* is obtained from a glowing gas under low or moderate pressure. Narrow rectangles or lines of light appear with gaps in between where there is no light. These lines of light can be thought of as images of the rectangular slit. Different elements in gaseous form produce different spectra. We say each element has a *characteristic spectrum* and use it for identification of the element. A *dark-line spectrum* is a continuous spectrum which is interrupted by thin dark lines. The dark lines result from the absorption of the energy of the missing wavelengths by gases that were between the hot source and the spectroscope. When a gas is cool, it can absorb some of the wavelengths which it emits when it is hot. When the sun's spectrum is examined superficially, it seems continuous. Actually it is a dark-line spectrum. The dark lines in the sun's spectrum are known as *Fraunholer* lines. They are produced mostly by gases in the sun's atmosphere which absorb some of the energy emitted by the hotter core. (Spectra will be discussed further in Chapter 14.)

Doppler Effect with Light

When we studied sound, we noticed that the pitch we hear depends on the frequency of the vibration of the source. The pitch is affected by the relative motion between the source and the observer. A similar phenomenon is observed in the case of electromagnetic waves.

If the distance between the source and the observer is decreasing, the observed frequency is greater than that of the source. In the case of light, frequency determines the color of light we see. If the frequency is greater than the source frequency (wavelength is smaller), the light is more violet than it would have been if there were no relative motion.

If the distance between the source and the observer is increasing, the observed frequency is lower than that of the source. In the case of light, this means that the observed light would be shifted towards the red.

There are some interesting applications of the Doppler effect with electromagnetic waves. Radar may be used to measure the velocity of approach of airplanes, automobiles, and similar objects. At a radar installation a transmitter sends out an electromagnetic wave in a narrow beam. The beam is reflected back by many objects, especially metallic ones. The reflected wave is picked up by a radar receiver. If the object is stationary, the reflected wave has the same frequency as that sent out by the transmitter. If the object's distance from the radar is increasing, the reflected frequency is less than the radar frequency. If the object's distance is decreasing, the reflected frequency is greater. The change in frequency depends on the velocity of approach. The greater the velocity, the greater the change in frequency.

The famous *red shift* is explained by the *Doppler principle* as being due to an expanding universe. What does that mean? The light from the sun, stars, and other heavenly objects has been analyzed with a spectroscope. Present are the characteristic spectra of many elements we know on earth. By comparing the spectrum of an element on earth with the corresponding spectra from stars, it has been found that the spectra from some stars are shifted towards the blue end of the spectrum; this means that these stars must be approaching the earth. The spectra from some other stars have been found to be shifted towards the red end of the spectrum. This means that these stars are moving away from the earth. There are some very distant objects in the sky known as *nebulae* (singular is nebula). Some are galaxies similar to our Milky Way galaxy. The spectra from these nebulae are shifted towards the red. The further the nebulae are, the greater the shift. This has been interpreted to mean that the distant parts of the universe are moving further and further away from us and from each other: the universe is expanding.

ILLUMINATION

A *luminous* body is one that emits light of its own. An *incandescent* object is one that emits light because it has been heated. The filament in electric light bulbs is incandescent; the firefly is luminous, but not incandescent. An *illuminated* object is one that is visible by the light it reflects.

If a point source of light is used, the illumination on a screen at right angles to the light varies inversely as the square of the distance from the source and is proportional to the luminous intensity of the source.

$$\text{illumination} = \frac{\text{intensity of source}}{\text{distance}^2}$$

ANSWERING THE QUESTIONS Let us return to the questions at the beginning of the chapter. The size of an object doesn't change as it moves further away from us, but it looks smaller to us. The explanation for this lies in the characteristics of images produced by convex lenses, of which there is one in the eye. The further the object, the smaller the image on the retina. This is also true of the plane mirror image. Its size is the same as the size of the object, but it is further from the eye, and so forms a smaller image on the retina.

Incidentally, if you look at the diagram of the plane mirror image, you will observe that we see the virtual image by means of diverging rays which come to our eye. (This is also true of rays coming to us from any point of a real object.) The convex lens in the eye brings these rays to a focus on the retina, thus producing a real image there. The convex lens in a camera acts in a similar way.

QUESTIONS Chapter 9

Select the choice that best completes the sentence.

1. In the light wave **(A)** the vibrations of the electric and magnetic fields are transverse **(B)** the vibrations of the electric field are transverse; those of the magnetic field are longitudinal **(C)** the vibrations of the magnetic field are transverse; those of the electric field are longitudinal **(D)** all vibrations are longitudinal **(E)** longitudinal vibrations alternate with transverse

2. If the distance between a point source of light and a surface is tripled, the intensity of illumination on the surface will be **(A)** tripled **(B)** doubled **(C)** reduced to $1/2$ **(D)** reduced to $1/3$ **(E)** reduced to $1/9$

For 3–5. X and Y are each 6 ft tall. X stands 4 ft from a vertical plane mirror, and Y 8 ft from the same mirror.

3. The size of X's image as compared with Y's is **(A)** 4 times as great **(B)** 2 times as great **(C)** the same **(D)** $1/2$ as great **(E)** $1/4$ as great

4. It will seem to X that Y's image, as compared with his own, is **(A)** 4 times as great **(B)** twice as great **(C)** the same size **(D)** smaller **(E)** beyond compare

5. The distance between X's image and Y's image **(A)** is 4 ft **(B)** is 8 ft **(C)** is 12 ft **(D)** is 16 ft **(E)** can't be calculated because of insufficient data

For 6–8. A candle 6 in. long is placed upright in front of a concave spherical mirror whose focal length is 10 cm. The distance of the candle from the mirror is 30 cm.

6. The radius of curvature of the mirror is **(A)** 5 cm **(B)** 10 cm **(C)** 15 cm **(D)** 20 cm **(E)** 6 in.

7. The image will be **(A)** virtual and smaller than the candle **(B)** virtual and larger than the candle **(C)** virtual and the same size as the candle **(D)** real and smaller than the candle **(E)** real and larger than the candle

8. If the top half of the mirror is covered with an opaque cloth, **(A)** the whole image will disappear **(B)** the whole image will be approximately one-half as bright as before **(C)** the top half of the image will disappear **(D)** the bottom half of the image will disappear **(E)** one cannot predict what will happen

9. Real images formed by single convex lenses are always **(A)** on the same side of the lens as the object **(B)** inverted **(C)** erect **(D)** smaller than the object **(E)** larger than the object

10. A virtual image is formed by **(A)** a slide projector **(B)** a motion-picture projector **(C)** a duplicating camera **(D)** an ordinary camera **(E)** a simple magnifier

11. A person on earth may see the sun even when it is somewhat below the horizon primarily because the atmosphere **(A)** annuls light **(B)** reflects light **(C)** absorbs light **(D)** refracts light **(E)** polarizes light

12. Incident rays of light parallel to the principal axis of a convex lens, after refraction by the lens, will **(A)** converge at the principal focus **(B)** converge inside the principal focus **(C)** converge outside the principal focus **(D)** converge at the center of curvature **(E)** diverge as long as they are close to the lens.

13. A red cloth will primarily **(A)** reflect red light **(B)** refract red light **(C)** absorb red light **(D)** transmit red light **(E)** annul red light

14. Yellow light of a single wavelength can't be **(A)** reflected **(B)** refracted **(C)** dispersed **(D)** focused **(E)** diffused

15. Some gold is heated to a temperature of 2000°C. (The melting point of gold is 1063°C; its boiling point is 2600°C.) The light emitted by this gold is passed through a triangular glass prism. The result will be **(A)** a continuous spectrum with a golden hue all over **(B)** a line spectrum with a golden hue all over **(C)** a continuous spectrum with a bright gold line **(D)** a line spectrum with a bright gold line **(E)** none of the above

16. The diagram shows 4 layers of different transparent liquids on top of each other. The liquids do not mix. The path of an oblique ray of light through the liquids is shown. The medium in which the speed of the wave is lowest is **(A)** I **(B)** II **(C)** III **(D)** IV **(E)** indeterminate on the basis of the given information

17. The speed of light in a certain transparent substance is two-fifths of its speed in air. The index of refraction of this substance is **(A)** 0.4 **(B)** 1.4 **(C)** 2.0 **(D)** 2.5 **(E)** 5.0

18. A camera of 6-in. focal length is used to photograph a distant scene. The distance from the lens to the image is approximately **(A)** 0.5 ft **(B)** 1 ft **(C)** 2 ft **(D)** 4 ft **(E)** 6 ft

19. A film 2.0 cm wide is placed 6.0 cm from the lens of a projector. As a result a sharp image is produced 300 cm from the lens. The width of the image is **(A)** 12 cm **(B)** 50 cm **(C)** 100 cm **(D)** 300 cm **(E)** 600 cm

20. If an object is placed 30 cm from a convex lens whose focal length is 15 cm, the size of the image compared to the size of the object will be approximately **(A)** twice as large **(B)** more than twice as large **(C)** 1.5 times as large **(D)** smaller **(E)** the same

21. A small beam of monochromatic light shines on a plate of glass with plane parallel surfaces. The index of refraction of the glass is 1.60. The angle of incidence of the light is 30°. The angle of emergence of the light from the glass is **(A)** 18° **(B)** 30° **(C)** 45° **(D)** 48° **(E)** 60°

22. In an experiment, an object was placed on the principal axis of a convex lens 25 cm away from the lens. A real image 4 times the size of the object was obtained. The focal length of the lens is **(A)** 20 cm **(B)** 25 cm **(C)** 33 cm **(D)** 50 cm **(E)** 100 cm

23. A ray of light goes obliquely from water into glass. The angle of incidence in the water is θ_1, the angle of refraction in the glass in θ_2, the index of refraction of water is n_1, and the index of refraction of the glass is n_2. Which of the following is a correct relationship for this case? **(A)** n_1, sin $\theta_1 =$ sin θ_2 **(B)** n_1 sin $\theta_2 =$ sin θ_1 **(C)** n_2 sin $\theta_1 =$ sin θ_2 **(D)** n_2 sin $\theta_2 =$ sin θ_1 **(E)** n_2 sin $\theta_2 = n_1$ sin θ_1

EXPLANATIONS TO QUESTIONS Chapter 9

Answers

1. **(A)**	6. **(D)**	11. **(D)**	16. **(D)**	21. **(B)**
2. **(E)**	7. **(D)**	12. **(A)**	17. **(D)**	22. **(A)**
3. **(C)**	8. **(B)**	13. **(A)**	18. **(A)**	23. **(E)**
4. **(D)**	9. **(B)**	14. **(C)**	19. **(C)**	
5. **(E)**	10. **(E)**	15. **(E)**	20. **(E)**	

Explanations

1. **(A)** Light is an electromagnetic wave. In all electromagnetic waves the electric and magnetic fields vibrate at right angles (transverse) to the direction in which the wave is traveling.

2. **(E)** (The intensity of) illumination from a point source varies inversely as the square of the distance. As the distance from the light source increases, the illumination decreases. When the distance is 3 times as great, the illumination is $(1/3)^2$ (or $1/9$) as much as before.

3. **(C)** The size of the image in a plane mirror is the same as the size of the object. Therefore, X's image is 6 ft tall and so is Y's.

4. **(D)** Although the actual size of the images is the same (see question 4), their apparent sizes will depend on the distance of the image from the observer, just as the apparent sizes of real objects will depend on their distances from the observer. The further an object or image is from the observer, the smaller it will *seem*. In this problem, since the image in a plane mirror is as far behind the mirror as the object is in front, X's image is 4 ft behind the mirror and 8 ft from X. For the same reason, Y's image is 8 ft behind the mirror and therefore at least 12 ft from X, who is 4 ft in front of the mirror. (Also see the next question.) Therefore to X, Y's image will seem smaller.

5. **(E)** The distance between the two images is the same as the distance between X and Y. This may be 4 ft or anything greater than 4 ft, as illustrated in the diagram, depending on how far over to one side Y stands.

6. **(D)** For a spherical mirror, the focal length = $1/2$ of the radius of curvature. $R = 2f = 2 \times 10$ cm = 20 cm.

7. **(D)** The situation described in this problem is similar to one for which the ray diagram is drawn in the chapter and a real image is obtained. Be able to draw such a ray diagram quickly and to deduce pertinent information from it. In this diagram the image is definitely smaller than the object. In the next chapter you will see how numerical calculations can be made rather quickly.

8. **(B)** All the rays starting from one point on the object will, after reflection from a spherical mirror, converge towards one point (for real image), or will diverge from one common point (for virtual image). This is the way points on the object are reproduced as points on the image, producing a sharp image. If part of the mirror is covered, less light will be available for each point reproduction, making the image dimmer.

9. **(B)** Note from the ray diagrams in the chapter that real images formed by single convex lenses are always inverted and on the other side of the lens from the object. The real images may be larger, smaller, or the same size as the object, depending on the distance of the object from the lens.

10. **(E)** Projectors and cameras are used to put images on screens or film; images that appear on screens are real images. The simple magnifier (also called magnifying glass or simple microscope) is used to view something without projecting an image on a screen (other than the eye's retina); it produces a virtual image as shown in the ray diagram in the chapter.

11. **(D)** Light travels somewhat more slowly in air than in vacuum. Sunlight entering the atmosphere obliquely is refracted towards the normal. Since the atmosphere's density increases as it

gets closer to the earth, the path of the light in the atmosphere is slightly curved. The drawing is not to scale and the effect is exaggerated. The observer projects a line backward to an imaginary position S' where the sun will appear to him: somewhat higher in the sky.

12. **(A)** This situation gave us the definition for the principal focus of a convex lens: rays parallel to the principal axis, after refraction by a convex lens, pass through a common point on the principal axis called the *principal focus*. The ray diagram in the chapter shows these refracted rays converging on the principal focus. (If these rays pass the principal focus and are not stopped, they will diverge *after* having converged.)

13. **(A)** Opaque objects are seen by the light they reflect. We say a cloth is red if it appears red when viewed in natural white light; it must, therefore, reflect red light, which is a component of the white light.

14. **(C)** All light can be reflected, refracted, polarized, and diffused. However, if it contains only one wavelength, it can produce only one color and can't be dispersed. (Definition of dispersion: breaking up of light into its component colors.)

15. **(E)** At the temperature given, gold is an incandescent liquid. The light from incandescent solids or liquids produces a continuous spectrum without any special bright lines due to the color of the cold solid or liquid. The various colors, such as yellow and orange, gradually change from one to the other.

16. **(D)** A ray passing obliquely into a medium is bent towards the normal if it travels more slowly in the new medium; it is bent away from the normal if it travels faster in the new medium. In the diagram, if the ray is directed from medium I toward medium IV, it is bent closer to the normal in each successive medium. Therefore the ray travels most slowly in medium IV. If the ray is directed from medium IV toward medium I, we may notice that the ray is bent further away from the normal in each successive medium, again indicating that the wave travels fastest in medium I, slowest in medium IV.

17. **(D)** Index of refraction $= \dfrac{\text{speed of light in air}}{\text{speed of light in medium}} = \dfrac{v}{2/5\,v} = 5/2 = 2.5$

18. **(A)** You may just recall that, if the object is very far from a convex lens, the image is formed practically one focal length away from the lens. Or, you may use the lens equation: $1/p + 1/q = 1/f$; the object distance p is very large, so we'll use the infinity symbol (∞) for it.

$$1/\infty + 1/q = 1/f, \ 1/\infty = 0$$

$$1/q = 1/f; \text{ and } q = f$$

That is, the image distance equals the focal length, in this case 6 in., which equals 0.5 ft.

19. **(C)** $s_1/s_0 = q/p$

$$s_1 = \frac{q}{p} \times s_0 = \frac{300 \text{ cm}}{6 \text{ cm}} \times 2 \text{ cm} = 100 \text{ cm}$$

20. **(E)** You should know that, if an object is 2 focal lengths away from a convex lens, a real image is formed 2 focal lengths away from the lens (on the other side from the object) and the image is the same size as the object. Otherwise you would have to use valuable time on calculations with the lens equation and size relationship.

21. **(B)** The angle which the emerging ray makes with the normal is the angle of emergence. We assume here that the entering ray and emerging ray are both in air. Then the two rays are par-

allel since the glass surfaces are parallel. Therefore, the angle of incidence equals the angle of emergence.

22. **(A)** $s_i/s_0 = 4 = q/p$

$$q = 4p; \text{ and } p = 25 \text{ cm}$$

$$\therefore q = 100 \text{ cm}$$

$$1/f = 1/p + 1/q$$

$$1/f = 1/25 + 1/100 = 5/100$$

$$f = 100/5 \text{ cm} = 20 \text{ cm}$$

Also *note* that the object distance is between f and $2f$, since a real, enlarged image was produced. The only choice that fits this is (A).

23. **(E)** In refraction, if one of the two media is vacuum, we need only one index of refraction, that of the substance used. This is its absolute index of refraction, or its index of refraction with respect to vacuum. This is also usually adequate if the substance is solid or liquid and we use air instead of vacuum. However, for the general case we have to use the index of refraction of both substances, as pointed out in the text.

10

Physical Optics: Interference and Diffraction

You may have noticed that the principles of reflection, refraction, illumination, and the Doppler effect would apply with equal validity to particles or waves. Which is light? There is a test for determining whether light is behaving like a particle or a wave. It is *interference*.

INTERFERENCE OF LIGHT

Coherent Sources

In the chapter on Wave Motion and Sound we noted that when two waves go through the same portion of the medium at the same time, interference occurs. The two waves are superposed. They may reinforce each other, giving constructive interference; or they may annul each other, giving destructive interference. This is readily observed in sound, where we can easily hear beats. It is also readily observed in standing waves in a string, or in water waves.

In order to observe interference we need two *coherent sources*, sources that produce waves with a constant phase relation. For example, two waves that are always in phase will always reinforce each other. If two waves are of opposite phase—that is, one wave is 180° out of step with the other—they will tend to annul each other. We have no trouble maintaining this constant phase relationship with mechanical vibrations. If we strike a tuning fork, both prongs will keep vibrating at the same frequency and in step. If we hold the vibrating fork vertically and rotate it around the stem as an axis, we can observe the interference caused by the waves produced by the two prongs. The two prongs are coherent sources.

Until recently it has been impossible to get two independent light sources which are coherent. The reason for this is that most sources of light emit it in short bursts of unpredictable duration. This would be like a tuning fork, momentarily stopping every few cycles. Two light sources might be out of phase during one burst but not during the next one. Annulment would be masked by the rapid change in phase relationship. For most purposes, if we want interference of light, we take light from one source and have it travel by two different paths to the same place.

Young's Double Slit—Division of Wavefront

In 1801 Thomas Young performed a famous experiment which suggested the interference of light. Its essential features are similar to the setup described: Light from a small source F illuminates a barrier which has two narrow slit openings, S_1 and S_2, very close to each other. The light which gets through these two slits falls on a screen. The screen may be thought of as the retina of our eye, because we usually look at the light source through the two slits. Assume that the light source is monochromatic. What we see on the screen is surprising. We see a whole series of bright lines alternating with dark regions. The technique we used for drawing ray diagrams with lenses and mirrors is inadequate. On that basis we might have expected to see two bright lines, one for each slit which lets light through.

We apply *Huygens' principle* and the wave theory of light to explain what we actually see. Imagine that we are looking down at the above setup. The light from the source spreads out and the wave fronts are represented by circles with source F at the center. The two slits are equidistant from the source. Each wave front reaches S_1 and S_2 at the same time. According to *Huygens' principle*, we can think of each point on a wavefront as a source of a *wavelet*. The *envelope* or curve tangent to all the wavelets is the new wavefront.

Huygen's Principle

Since there are two "source points" at the slits, two sets of waves are generated. These are represented as two sets of circles with S_2 being the center of the top set and S_1 the center of the bottom set. Since the light originally came from a single source, F, the waves produced by S_1 and S_2 are coherent.

The waves overlap on the screen and interfere with each other. In some places the waves arrive in phase, reinforce each other producing antinodes, and give a bright region or line. One such place is B, which is equidistant from S_1 and S_2; at this place we have the central maximum, or the central bright line. There are other places, on either side of the central maximum, where we get bright lines, places where the two waves are in phase and reinforce each other. The waves are in phase, but one is a whole number of wavelengths behind the other.

In between the bright lines we have dark regions. The two waves cancel each other, producing nodes, where they are out of step by ½ of a wavelength, ¾ wavelengths, or any other odd number of half-wavelengths.

Let us see if we can calculate the distance between bright lines or fringes. Let us look at the right half of the previous diagram in a slightly different way. Let us think of the first bright line on one side of the central maximum and represent it as point P. It is bright because the wave from S_2, traveling in the

direction S_2P, arrives in phase with the wave from S_1 which travels in the direction S_1P. The length of path S_1P is greater than S_2P; how can the waves arrive in phase? This is possible if the difference in the lengths of the two paths is exactly one wavelength. For the second bright fringe, the difference in path lengths is two wavelengths; for the third bright fringe, the difference is three wavelengths, etc.

If d is the distance between the two slits, L the distance between the barrier and the screen, λ the wavelength, and x the distance between the central maximum and the first bright fringe, it can be shown by selecting two triangles and making some approximations, that

$$\frac{\lambda}{d} = \frac{x}{L}$$

It can also be shown that the distance between any two adjacent bright fringes has the same value of x.

Complete annulment occurs midway between the bright fringes; the distance between adjacent nodes is also x.

Let us look at the important relationship shown above to see what predictions we can make. Since

$$\frac{\lambda}{d} = \frac{x}{L}$$

1. if the wavelength of light (λ) is increased, the distance between fringes increases; if we use red light instead of blue light, the distance between successive red lines on the screen is greater than between successive blue lines;
2. if the distance between the two slits (d) is decreased, the distance between the bright fringes increases;
3. if white light is used, the central maximum (at B) is white, since all the wavelengths are reinforced there. On either side of the central maximum we get bright fringes consisting of all the colors of the spectrum, with violet closest to the central maximum;
4. if the distance between the screen and the slits (L) is increased, the distance between the bright fringes increases.

Example: Calculate the distance between adjacent bright fringes if the light used has a wavelength of 6000 angstroms and the distance between the two slits is 1.5×10^{-3} meter. The distance between the screen and the slits is 1.0 meter.

$$\frac{\lambda}{d} = \frac{x}{L}$$

$$\frac{6000 \times 10^{-10} \text{ meter}}{1.5 \times 10^{-3} \text{ meter}} = \frac{x}{1.0 \text{ meter}}$$

$$x = 4000 \times 10^{-7} \text{ m, or } 0.00040 \text{ m}$$

In the diagram on the bottom of page 92, the pattern to the right of the barrier is very similar to the pattern obtained on the surface of water by two small sources vibrating in phase with the same frequency at S_1 and S_2, as in a ripple tank. A succession of nodes (and antinodes) is produced in the whole region as the waves move to the right and interfere with each other. This succession produces *nodal* (and *antinodal*) lines.

Diffraction Grating

If instead of having only two parallel slits, as above, we have many such slits close together, we have a diffraction grating. It is possible now to have cheap gratings with thousands of slits per inch. The full analysis of how a diffraction grating works is complicated, but in some respects it is similar to the double slit. However, the more slits we have, the brighter is the pattern. For approximate calculations, the above formula (for the double slit) may be used. It provides a convenient method for measuring the wavelength of light. Instead of the triangular glass prism the grating may be used in the spectroscope.

As with the double slit, the pattern obtained on the screen with a grating has a central maximum which is the same color as the light used. On either side of the central maximum we get bright fringes; if white light is used, the bright fringes are continuous spectra. The spectrum closest to the central maximum is known as the first-order spectrum. Notice there is a first-order spectrum on either side of the central maximum. If the source of light is a luminous gas, each "bright fringe" is the characteristic spectrum of the element.

DIFFRACTION

Wave Characteristic

When we deal with a wave, we expect to find *diffraction:* the bending of a wave around obstacles. We know that this happens in the case of sound because, for example, we can hear a speaker even if our direct view of him is blocked by a crowd of people. In the case of a water wave we can see the wave going around objects on the surface of the water, so that after a short distance the wave looks again as though there had been nothing in the way.

If light is a wave, why do objects cast sharp shadows? Why doesn't the light bend around the object and illuminate the region behind it? Theory shows that the smaller the wavelength the smaller the diffraction effects. We already know that the wavelength of light is only a small fraction of a millimeter, while the wavelengths of radio and sound waves are many centimeters (and even meters for radio waves). It is due to the very short wavelength of light that shadows are so sharp and that a beam of light tends to travel along straight lines.

However, diffraction of light does occur; because its wavelength is so small, we must look very carefully. For example, if we photograph the shadow of a small ball, using a suitable light source, we find a small illuminated spot in the center of the shadow.

Single Slit Diffraction

Suppose we shine a beam of monochromatic light on an opaque barrier which has a narrow rectangular opening cut into it, a single narrow slit. Let the light which goes through the slit fall on a screen held parallel to the barrier. On the basis of what we did with ray diagrams, we might expect that the part of the beam which gets through the slit will have the same cross section as the slit and that the illuminated part of the screen will look exactly like the slit in shape and size.

If the slit is narrow and we look carefully, what we actually see on the screen is many rectangular, parallel bands of light (*images of the slit*). Each band may be a little wider than the slit. The central band is very bright; to either side are bands of decreasing brightness. (The central band's intensity is about 20 times as great as the first bright band to either side.) Below is a rough graph of the intensity of the observed pattern plotted against distance along the screen.

In the diffraction pattern, the central band is also called the central bright line or the central maximum. Careful analysis shows that
1. the width of the central maximum varies inversely as the width of the slit; that is, if we make the slit narrower, the central bright line becomes broader, or, in other words, there is more and more diffraction, more and more bending of the light around the edges of the slit;
2. the width of the central maximum varies directly as the wavelength; if we use red light, we get a wider or broader central line than if we use blue light;
3. the distances between successive dark bands are approximately the same.

If the opening is large compared with the wavelength, light practically travels along straight lines; diffraction is negligible.

The Wave Theory and Single Slit Diffraction

As in the case of the double slit interference pattern, we can apply Huygens' principle and the wave theory of light to explain the single slit diffraction pattern. Let us view the barrier and screen edge-on. Assume that the slit has a width d and that the barrier is a distance L from the screen. Think of a wave front arriving at the slit opening. According to *Huygens' principle,* every point on the wave front can

For P to be minimum
$$\sin \theta = \frac{n\lambda}{d}, \; n = 1, 2, 3, \ldots$$

be thought of as sending out its own little waves. Two such points are shown at A and B. Think of the waves from A and B going towards P, a point on the screen. If P is to be a dark spot on the screen, the two waves traveling along AP and BP must annul each other; and, similarly, the waves from the two points just below A and B on the wave front at the slit, etc. Now path BP is larger than path AP. If this difference in path length is one-half wavelength, the two waves will annul each other.

With a little geometry it can be shown that for a dark point on the screen $\sin \theta = n\lambda/d$, where the letters have the values shown in the diagram, and λ is the wavelength of the light used. When $n = 1$, P gives us the point of minimum intensity for the central line. In other words, the distance OP gives half of the width of the central band. By looking at the relation $\sin \theta = \lambda/d$, we can see that, if the wavelength λ increases, $\sin \theta$, and therefore the width of the central band, must increase. Also, if the width of the slit d decreases, $\sin \theta$, and therefore the width of the central band, must increase.

Diffraction and Lens Defects

We have already indicated that even a perfectly made spherical lens suffers from chromatic aberration. Spherical lenses have other defects even if monochromatic light is used. One of these is due to diffraction. As with a single slit, the light going through a lens is diffracted. The amount of diffraction is usually negligible, but one effect is that parallel light entering the lens is brought, not to a point focus, but to a disk focus. Around this bright diffraction disk we may be able to see bright diffraction rings. The fact that we get a disk diffraction pattern instead of a point focus with a lens sets a practical limit to the magnification we can get with a lens.

Resolving Power

The ability of a lens or optical instrument to distinguish between two point sources is its *resolving power*. Resolution or resolving power is increased by increasing the diameter of the lens; it works similarly for spherical mirrors. Suppose, for example, we look through a telescope at two stars that are close to each other in the sky. If the objective lens has a small diameter, the diffraction pattern of each star will be large and the two disks will overlap as in diagram A. The resolution is poor: it is hard

A   B

to tell whether we are looking at one star or two. If we try to use greater magnification we will not improve resolution, because we also magnify the size of the disk. If, instead, we use an objective lens with a larger diameter, we decrease the amount of diffraction, we decrease the size of the diffraction disk, and we increase the resolving power. The effect of using a larger diameter lens is shown in diagram B.

Interference with Thin Films—Division of Amplitude

The beautiful colors of soap bubbles and of thin films of oil on a city pavement or highway are due to interference of light and give further evidence that light behaves like a wave. Let us assume that we have monochromatic light incident on a thin film. The film may be oil, soap solution, or even air trapped between two flat glass plates. Some of the light is reflected at the top surface of the film and is represented by ray 1. Most of the light goes through the film; some of this is reflected at the bottom surface of the film and comes out again. This is represented by ray 2. If we look down on the film, rays 1 and 2 may enter our eye and be focused on our retina. Coherent monochromatic light is coming to our eye by two different paths. Ray 2 had to go back and forth through the film. The two rays (or light waves) arriving simultaneously on our retina will interfere with each other. (Refraction is not shown in the diagram because it is negligible in a thin film.)

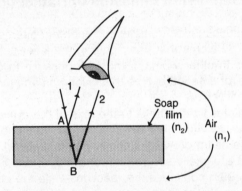

When a wave encounters a denser medium, its reflection at that point will undergo a phase change of 180°. Thus the ray reflecting at point A is exactly out of phase with the ray that continues through the soap film. When the ray gets to point B it encounters a less dense medium, so no phase change occurs. The waves continue on out of phase with one another. However, if the thickness of the soap film is $1/4\ \lambda$ and the incident ray is almost perpendicular to the surface, the total path through the soap will be $\lambda/2$. The crest of a wave from B will meet the *next* crest of a wave from A, and there will be constructive interference. If the film is thicker by any odd number of quarter wavelengths, crests will still meet crests, and constructive interference will be seen. If the film is thicker by any even number of quarter wavelengths, crests will meet troughs, and destructive interference will be seen.

In ordinary daylight the film is illuminated by many different wavelengths. The thickness of the film may be just right in one direction to cause annulment of one color. All the other wavelengths will combine to give a colored spot. In another direction the thickness may be just right for the cancellation of a different wavelength, and the complement of the canceled color will be seen. As a result, when viewing a soap bubble or an oil film we see the full colors of the rainbow.

In the above case, ray 1 undergoes a phase change as before, but so does ray 2 since $n_3 > n_2$. Thus, if the film thickness is any odd multiple of $\lambda/4$, crests will meet troughs, and cancellation will occur. This idea is applied in the coating of expensive photographic lenses to minimize undesirable reflections. (Of course, if a manufacturer carelessly applies a coating with a thickness of $\lambda/2$, the undesirable reflections will be exaggerated by constructive interference!)

Light Amplification by Stimulated Emission of Radiation (LASER)

Lasers are devices that produce monochromatic and coherent beams of light. They are formed by cylinders with parallel ends. The atoms that participate in the laser action must be capable of sustaining a *population inversion*. In other words, it must be possible to *pump* more than 50% of the atoms above the ground state for a period of time that is long on an atomic time scale. This is usually done by applying an electrical voltage.

When one of the atoms radiates light parallel to the axis of the cylinder, that light will stimulate a nearby atom to emit light, coherent with the first wave, and in the same direction. This process continues, with the strength of the beam growing, until an end is reached. At that point, about 99% of the beam will be reflected, but a partially-silvered mirror at the end will allow about 1% of the beam to leak through. The reflected 99% continues the reaction, while the output 1% can be used in the laboratory. Because only light parallel to the axis can continue lasing, the output beam is highly *collimated*. That is, it diverges very little from its exit diameter. Because the beam is highly collimated, it has a very high energy density.

Light Amplification by Stimulated
Emission of Radiation (LASER)

It is now possible to get two lasers to be coherent.
Interference and diffraction experiments are much easier now than they were in 1801!

POLARIZATION

We have been saying that light behaves like a transverse wave. What is the evidence? We have already shown how light behaves like some kind of wave. We explained interference and diffraction of light by making use of wave theory. We can readily see how two waves can get to the same place at the same time and annul each other. We cannot explain this annulment if we think of the energy as arriving as streams of particles. However, this did not tell us whether the wave is longitudal or transverse. We observed interference and diffraction with sound and decided that the sound wave is longitudinal.

An effect observed with light and not with sound is polarization. *Polarized light* is light whose direction of vibration has been restricted in some way. The direction of a longitudinal wave cannot be restricted; either it vibrates in the direction in which the energy is traveling (the direction of propagation), or it doesn't vibrate at all and we have no wave. On the other hand, in a transverse wave there is an infinite number of ways in which we can have vibrations at right angles to the direction of propagation of the wave.

In the diagram, imagine a ray coming out of the paper. Vibration can be towards the top and bottom edges of the paper, towards the right and left, and in all other directions in between. We think of ordinary natural light, such as we get from our tungsten filament bulbs, as a transverse wave with all directions of vibrations present. Some crystals, natural and synthetic, allow only that light to go through whose vibration is in the direction of the axis of the crystal. Such light is then polarized:

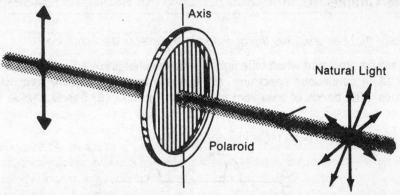

Polaroid is a synthetic material that does this. It consists of plastic sheets with special crystals embedded in them. If we let ordinary light shine through one Polaroid disk, the light is polarized but the human eye can't tell the difference. If we allow this polarized light to shine through a second Polaroid disk kept parallel to the first one, the amount of light transmitted by the second disk depends on how we rotate the second disk with respect to the first one. If we rotate the second disk so that its axis is at right angles to the axis of the first disk, practically no light is transmitted. The maximum amount of light is transmitted when the two axes are parallel to each other.

In many ways light behaves like a wave. We have seen that it is possible to have two light beams interfere with each other so that their combination is dimmer than either beam alone. In fact, polarization experiments suggest that light is a transverse wave. (Later we shall consider other experiments which the wave theory does not explain.) Since light comes to us from the sun through an excellent vacuum, one would like to know what vibration represents the wave. Until about 1900 it was customary to talk about some ether filling all of space and to describe light as a wave in this ether. Now when we think of light as a wave, we describe it as an *electromagnetic wave;* we think of electric fields and magnetic fields which vibrate (fluctuate in magnitude) at right angles to the direction in which the light travels. These fields can exist in a vacuum. Light is one type of electromagnetic wave; its wavelength is rather short: about 5×10^{-5} cm. The exact wavelength depends on the color of the light. X rays are also electromagnetic waves—their wavelength is about 10^{-8} cm or 10^{-10} m. (One angstrom unit = 10^{-10} m.) Radio waves are electromagnetic waves with rather long wavelengths; they may be many meters long.

According to *Maxwell's theory,* light is a transverse wave in which electric and magnetic fields vibrate or fluctuate at right angles to the direction of propagation. Electric and magnetic fields will be discussed further in later chapters.

QUESTIONS Chapter 10

Select the choice that best answers the question or completes the sentence.

1.   Which will be produced when blue light with a wavelength of 4.7×10 meters passes through a double slit? **(A)** a continuous spectrum   **(B)** two narrow bands of blue light   **(C)** alternate blue and black bands   **(D)** bands of blue light fringed with green   **(E)** bands of blue light fringed with violet

2.   Two pulses approach each other in a spring, as shown.

Which of the following diagrams best represents the appearance of the spring shortly after the pulses pass each other at point *P*?

3.   The diagram represents straight wave fronts passing through a small opening in a barrier. This is an example of **(A)** reflection   **(B)** refraction   **(C)** polarization   **(D)** dispersion   **(E)** diffraction

4. If light of wavelength 5.0×10^{-7} m shines on a pair of slits 1 mm apart, how far from the central maximum will the first bright band appear on a screen 1 m away? **(A)** 5×10^{-4} m **(B)** 5×10^{-10} m **(C)** 2×10^3 m **(D)** 2×10^{-4} m **(E)** 2×10^{-10} m

5. Newton's rings may be observed if you place a curved glass surface on a flat glass surface. A thin film of air is wedged between the glass surfaces. Looking down, one can see several rings around the point where the two glass surfaces touch. Newton's rings are produced by **(A)** interference **(B)** diffraction **(C)** polarization **(D)** absorption **(E)** a lighted cigarette falling with nonuniform acceleration.

6. Water waves **(A)** can be polarized **(B)** are polarized **(C)** cannot be polarized because they are longitudinal **(D)** cannot be polarized because of their frequencies **(E)** cannot be polarized because of their amplitudes

EXPLANATIONS TO QUESTIONS Chapter 10

Answers

1. **(C)**   3. **(E)**   5. **(A)**
2. **(B)**   4. **(A)**   6. **(B)**

Explanations

1. **(C)** When light passes through a double slit, the pattern which forms on the screen where the light falls consists of alternating bands of light separated by black regions. If white light is used, the central band is white and on either side each of the bright bands consists of the spectrum of colors of which the white light is composed. In this question blue light of a single wavelength is used. Such light cannot be dispersed. Therefore all bands of light on the screen, including the central band, consist of this blue light. These bands are separated by bands of black regions.

2. **(B)** When two pulses or waves pass each other in a medium, each continues on as though there had been no interference from the other. In this question, therefore, the pulse with the larger amplitude will appear on the right side of P and continue traveling towards the right. The pulse with the smaller amplitude appears on the left and continues traveling towards the left.

3. **(E)** *Diffraction* is the bending of a wave around an obstacle. The shaded parts of the diagram represent the obstacle. As the wave goes through the small opening in the obstacle, it spreads behind the obstacle. The small opening acts like a point source of a wave.

4. **(A)**
$$\frac{\lambda}{d} = \frac{x}{L} \qquad \frac{5.0 \times 10^{-7} \text{ m}}{10^{-3} \text{ m}} = \frac{x}{1 \text{ m}}$$

$x = 5.0 \times 10^{-4}$ m or 0.5 mm

Don't forget to change all units to SI!

5. **(A)** The production of Newton's rings is an interference phenomenon. The rings are produced by interference between the light reflected from the top surface of the thin air film and the light reflected from the bottom.

6. **(B)** While water waves are transverse, and thus can be polarized (A), (B) is the better choice, as water waves are already restricted to one plane of vibration (up and down).

11

Static Electricity—Electric Circuits

Does a short circuit between A and B or C and D blow the fuse? What is the potential difference between A and B in the circuit as drawn? What is the potential difference there when there is a short circuit between A and B?

To answer these questions you obviously must know and understand Ohm's law and associated definitions and concepts. Don't assume that you do. Carefully study the material below and check your real understanding. The problem will be considered in detail later.

KINDS OF ELECTRIC CHARGE AND FORCE BETWEEN CHARGES

You should remember that a rubber rod rubbed with a piece of fur or wool acquires a negative charge; a smooth glass rod rubbed with silk becomes positively charged. Of course, the other material in the pair acquires an opposite charge, i.e., the silk becomes negative and the fur or wool becomes positive. Lucite may be used instead of glass; polystyrene instead of rubber.

Like charges repel; unlike charges attract. *Coulomb's law* applies to this force of attraction and repulsion if the charges are concentrated at points or small objects; the force is proportional to the product of the two charges and varies inversely as the square of the distance between them.

$$F = \frac{kq_1q_2}{d^2}$$

In SI units, charge q is the coulomb (C), the distance d is in meters, and k is a proportionality constant which has the value 9×10^9 N • m²/C² in vacuum or air. It is sometimes called the electrostatic or Coulomb's law constant.

METHODS OF CHARGING AND ELECTROSTATIC INSTRUMENTS

Charging an object results in a gain or loss of electrons. In a solid, the positive charges usually do not move readily. A gain of electrons results in making an object more negative; a loss of electrons in making it more positive. A neutral object usually acquires the same kind of charge as that of the charged object it touches (unless it is grounded). In *charging by induction,* a charged object is held near (but not touching) a neutral conductor while the latter is grounded. The latter thus acquires a charge opposite to that of the original charged object. The ground connection is broken before the charged object is removed. (See illustration below.)

The *electroscope* is an instrument used to determine the presence and sign of small electrical charges by the deflection of very thin metal leaves; in this type, gold leaf is frequently used. The *electrophorus,* the *Wimshurst machine,* and the *Van de Graaff* generator are devices for producing electrical charges by induction.

Nearly all the mass of an atom is concentrated in the *nucleus* which contains protons and, except in the case of the common hydrogen atom, neutrons. The *electrons* move in orbits around the nucleus and are imagined to form "shells." Electrons in all atoms are alike: they have the same negative charge and small mass. The *proton* has a positive charge equal in magnitude to that of an electron; its mass is approximately 1836 times as much as the mass of the electron. The *neutron* is electrically neutral; its mass is slightly greater than that of the proton. In the neutral atom the number of protons equal the number of electrons. An *ion* is a charged atom (lost or gained electrons) or group of atoms. Metals are good conductors of electricity because their outermost electrons move readily.

Illustrations and Additional Facts

B and C are metal spheres mounted on insulating stands. The metal portions are initially in contact with each other. A is a smooth glass rod that has been rubbed with silk and is held near B. If C is touched by hand momentarily and A is then removed, C and B are both charged negatively by induction because electrons were attracted from the hand due to the nearness of the positive glass rod. What would have been the charge on C and B if the procedure had been to separate C and B slightly without touching the metallic portion and then removing A? Electrons would have been attracted to the end of B closest to A, leaving C positive. After separation B remains negative, C positive.

If we move a charged metallic sphere so that it will not be affected by any external charges, the excess charge, positive or negative, will be distributed uniformly on the outside of the sphere. In general, if the metallic object is not a sphere, the excess charge will distribute itself so that the greatest charge will be on the most pointed portion.

Electric discharge takes place readily from sharp points. This is often demonstrated with the *electric whirl,* which consists of a wire with sharp points bent as shown in the diagram and pivoted at its center of gravity so that it is free to rotate in a horizontal plane. No matter which terminal of a static machine the whirl is connected to, it always rotates in the direction shown, away from its points. The air always contains some ions. When the whirl is positively charged, its points are strongly repelled by positive charges in the air; when negatively charged, by negative charges in the air. Why isn't this effect neutralized by ions in the air of opposite charge? Opposite charges are attracted to the points and by successive collisions overcome the friction and inertia of the whirl. This produces rotation in the same direction as before.

ELECTRIC FIELDS

We noticed above that two charged objects exert a force on each other without touching. Physicists have found it desirable to introduce the concept of an *electric field* in order to visualize better and describe more precisely this force acting at a distance. An electric field is said to exist wherever an electric force acts on an electric charge. Note the similarities of the following to the material on gravitational fields in Chapter 2.

Electric Field Intensity

The strength of an electric field, or the *electric field intensity*, at a certain point is the force per unit positive charge placed there. It is a vector quantity. Its direction is the direction of the force on a small *positive* test charge; if this is to the right, the direction of the field intensity at that point is to the right. If we use a negative test charge, the direction of the force on it is opposite to the direction of the field intensity

$$E = F/q$$

where E is the electric field intensity (N/C) and F is the force (N) exerted on positive charge q (C).

We can represent the electric field intensity around a charge by drawing vectors with suitable direction and length. Frequently we represent the field by merely drawing lines whose direction is the same as the direction of the field intensity at the various points along the lines, but whose length is independent of the magnitude. These lines are called *lines of force* or *lines of flux*. The stronger the field, the more the number of lines drawn in that area.

A few patterns representing electric fields are shown below.

Positive Point Charge   **Negative Point Charge**

Field around Positively Charged Metal Rod

Field is Greatest Near the Most Pointed Portion

Uniform Field between Parallel Plates

For point charges and metallic spheres, the electric field intensity varies inversely as the square of the distance from their centers. Note the similarities between these cases and the gravitational field of the earth. Note also that there is no field inside the metallic sphere. In fact, there is no net charge or field inside *any* charged conductor. All excess charge is on the outside surface. This effect, discovered by Michael Faraday, is responsible for the shielding effects of metal buildings and coaxial cables on radio waves.

The field intensity around a long charged rod varies inversely as the distance (not the square of the distance) from the rod. The field between two oppositely charged parallel metallic plates is uniform; the intensity is the same everywhere between the plates except near the edges. Again, note the similarity between this field and the gravitational field at sea level.

ELECTRIC POTENTIAL AND POTENTIAL DIFFERENCE

In the diagram below an electric field is represented by three curved lines. Let *A* and *B* be two points in the field, as shown. If we put a positive charge *q* at point *A*, the field will exert a force *F* on the

**Work Is Required To Move
a Charge from A to B**

charge in the direction of the field. If we want to move the charge from *A* to *B*, we must do work. (Recall that work done equals the product of the force and the distance moved in the direction of the force.)

We define the potential difference, *V*, between two points in an electric field as the work per unit charge required to move a charge between the points.

$$\text{potential difference} = \frac{\text{work}}{\text{charge}}$$
$$V = \frac{\text{work}}{q}$$

The SI unit of work is the joule, and the unit of charge is the coulomb. Therefore the unit of potential difference is the joule per coulomb.

$$1 \text{ volt} = 1 \text{ joule/coulomb}$$

Example: The potential difference between two points is 40 volts. What is the work required to move a charge of 800 microcoulombs between these points?

$$40 \text{ volts} = \text{work}/(800 \times 10^{-6} \text{ coulomb})$$
$$\text{work} = 0.032 \text{ joule}$$

Electric Potential

Electric potential is really the same thing as potential difference, except that we arbitrarily select a special point as reference. In some practical work the special reference "point" is the ground. In some of our work the special reference point is any point at infinity. We then define the *electric potential* at any point in the electric field as the work required to bring a unit positive charge from infinity to that point.

Note that, if a positive charge is released in an electric field, by definition of the direction of the electric field, the positive charge will move in the direction of the electric field. On the other hand, a negative charge released in an electric field will move in the direction opposite to that of the field. (If this bothers you, think of the field as being produced by a positive charge.) However, all objects released in the earth's gravitational field move in the direction of the field, namely towards the earth.

As will be discussed in more detail under Electric Currents, the two terminals of a battery are oppositely charged; there is a definite difference of potential between them. If two parallel metallic plates of the same size are connected to these terminals, one plate to a terminal, the two plates will acquire opposite and equal charges. (Such an arrangement is known as a *capacitor* and is discussed in Chapter 13.) There will be a difference of potential between them, the same as the difference of potential between the two terminals of the battery. We already mentioned that there is a uniform field between *oppositely charged parallel plates.* The intensity of this field (E) is proportional to the difference of potential between the plates (V) and inversely proportional to the distance (d) between them:

$$E = V/d$$

Defined this way, electric field intensity is known as *potential gradient.* As with gravitational field intensity and acceleration, the optimum usage is clear from context. However, both yield correct answers.

$$1 \text{ newton/coulomb} = 1 \text{ volt/meter}$$

POTENTIAL DIFFERENCE; ELECTRIC CURRENTS— DIRECT CURRENT (DC)

Potential Difference

Potential difference is also referred to as difference of potential or voltage. Electromotive force is a special kind of potential difference.

1. The concept—Batteries (also dynamos, electrostatic generators, etc.) have two terminals: one positive, the other negative. The positive terminal has a deficiency of electrons; the negative terminal an excess of electrons. Energy (chemical energy in the case of the battery) had to be used to attain this charged condition of the terminals; e.g., work had to be done to push electrons onto the negative terminal against the force of repulsion of electrons already there. *Potential difference (V) is the work per unit charge* that was done to get the terminals charged and that is therefore potentially available for doing work outside the battery.

Electromotive force (emf) is the potential difference between the terminals of the source when no current flows. When current flows, as when a lamp is connected to a battery, the potential difference between the terminals of a battery is sometimes significantly less than its *emf* because of the battery's internal resistance (see page 108). Thus the term electromotive force or *emf* is used only when energy is put into a circuit. Potential difference is often referred to as *voltage* when energy is removed.

2. Unit of potential difference—the *volt;* e.g., the common flashlight cell supplies $1\frac{1}{2}$ volts, the outlet at home 115 volts.

$$V = \frac{\text{work}}{q} \ , \qquad \text{volts} = \frac{\text{joules}}{\text{coulomb}}$$

Current

1. The concept—*Current* is the rate of flow of electric charge. In a metallic conductor (e.g., copper wire) the motion of electrons is the electric current; in liquids the electric current consists of moving negative and positive ions (an *ion* is a charged atom or group of atoms); in gases the electric current consists of moving ions and electrons.

2. Direction—If a copper wire is connected to the terminals of a battery or generator, electrons will go through the wire from the negative terminal to the positive terminal. This is the direction of the *electron current* in the wire, and will be used in this book.

Dating back to the days of Benjamin Franklin, the opposite direction (+ to –) has also been used. Called *conventional current*, the flow of positive charge actually occurs only in specific situations. However, because of its long history, it is often referred to "by convention." Usually on nationwide examinations, questions that depend on a specific definition of current direction have been avoided. Your knowledge of a consistent set of rules based on one definition is expected (see left-hand rules, page 117). One way or the other, you must be able to explain real-world phenomena.

3. SI Units—the ampere (A);

$$1 \text{ ampere} = 1 \text{ coulomb/second};$$

$$1 \text{ coulomb} = 6.25 \times 10^{18} \text{ electrons.}$$

Resistance

1. The concept—The amount of current in a device when it is connected to a given source of potential difference depends on the nature of the device. Resistance of a device is its opposition to the flow of electric charges, converting electrical energy to heat because of this opposition. (Note that in alternating current (ac) *impedance* is the *total* opposition to the electric current, and that portion of it which converts electrical energy to heat is the resistance.)
2. Unit—the ohm (Ω).

FACTORS AFFECTING RESISTANCE These are temperature, length, cross section, and material.

1. Effect of temperature: The resistance of most metallic conductors goes up when the temperature goes up.
2. Effect of other factors: The resistance of a conductor is directly proportional to its length and inversely proportional to its cross-sectional area, at constant temperature. This is expressed by the formula:

$$R = \frac{kL}{A}$$

L = length in meters
R = resistance in ohms
A = cross-sectional area in meters^2
k = a constant for the material and is called resistivity; unit is ohm-meter

Conductivity. This is the reciprocal of resistivity. The resistivity of good conductors is low; their conductivity is high.

Superconductivity. Since 1911 various conductors have been found whose resistivities become zero or nearly so at extremely low temperatures. Once current is started in a loop made of such a superconductor, it will continue indefinitely without a potential difference being applied to the circuit. The goal is to produce conductors which have this property at room temperature.

Conductance

Conductance is the reciprocal of resistance, and its unit is the *mho*. (The higher the resistance, the lower or poorer is the conductance.)

OHM'S LAW AND ELECTRIC CIRCUITS—DC

Ohm's Law

The current in a circuit (I_T) is directly proportional to the potential difference applied to the circuit (V_T) and inversely proportional to the resistance of the circuit (R_T).

Formulas:

$$I_T = V_T/R_T; \quad R_T = V_T/I_T; \quad V_T = I_T R_T$$

Series Circuit   Parallel Circuit   Series-Parallel Circuit

	Series Circuit	Parallel Circuit	Series-Parallel Circuit
Current	$I_T = I_1 = I_2$	$I_T = I_1 + I_2$	$I_T = I_3 = I_1 + I_2$
Resistance	$R_T = R_1 + R_2$	$\dfrac{1}{R_T} = \dfrac{1}{R_1} + \dfrac{1}{R_2}$ *	$R_T = R_3 + \dfrac{R_1 R_2}{R_1 + R_2}$ *
Voltage	$V_T = V_1 + V_2$	$V_T = V_1 = V_2$	$V_T = V_1 + V_3 = V_2 + V_3; \; V_1 = V_2$
IR-drop	$V_T = I_T R_T; \; V_1 = I_1 R_1; \; V_2 = I_2 R_2,$ etc.		
Symbols	I_1 = current through R_1; V_2 = potential difference across R_2, etc.		

*If only two resistors are connected in parallel, the combined resistance is equal to their product divided by their sum: $R_T = \dfrac{R_1 R_2}{R_1 + R_2}$.

For a PORTION OF A CIRCUIT the same formulas apply, but I, V, and R have to be selected for that part of the circuit. The potential difference across a resistor is sometimes called *potential drop, IR-drop, or voltage drop.*

If n equal resistors are connected in parallel, their combined resistance is $R_T = \left|\dfrac{R}{n}\right|$, where R is the resistance of one of them. The combined resistance of resistors in parallel is always less than the smallest resistance.

Notes: 1. V_T = potential difference at terminals of source = emf of source if internal resistance of source is negligible. 2. The *internal resistance* of the source can be treated as an external resistance in series with the rest of the circuit; to all of this is applied the emf of the source. 3. When the internal resistance is not negligible,

$$V_T = \text{emf} - Ir$$

where I is the total current, r is the internal resistance of the source of electrical energy, V_T is the potential difference across the external circuit = voltage at terminals of source.

LINE DROP This is the voltage across wires connecting the source to devices getting energy. This may be negligible; if not, it can be represented and treated like R_3 in the above series-parallel circuit.

EXAMPLE 1   Series Circuit

20 Ω 100 V

30 Ω

$V_T = 100$ V

$R_T = R_1 + R_2 = 20\ \Omega + 30\ \Omega = 50\ \Omega$

$I_T = \dfrac{V_T}{R_T} = \dfrac{100\ V}{50\ \Omega} = 2.0$ A

$I_1 = I_T = 2.0$ A: this is current through each resistor

EXAMPLE 2   Parallel Circuit

$$V_T = 100\ V = V_1 = V_2$$

$$R_T = \frac{R_1 R_2}{R_1 + R_2} = \frac{20\ \Omega \times 30\ \Omega}{20\ \Omega + 30\ \Omega} = 12\ \Omega$$

$$I_T = \frac{V_T}{R_T} = \frac{100\ V}{12\ \Omega} = = 8.3\ A\ or\ 8\tfrac{1}{3}\ A$$

$$I_1 = \frac{V_1}{R_1} = \frac{100\ V}{20\ \Omega} = 5.0\ A\ through\ 20\ \Omega$$

$$I_2 = \frac{V_2}{R_2} = \frac{100V}{30\ \Omega} = 3\tfrac{1}{3}\ A\ through\ 30\ \Omega$$

$$N.B.:\ I_1 + I_2 = (5.0 + 3\tfrac{1}{3})\ A = 8\tfrac{1}{3}\ A = I_T$$

EXAMPLE 3

Assume same circuit as for Example 2, except that battery has emf of 120 V and internal resistance of battery is 3 Ω.

On the basis of calculations for Example 2, this circuit is equivalent to:

$$I_T = \frac{V_T}{R_T} = \frac{120\ V}{(12 + 3)\ \Omega} = \frac{120}{15}\ A = 8.0\ A$$

$V_{AB} = IR = (8.0\ A)\ (12\ \Omega) = 96\ V$. The potential difference between A and B is 96 V. This is also the voltage across the 20 Ω resistor, as well as the voltage across the 30 Ω resistor. It is also the terminal voltage of the battery when used in this circuit.

SHORT CIRCUIT A low resistance path between two points where there is normally a relatively high resistance. This *may* result in an excessive current, known as an *overload*. If the circuit is overloaded, a fuse properly placed in the circuit will burn out.

In a parallel connection any device may be disconnected without breaking the circuit for the others.

ELECTRICAL ENERGY AND POWER

Joule's Law

The heat produced by current in a given resistor is proportional to the square of the current through the resisitor, the resistance, and the time that the current flows through the resistor:

$$\boxed{H = 0.24\ I^2 Rt}$$

where H = heat in calories, I = current in amperes, R = resistance in ohms, t = time in seconds.

To get the heat produced, in joules, use $\boxed{H = I^2 Rt}$ with t in seconds. Heat produced is proportional to the square of the current if R remains fixed; then, if I is doubled, H is quadrupled, provided R and t remain the same.

In *Parallel Circuits* the same formula for heat produced applies, but note that in a parallel circuit the device with the least resistance draws the most current and produces the most heat.

Power

Power is the rate of using or supplying energy. The power consumption P of a resistor is:

$$P = VI; \qquad P = I^2R; \qquad P = V^2/R;$$

where P = power in watts, V = potential difference across resistor in volts, I = current through resistor in amperes, R = resistance in ohms.

ADDITIONAL ENERGY AND POWER UNITS Since power = energy/time

$$\text{energy} = \text{power} \times \text{time},$$

if power is expressed in watts, appropriate energy units are watt-second; watt-minute; and watt-hour.

$$1 \text{ watt-second} = 1 \text{ joule}$$

ANSWERING THE QUESTIONS Now let us return to the electric circuit at the beginning of the chapter. Note again that *some questions can be answered without detailed calculations.* You can't afford to take time for precise calculations when only an estimate is needed. QUICKLY EXAMINE THE SUGGESTED ANSWERS BEFORE MAKING CALCULATIONS. If there is a big difference between suggested answers, a rough estimate on your part may be adequate.

To determine whether the fuse will blow we need to know whether the current exceeds 3 A. Any short circuit to the right of E or F in the diagram can at most reduce the resistance of the circuit to the right of EF to zero. Then the total resistance of the circuit would be 90 Ω (IF we neglect the internal resistance of the generator) and, using Ohm's law, $I_T = 120$ V/90 Ω, the current would be less than 2 A. Therefore the fuse will not blow because of a short circuit from A to B or from C to D. To produce a *short circuit between A and B,* a copper wire may be connected between A and B. The resistance of such a wire is usually assumed to be negligible; i.e., equal to zero. Therefore the IR-drop across the short circuit is zero. (Also note from above that the current through this short circuit would have to be something less than 2 A.)

When there is *no connection from A to B,* no current flows through the 120-ohm resistor and the IR-drop across this resistor is therefore zero. The potential difference between A and B will then be the same as between E and B, or E and F. The simplified circuit will then be a fairly simple series-parallel circuit:

There are two parallel branches containing 60 Ω each. Their combined resistance is 60/2 or 30 Ω. R_T then is 120 Ω, $I_T = 120$ V/120 Ω = 1 A, and the IR-drop across the 30-ohm resistance is 30 V. This is therefore also the voltage across each of the 40-ohm, 20-ohm branches; the current through each is 30 V/60 Ω = ½ A. The IR-drop across the 40-ohm resistor is ½ A × 40 Ω = 20 V, etc.

When there is a short circuit from A to B, the simplified circuit is indicated below, and the calculations can be carried out, if necessary, as indicated above, by using the appropriate relations as tabluated on p. 108.

F, B, A

QUESTIONS Chapter 11

Select the choice that best answers the question or completes the statement.

1. The leaves of a negatively charged electroscope diverged more when a charged object was brought near the knob of the electroscope. The object must have been **(A)** a rubber rod **(B)** an insulator **(C)** a conductor **(D)** negatively charged **(E)** positively charged

For 2-3. Two point charges repel each other with a force of 4×10^{-5} newton at a distance of 1 meter.

2. The two charges are **(A)** both positive **(B)** both negative **(C)** alike **(D)** unlike **(E)** equal

3. If the distance between them is increased to 2 meters, the force of repulsion will be, in newtons, **(A)** 1×10^{-5} **(B)** 2×10^{-5} **(C)** 4×10^{-5} **(D)** 8×10^{-5} **(E)** 16×10^{-5}

4. A proton (electric charge $= 1.6 \times 10^{-19}$ coulomb) is placed midway between two parallel metallic plates which are 0.2 meter apart. The plates are connected to an 80-volt battery. What is the magnitude of the electric force on the proton, in newtons? **(A)** 3.2×10^{-20} **(B)** 6.4×10^{-17} **(C)** 400 **(D)** 16 **(E)** 80

5. In the circuit shown, R_1 and R_2 are 30 Ω and 60 Ω, resp., and $I_1 = 4$ A. The potential difference across R_2 is equal to **(A)** 30 V **(B)** 60 V **(C)** 120 V **(D)** 240 V **(E)** a quantity which can't be calculated with the given information.

For 6-9. In the circuit shown, 4 A is the current through R_1.

6. The potential difference across R_1 is, in volts, **(A)** 7.5 **(B)** 30 **(C)** 60 **(D)** 120 **(E)** 160

7. V_T is equal to, in volts, **(A)** 90 **(B)** 160 **(C)** 400 **(D)** 500 **(E)** 540

8. The rate at which R_1 uses electrical energy **(A)** is 120 watts **(B)** is 240 watts **(C)** is 360 watts **(D)** is 480 watts **(E)** can't be calculated with the given information

9. The heat developed by R_1 in 5 seconds is **(A)** 120 joules **(B)** 600 joules **(C)** 1800 joules **(D)** 2400 joules **(E)** none of the above

10. One thousand watts of electric power are transmitted to a device by means of two wires, each of which has a resistance of 2 ohms. If the resulting potential difference across the device is 100 volts, the potential difference across the source supplying the power is   **(A)** 20 V **(B)** 40 V **(C)** 100 V **(D)** 140 V **(E)** 500 V

For 11-12. A battery has an emf of 6.0 volts and an internal resistance of 0.4 ohm. It is connected to a 2.6-ohm resistor through a SPST (single pole, single throw) switch.

11. When the switch is open, the potential difference between the terminals of the battery is, in volts,   **(A)** 0 **(B)** 0.8 **(C)** 2.6 **(D)** 5.2 **(E)** 6.0

12. When the switch is closed, the potential difference between the terminals of the battery is, in volts,   **(A)** 0 **(B)** 0.8 **(C)** 2.6 **(D)** 5.2 **(E)** 6.0

13. The current through the 10-ohm resistor is, in amperes,   **(A)** 6 **(B)** 2 **(C)** 1 **(D)** $^2/_3$ **(E)** 0

14. In the circuit shown, a good lead-acid storage battery (negligible internal resistance) is used. The battery supplies 6.0 volts. F_1, F_2 and F_3 are fuses with ratings of 10 A, 10 A, and 2 A, respectively. When switches S_1, S_2, and S_3 are closed, the fuse(s) that will blow is (are)   **(A)** F_1 only   **(B)** F_2 only   **(C)** F_3 only   **(D)** F_1 and F_2 **(E)** F_1 and F_3

EXPLANATIONS TO QUESTIONS Chapter 11

Answers

1. **(D)**	4. **(B)**	7. **(E)**	10. **(D)**	13. **(B)**
2. **(C)**	5. **(D)**	8. **(D)**	11. **(E)**	14. **(A)**
3. **(A)**	6. **(D)**	9. **(D)**	12. **(D)**	

Explanations

1. (D) The leaves of a negatively charged electroscope have an excess of electrons. Since like charges repel, the negatively charged object will repel some (negatively charged) electrons from the knob of the electroscope to the leaves, increasing the amount of negative charge on the leaves. Since the force of repulsion increases with the charge, the leaves will diverge more. The negatively charged object may be rubber, but it may also be some other insulator or a metal.

2. (C) Two like charges repel each other. Both may be positive or both may be negative. They may be equal or unequal.

3. (A) The force between two point charges varies inversely as the square of the distance between them. Since the distance is doubled, the force becomes ¼ as great.

4. (B) The plates are charged oppositely by the battery and this produces a uniform electric field between the plates. Its intensity is equal to the ratio of the difference of potential between the plates to the distance between the plates:

$$E = V/d$$
$$= (80 \text{ V}/0.2 \text{ m}) = 400 \text{ N/C}$$

The field intensity is defined as the force on a unit positive charge placed in the field:

$$E = F/q$$
$$400 \text{ N/C} = F/(1.6 \times 10^{-19} \text{ C})$$
$$F = 6.4 \times 10^{-17} \text{ N}$$

5. (D) This is a series circuit and the current is the same in every part of the circuit: $I_1 = I_2 = 4$ A. The potential difference across $R_2 = I_2 R_2 = 4$ A $\times$ 60 $\Omega = 240$ V

6. (D) The potential difference across R_1 is merely the IR-drop.
$$V_1 = I_1 R_1$$
$$V_1 = 4 \text{ A} \times 30 \text{ }\Omega = 120 \text{ V}$$

7. (E) Since R_1 and R_2 are in parallel, $V_1 = V_2$

$$\therefore I_1 R_1 = I_2 R_2$$
$$4 \text{ A} \times 30 \text{ }\Omega = I_2 \times 60 \text{ }\Omega$$
$$I_2 = 2 \text{ A}$$
$$I_3 = I_1 + 2 \text{ A} = 6 \text{ A}$$
$$V_3 = I_3 R_3 = 6 \text{ A} \times 70 \text{ }\Omega = 420 \text{ V}$$
$$\text{But } V_T = V_3 + V_1 = 420 \text{ V} + 120 \text{ V} = 540 \text{ V}$$

8. (D) The rate of using energy is power.
$$P_1 = I_1{}^2 R_1 = (4 \text{ amperes})^2 \times 30 \text{ }\Omega = 480 \text{ watts}$$

9. (D) Energy = power $\times$ time = 480 watts $\times$ 5 seconds
$$= 2400 \text{ watt-seconds} = 2400 \text{ joules}$$
The energy used by a resistor is converted to heat. Therefore the heat developed by the resistor is 2400 joules. Notice that any unit of energy may be used. If desired, we may convert to calories.

10. (D) The power used by the device, $P = VI$.
$$1000 \text{ watts} = 100 \text{ volts} \times I$$
$$I = 10 \text{ A}$$
Since this is a series circuit, the current in each of the wires is also 10 A. The voltage across each of these wires is an IR-drop = 10 amperes $\times$ 2 ohms = 20 volts. The voltage across the source = voltage across device + voltage across the wires = 100 V + 20 V + 20 V = 140 V.

11. (E) When the switch is open, the circuit is incomplete and no current flows. When a battery supplies no current, the potential difference across its terminals is the emf.

12. (D) When the switch is closed, current flows. The terminal voltage = emf - Ir, where I is the current flowing and r is the internal resistance of the battery.

$$I = \frac{\text{total voltage}}{\text{total resistance}} = \frac{6.0 \text{ V}}{(2.6 + 0.4) \text{ }\Omega}$$
$$I = 2 \text{ A}$$
$$\text{terminal voltage} = 6.0 \text{ V} - (2 \text{ A} \times 0.4 \text{ }\Omega) = 5.2 \text{ V}$$

13. **(B)** This is really a parallel circuit with the two branches drawn on opposite sides of the battery. You may be able to see it better if you draw both branches on the same side of the battery. In any case, the full 60 V is applied across the branch containing the 10-ohm and the 20-ohm resistors in series. For that branch $R_T = 30\ \Omega$, $V_T = 60$ V, and $I = V/R = 60$ V/30 $\Omega = 2$ A.

14. **(A)** The fuse rating gives the maximum current that the fuse can carry continuously. The resistance of the fuses is usually quite small—a fraction of an ohm at these current ratings. When switches S_1 and S_2 are closed, F_1 is directly across the battery; with practically no resistance in the circuit, a current much larger than 10 A will flow momentarily through F_1, burning out the fuse. The additional closing of S_3 closes the circuit for F_2 and the 3-ohm resistor. The current in this circuit is $V/R = 6$ V/3 $\Omega = 2$ A. This current is handled safely by fuse F_2.

12

Magnetism; Meters, Motors, Generators

What happens to an ammeter when it is connected across a generator? What happens when a dc generator is connected across a battery? To answer these questions we need to understand the principle of operation of the generator and meters. This requires a knowledge of magnetism.

SOME BASIC TERMS

A magnet attracts iron and steel; when freely suspended it assumes a definite position (because of the earth's magnetism). *Ferromagnetic* substances (iron, nickel, and cobalt) and alloys of iron (like Alnico) are strongly attracted by a magnet. All other materials are often referred to as nonmagnetic, yet every atom exhibits some form of magnetism. *Paramagnetic* substances are attracted feebly; *diamagnetic* ones are repelled feebly. A *magnetized* substance is a ferromagnetic substance that has been made into a magnet. A magnetic *pole* is the region of a magnet where its strength is concentrated; every magnet has at least two poles. The *north* pole (*N-pole*, or *north-seeking pole*) of a suspended magnet points towards the earth's magnetic pole in the northern hemisphere. A *lodestone* is a natural magnet. Usually we use artificial (laboratory-made) magnets.

FACTS AND THEORY OF MAGNETS

The *law of magnets* states that like poles repel; unlike poles attract. If the poles are concentrated at points, this force between two poles is proportional to the product of their strengths and varies inversely as the square of the distance between them. (Note similarity to Coulomb's law of electric charges.) The old *molecular theory of magnetism* states that every molecule of a *magnetic* substance is a magnet with an N- and an S-pole. When the substance is fully magnetized, all the like poles face in the same direction. When it is not magnetized, the molecules are arranged in helter-skelter fashion. A more modern theory speaks about *domains* rather than molecules. A domain is about 0.01 mm long and consists of many, many atoms; some of its properties are like those of the above-described molecular magnets. In general, a moving electric charge produces a magnetic field. In the atoms the spinning of the electrons produces the magnetism. (The explanation of para- and diamagnetism involves the orbital motion of the electrons around the nucleus.)

Magnetic Field and Magnetic Flux

The *magnetic field* is the region around the magnet where its influence can be detected as a force on another magnet. The direction of the field at any point is the direction in which the N-pole of a compass would point. The magnetic field can be represented by fictitious *lines of flux* with the following properties: they are closed curves; they leave the magnet at an N-pole and enter at an S-pole; they never cross each other; they are more crowded at the poles; and, in general, the greater the crowding, the greater is the force on the pole placed at that point. A *permeable* substance is one through which magnetic lines of force go readily; e.g., soft iron. A representation of the magnetic field can be obtained by sprinkling iron filings on a horizontal surface in the field. A compass needle takes a position in the direction of the magnetic field in which it is located and can be used to get a point-by-point representation of the magnetic field. By now, this should be sounding very familiar. Indeed, you should be finding many similarities between gravitational, electric, and magnetic fields.

Typical Magnetic Field Diagrams

Terrestrial Magnetism

In a rough way the earth acts as if it had a huge bar magnet inside with its S-seeking pole in the northern hemisphere. (However, this pole is called the North Magnetic Pole.) Remember that it attracts the N-pole of the compass needle and that the magnetic poles do not coincide with the geographic poles, which are the points where the earth's axis of rotation intersects the surface of the earth.

The angle between the direction of the compass needle at a particular location and the direction to geographic north (or true north) is the *angle of declination* or compass *variation* of that location. *Isogonic lines* are the irregular lines drawn through locations having the same angle of declination. The *agonic line* is the isogonic line drawn through points having zero declinatoin. Places east of the agonic line have west declination because the compass needle points west of the direction to true north.

The *dipping needle* is a compass needle mounted on a horizontal axis; it measures the *angle of dip* or angle of *inclination* at a given place. At the magnetic poles the angle of dip is 90° The magnetic equator is the line drawn through points of zero dip. *Isoclinic lines* are lines drawn through points having the same dip.

Electromagnetism

Oersted discovered that a wire carrying current has a magnetic field around it. The magnetic field around a long straight wire carrying current is represented by lines of magnetic flux which are concentric circles (in the plane perpendicular to the wire) with the wire at the center. (The magnetic lines of flux are somewhat analogous to the electric lines of force.) To determine the direction of these magnetic lines of flux we may use the *left-hand rule:* Grasp the wire with the left hand so that the thumb will point in the direction of *electron flow;* the fingers will then circle the wire in the direction of the lines of flux. (If conventional current is used, the right hand will be employed with the thumb pointing in the direction of the conventional current. The direction of the lines of flux is the same, no matter what the convention of current.)

Left-Hand Rule for Straight Conductor

The strength of a magnetic field can be given a number of ways. The unit of *magnetic flux densi-ty*, or *magnetic induction* can be specified with its SI unit (the *Tesla*), or as the number of flux lines perpendicular to a unit area (*webers/m²*), or with reference to its causative factors: a magnetic force, created by a current flowing through some distance. In such case, the SI units are newtons/ampere • meter.

$$1\,T = 1\frac{Wb}{m^2} = 1\frac{N}{A \bullet m}$$

The symbol **B** is used to denote magnetic induction. In the CGS system, the unit is the gauss. Note that the term "magnetic field intensity" cannot be used here. For historic reasons, it belongs to a slightly different quantity.

In a metallic solid the electric current does consist of moving electrons, and the left-hand rule is natural for determining the direction of the magnetic field. In a liquid and gas the electric current usually consists of moving negative and positive ions. What is the direction of the magnetic field produced by the moving ions? For the negative ions we use the left-hand rule just as for electrons. For the positive ions we may still use the left-hand rule, but we must have the thumb point in the direction opposite to the flow of the positive ions; the other fingers will then point in the direction of the magnetic lines of the flux.

A *solenoid* is a long spiral coil carrying electric current. It produces a magnetic field similar to that of a bar magnet, and has an N-pole and S-pole at each end, respectively. Its strength is increased by the use of a permeable core such as soft iron. The location of the poles can be found by the use of

another *left-hand rule* for solenoids and electromagnets: grasp the coil with the left hand so that the *fingers* will circle the coil in the direction of *electron flow;* the extended thumb will then point to the N-pole and in the direction of the lines of flux. An *electromagnet* is a solenoid with a permeable core such as soft iron. The *strength* of an electromagnet depends on the number of turns in the coil, the current through the coil, and the nature of the core. The first two effects are combined in the concept of *ampere-turn:* it is the product of the number of turns and the number of amperes of current through the wire. A solenoid with 50 turns and 2 amperes going through it has 100 ampere-turns. Over a wide range the strength of an electromagnet is proportional to its ampere-turns. This is affected by the nature of the core. Iron is said to have a high permeability; it helps to give a strong electromagnet. Air, wood, paper, etc. have a low permeability; their presence does not affect the strength of the solenoid. (*Strength* here refers to the magnet's ability to attract iron.) The electro-magnet can be made very strong; its strength can be changed by changing the current; its strength becomes practically zero when the current is turned off; it is, therefore, a temporary magnet. The electromagnet has many practical applications: electric motor, meter, generator, relay, telegraph sounder, bell, telephone.

It is now appropriate to reconsider bar magnets and terrestrial magnetism. Note that we said that the earth behaves *as though* it had a huge bar magnet inside. Note also that bar magnets have fields shaped like objects with circulating currents. This is appropriate, because bar magnets *have* circulating currents—in their constituent atoms. In ferromagnetic substances, it is possible for the atoms to line up in domains. Of course there is no huge bar magnet in the earth. Terrestrial magnetism arises from circulating currents of ions in magma, deep in the earth.

Circular Loop

The magnetic field around a long straight wire carrying current does not have any poles. As we saw above, when the wire is wound in the form of a coil, magnetic poles are produced. The magnetic field around a single circular loop carrying current is such that the faces show polarity. We may apply the same left-hand rule as above to see this. Notice that both the left half and the right half of the loop produce lines of flux which have the same direction near the center of the loop. In this region the

two fields add up to give a relatively strong field. The face of the loop from which the lines are directed is the north pole: in this diagram, it is the face away from us.

Force on a Current-carrying Conductor

When electric charges move across a magnetic field, a force acts on the moving charges which is not present when the charges are stationary. In the diagram imagine the magnetic lines of flux between the north and south poles of some magnet. In this magnetic field is located a wire perpendicular to the paper and to the lines of flux. The current through the wire is shown going into the paper. We can determine the direction of the force on the wire by using the first left-hand rule we mentioned. Grasp the wire with the left hand with the thumb pointing (in this case) into the paper. The fingers then indicate that the lines of flux due to the current are counterclockwise around the wire; they oppose the magnet's lines of flux above the wire, but reinforce them below the wire.

Since opposite fields cause an attraction and like fields cause a repulsive force, the wire is pushed up. There is a hand rule that gives this result directly. If the fingers of the flat left hand point in the direction of the field (from N to S), and the thumb is in the direction of electron flow, the hand will push in the direction of the magnetic force. Note that the direction of force on the wire is at right angles to both the direction of the electron current and the lines of flux of the magnet.

Left Hand Rule for Force on a Current-carrying Conductor

The *magnitude of the force* depends on the direction of the wire in the magnetic field. It is maximum when the wire is at right angles to the field and zero when the wire is parallel to it. It is proportional to the current and the strength of the magnetic field. When the wire is at right angles to the field, the force on the wire is given by the following formula:

$$F = ILB$$

where I is the current in the wire, L is the length of wire in the magnetic field, and B is the flux density.

When two parallel wires carry current, a force acts on both wires. The reason for this is that each wire is in the magnetic field produced by the other. When the two currents are in the same direction, the two wires attract each other. When the currents are in opposite directions, the wires repel each other. The force is proportional to the product of the two currents and inversely proportional to the distance between them:

$$F \propto \frac{I_1 I_2}{d}$$

Force on a Moving Charge

The electric current consists of moving charges. We mentioned before that, when an electric charge moves across a magnetic field, a force acts on the moving charge that is not present when the charge is stationary. The direction of the force is perpendicular to the field and the velocity, and can be found with the hand rule given above. If the moving charge is positive, the direction will be opposite to the direction predicted by the left-hand rule. The force is at a maximum when the charge's velocity is at right angles to the flux. Its magnitude is then given by:

$$F = qvB$$

where q is the magnitude of the charge (in coulombs), v the velocity (in meters per second), and B the flux density (in teslas). The force will then be given in newtons. The path of this charge will be circular. Since the force will be at right angles to the velocity, the magnitude of the velocity will not change.

DC Meters

A *galvanometer* measures the relative strength of small currents. The common ones are of the moving-coil type; a coil free to rotate is placed in the magnetic field provided by a permanent magnet.

Galvanometer Operation

D'Arsonval Galvanometer

When current goes through the coil, the force on two sides of the coil produces a torque. A pointer attached to the coil rotates with it. In the Weston type of galvanometer a spiral spring keeps the coil from rotating too much; the deflection is usually proportional to the current. When the current stops, the spring restores the coil to its zero position. The resistance of the galvanometer coil is usually small (about 50 ohms); usually the coil can carry safely only small currents (a few milliamperes).

The *ammeter* is an instrument for measuring current; it is calibrated to give the actual magnitude of the current. The ammeter usually consists of a galvanometer with a low resistance in parallel with the moving-coil; this resistance is called a *shunt*. The ammeter is connected in series with the device

Ammeter

whose current is to be measured. All the current to be measured enters the ammeter. Internally the current divides: a part of the current goes through the coil; the rest goes through the shunt. We can calculate the required resistance of the shunt (R_s) if we apply the rules for a parallel circuit. The shunt is in parallel with the coil (R_c), and therefore the voltage drops are equal: $I_s R_s = I_c R_c$. If the coil has a resistance of 100 ohms and gives full-scale deflection for 10 milliamperes, we can convert it to a 0-1 ampere ammeter: remember that the coil gives full-scale deflection when 0.01 A goes through it. The other 0.99 A must then go through the shunt.

$$0.99\, R_s = 0.01 \times 100$$

and R_S is approx. 1 ohm.

A *voltmeter* is an instrument calibrated to measure the potential difference connected to its terminals. If we want to measure the potential difference across a lamp, we connect a voltmeter in

$R_c = 100\ \Omega$ R_m

Voltmeter

parallel with the lamp. A voltmeter usually consists of a galvanometer with a high resistance connected in series with it. This resistance is often called a *multiplier*. The range of a voltmeter can be changed by changing the multiplier. Suppose we want to convert the above galvanometer to a voltmeter with full-scale deflection at 100 V. (Range: 0-100 V.) At full-scale deflection 0.01 A goes through both the multiplier (R_m) and the coil. The IR-drop across both together is 100 V.

$$I_T R_T = 100$$
$$0.01\ R_T = 100$$

and R_T = 10,000 ohms. The coil supplies 100 ohms of this total resistance; therefore the required multiplier resistance is 9,900 ohms.

In general the resistance of voltmeters is high; ideally they behave like open switches. In general, the resistance of ammeters is low; ideally they behave like closed switches or wires.

The *wattmeter* measures power consumption. It is similar to the above voltmeter except that the permanent magnet is replaced by an electromagnet; its coil gets a current which is proportional to the current going through the device whose power consumption is being measured.

The *kilowatt-hour meter* measures energy consumption.

ELECTROMAGNETIC INDUCTION

Faraday in England and Henry in the United States independently discovered that a magnetic field can be used to produce an electric current. If a wire moves so that it cuts magnetic lines of flux, an electromotive force is induced in the wire. An *induced emf* is produced in a wire whenever there is relative motion between a wire and a magnetic field. If the wire is part of a complete conducting path, current flows in this circuit in accordance with Ohm's law; this current is referred to as *induced current*.

No emf is induced when the wire moves parallel to the magnetic flux. The emf is maximum when the wire moves at right angles to the magnetic flux, as in the second diagram below. In SI units, the magnitude of the maximum induced emf is given in volts by the following formula:

$$emf = lvB$$

where l is the length of wire cutting the flux, and v is the *relative* speed cutting the flux, and B is the flux density in teslas. The *magnitude* of the *induced emf* may be increased by increasing the length of the wire cutting the magnetic field, by increasing the relative speed of motion between the wire and the magnetic field, and/or by increasing the strength of the magnetic field. Note that the same result is obtained if the magnet is stationary and the wire moves, or if the magnet moves and the wire is stationary.

An emf is induced in a *single loop* of wire when the magnetic flux going through the loop changes. The magnitude of the induced emf is proportional to the speed with which the flux changes. The emf is 1 volt when the change in flux is 1 weber per second. If a coil has several turns of wire, the emf is proportional to the number of turns in the coil.

Lenz's Law

The *direction* of the induced current can be figured out by the use of *Lenz's law:* the direction of the

Direction of
induced electron flow

induced current is such as to produce a magnetic field which will hinder the motion that produced the current. For example, if a permanent magnet is moved away from a stationary coil, an emf is induced in the coil. In the diagram shown, the motion of the magnet is opposed if the induced current produces an S-pole to attract the retreating N-pole. This will happen if the induced current has the direction shown. Of course, an N-pole will be produced simultaneously at the left end of the coil. If we have a single wire moving across a magnetic field, we can determine the direction of the current this way: In the diagram assume that the wire is perpendicular to the page and pulled towards the bottom edge of the paper. If the induced current is directed into the paper, the left-hand rule tells us that the magnetic field is weakened above the wire, strengthened below it (closer to you). This tends to push the wire toward the top edge of the paper, opposing the motion which produced the induced current. Therefore we guessed the direction of the induced current correctly: into the paper. Note that Lenz's Law is a special case of the law of conservation of energy.

Motion
of wire

MUTUAL INDUCTION AND TRANSFORMERS

We saw before that an emf is induced in a coil if the current in that coil is changing. This is self-induction. We have *mutual induction* if an emf is induced in a coil because of current changes in a second coil. The current may be alternating or direct. As long as there is a change in the current there will be a change in the magnetic field surrounding the coil. If this changing magnetic field cuts the second coil, an emf is induced in the second coil. The *primary* coil (*P*) is the coil which is directly connected to the source of electrical energy, such as a dynamo. The *secondary* coil (*S*) is the coil from which electrical energy may be taken as a result of the emf induced in it. In the *induction coil* the source of energy is dc, usually a battery.

The purpose is to obtain a high voltage. In an automobile using a gasoline engine the induction coil is used as the *ignition coil:* it provides the high voltage which, at the spark plug, results in a spark that ignites the fuel mixture. A steady dc would produce no emf in the secondary. An interrupter is used to interrupt the current in the primary automatically. The changing magnetic field then cuts across the many turns of the secondary. The greater the number of turns, the greater the induced emf. In the diagram, *A* is springy, magnetic material. When the iron core is sufficiently magnetized, it will pull the springy armature (*A*) to the left, thus breaking the primary circuit. When, as a result of this, the current decreases, the magnetism becomes less and the spring (*A*) returns to its original position. This completes the primary circuit again; primary current and the magnetic field increase, inducing an emf in the secondary. Notice that the increase and decrease of the current result in an alternating emf in the secondary. Usually this emf is greater in one direction than in the other, and the gap in the secondary circuit can be arranged so that there will be current in only one direction in the secondary. A spark at the gap is evidence of current in the secondary. (In the automobile the armature (*A*) is opened by cams or projections on a rotating shaft.)

In the *transformer* we also depend on mutual induction; usually ac is applied to one coil and ac is obtained from a second coil. In transformers used on low-frequency ac (up to few thousand hertz), the following formulas apply:

$$\frac{\text{secondary emf}}{\text{primary emf}} = \frac{\text{number of turns on secondary}}{\text{number of turns on primary}}$$

$$\text{power supplied by secondary} = \text{efficiency} \times \text{power supplied to primary}$$

$$V_s I_s = V_p I_p \times \text{efficiency}$$

When the efficiency is 100%, $V_s I_s = V_p I_p$

The efficiency of practical transformers is high and constant over a wide range of power. When more power is used in the secondary circuit, more power is supplied to the primary circuit automatically. If we want a higher voltage than the generator supplies, we use a *step-up transformer:* more turns on the secondary than on the primary. A *step-down* transformer has fewer turns on the secondary than on the primary and therefore produces a lower voltage than the generator supplies.

Eddy Currents and Hysteresis

Some transformers are made with a silicon steel core and two coils of wire wound on the core. The coils are insulated from each other. Ac power is supplied to the primary winding. As more and more power is supplied by the secondary winding to devices connected to it, the current in the primary winding also increases. This can be explained by considering the magnetizing effect of the currents on the core and the emf induced in the coils. However, the changing magnetic field in the core also has two undesirable effects, eddy currents and hysteresis losses. Eddy currents result from the emf induced in the core. This current is reduced by making the core out of thin laminations insulated from each other. Hysteresis losses result from the fact that the magnetic domains tend to be twisted back and forth as the direction of the applied emf changes. This requires energy.

Electric Generators

The term *dynamo* is sometimes used to refer to an electric generator which converts mechanical energy to electrical energy. Usually a coil is made to rotate in a magnetic field, and an emf is induced in the coil. The source of the energy for turning the coil may be a waterfall, steam under pressure, etc. Imagine the coil in the diagram turning clockwise in the diagram. The axis of the coil's rotation is perpendicular to the paper and is represented by the dot. The coil is rotated clockwise. The

stationary magnet provides a magnetic field which is cut by the rotating coil; this magnet is called a *field magnet*. Because the rotating coil cuts across magnetic lines of flux, an emf is induced in it and electric energy can be taken from it; this coil is called an *armature* coil. We can use Lenz's law to figure out the direction of the current in the armature. At the instant shown the direction of the current in the armature must be such as to produce the poles marked in the diagram; then the motion will be opposed by the repulsion of like poles. If we use our left-hand rule for a solenoid, we will find that the direction of electron flow in the armature is as shown in the diagram. *Slip rings A and B,* insulated from each other, are on the same shaft as the armature and rotate with it. *Brushes C and D* are stationary and make wiping electrical contact with the slip rings. Current can therefore flow through an external circuit connected to the brushes.

However, a moment later the armature will be in a new position. In order for the motion to be opposed now, the polarity of the armature, and therefore the direction of the current in the armature, must change. This is repeated as the armature keeps rotating. Current whose direction is constantly reversing is known as *alternating current* (ac). In the generator described, using slip rings, the current in the external circuit is also alternating. One complete back-and-forth variation is known as a *cycle*. In the simple ac generator shown there would be one cycle for each revolution of the armature. The alternating current ordinarily used in the home is 60 hertz. The conservation of energy principle, of which Lenz's law is a special case, indicates that, as more current is drawn from the generator, more energy has to be used to turn the armature.

A *direct-current (dc) generator* can be constructed with a slight modification of the above ac generator. We use the same field magnet and armature coil, but instead of slip rings we use a *commutator,* a metallic ring split into two insulated parts of equal size. (In more complicated dc

generators the ring is split into several commutator segments.) Each end of the armature coil is connected to a commutator segment. As the armature rotates, the stationary brushes alternately make contact with one segment and then with the other. The brushes are set so that this change in contact occurs just when the direction of current in the armature coil changes. As a result, the current in the external circuit is always in one direction (dc), but its magnitude is constantly changing; such current is known as *pulsating* or *fluctuating dc.* This fluctuation is reduced in more complicated dc generators by the use of more commutator segments and more armature coils. The

| ac in armature | Pulsating dc in external circuit of dc gen. | dc with small ripple | Time or degree of rotation |

residual fluctuation is known as *ripple.* Notice that there is ac in the armature of both the dc and ac generators. The function of the commutator is described as changing ac to dc. Also note that the polarity of the field magnet does not change. This means that if it is an electromagnet, dc must be used. A *magneto* is a dynamo whose field magnet is a permanent magnet.

Electric Motors—DC

The dc motor is similar to the dc generator except that electrical energy is supplied to the motor to be converted to mechanical energy. The diagram shown is similar to the one for the dc generator. A *field winding* or field coil has been shown for the field magnet. The diagram is for a *shunt-wound motor;* again the commutator rotates with the armature.

The field winding is in parallel with the armature coil. (In a series-wound motor the field coil and armature coils are in series.) Notice that the connection has been made which will cause the armature to rotate counterclockwise. To keep the coil rotating that way, the current in the armature must reverse at the right instant to change the polarity of the armature. The interaction between the poles of the field magnet and the poles of the armature provides the force to keep the armature rotating. However, because the armature coil rotates in a magnetic field, an emf is induced in the armature. According to Lenz's law, this emf will be in such a direction as to oppose the rotation. Therefore this induced emf is called a *counter-emf* or *back emf.* This counter-emf tends to reduce the current in the armature. Because the counter-emf is greatest when the armature is rotating fastest, the current in the armature is less when the motor is running at full speed than when it is starting.

ANSWERING THE QUESTIONS Now let us return to the questions at the beginning of the chapter. What happens when an ammeter is connected across a generator? We saw that the resistance of an ammeter is small. The one we described had a resistance of about one ohm and a full-scale deflection for one ampere. If we connected the ammeter to a generator of 30 V, we could expect a current of 30 A (Ohm's law) to flow momentarily through the ammeter; momentarily, because the moving coil of the meter would burn out unless a protective fuse would burn out first. In general, don't connect an ammeter directly to a source of emf.

What happens when a dc generator is connected across a battery? If the emf of the generator is less than that of the battery (for example, when the armature is not rotating), the battery will turn the generator like a motor. In practice this is usually not desirable. If the emf of the generator is greater than the emf of a storage battery connected across it, the battery will be recharged. However, unless precautions are taken, this current may be excessive and damage the battery.

QUESTIONS Chapter 12

Select the choice that best answers the question or completes the statement.

1. Heating a magnet will **(A)** weaken it **(B)** strengthen it **(C)** reverse its polarity **(D)** produce new poles **(E)** have no effect

2. The emf produced by a generator operating at constant speed depends mainly on **(A)** the thickness of the wire on the armature **(B)** the thickness of the wire on the field magnet **(C)** the strength of the magnetic field **(D)** the length of time the generator operates **(E)** the size of the brushes

3. A factory gets its electrical power from a generator 2 km away. The two wires connecting the generator to the factory terminals have a resistance of 0.03 Ω/km. When the generator supplies 50 A to the factory, the terminal voltage at the generator is 120 V. A voltmeter connected to the factory terminals should then read **(A)** 100 V **(B)** 110 V **(C)** 114 V **(D)** 118 V **(E)** 120 V

For 4-6. In the circuit each of the three resistors has a resistance of 30 ohms.

4. When switch S_1 is open and S_2 is closed as shown, the potential difference across R_1 is, in volts, **(A)** 0 **(B)** 30 **(C)** 45 **(D)** 60 **(E)** 90

5. When switches S_1 and S_2 are closed, the potential difference across R_1 is, in volts, **(A)** 0 **(B)** 30 **(C)** 45 **(D)** 60 **(E)** 90

6. When switches S_1 and S_2 are open, a voltmeter connected across S_2 reads **(A)** 0 **(B)** 30 V **(C)** 45 V **(D)** 60 V **(E)** 90 V

7. X is a coil of wire with a hollow core. The permanent magnet is pushed at constant speed from the right into the core and out again at the left. During the motion **(A)** there will be no current in wire YZ **(B)** electron flow in wire YZ will be from Y to Z **(C)** electron flow in wire YZ will be from Z to Y **(D)** electron flow in wire YZ will be from Z to Y and then from Y to Z **(E)** electron flow in wire YZ will be from Y to Z and then from Z to Y

8. The soft-iron armature X is allowed to fall into position on top of the poles of the horseshoe magnet. While it falls,

(A) there will be no current in wire YZ **(B)** electron flow in wire YZ will be from Y to Z **(C)** electron flow in wire YZ will be from Z to Y **(D)** electron flow in wire YZ will be from Z to Y and then from Y to Z **(E)** electron flow in wire YZ will be from Y to Z and then from Z to Y

9. G is a sensitive galvanometer connected to coil 2. Coil 1 is insulated from coil 2. Both coils are wound on the same iron core and are insulated from it. When the variable contact on the rheostat is

moved half way to the left, the needle on the galvanometer   **(A)** moves to the left   **(B)** moves to the right   **(C)** moves momentarily and returns to its starting position   **(D)** doesn't move because coils 1 and 2 are insulated from each other   **(E)** doesn't move because coils 1 and 2 are insulated from the iron

10. A horizontal copper wire W is shown suspended between two magnetic poles by means of two flexible copper wires which are connected to a dc source through switch S'. A result of closing the switch will be   **(A)** a force on W toward the front   **(B)** a force on W toward the back   **(C)** a force on W toward the left   **(D)** a force on W toward the right   **(E)** no additional force on W

11. A 3-cm length of wire is moved at right angles across a uniform magnetic field with a speed of 2.0 m/s. If the flux density is 5.0 teslas, what is the magnitude of the induced emf? **(A)** 0.03 V **(B)** 0.3 V **(C)** 0.6 V **(D)** 10 V **(E)** 20 V

12. If a step-up transformer were 100% efficient, the primary and secondary windings would have the same **(A)** current **(B)** power **(C)** number of turns **(D)** voltage **(E)** direction of winding

For 13–14. When a transformer is connected to 120-volt ac, it supplies 3000 V to a device. The current through the secondary winding then is 0.06 A and the current through the primary is 2 A. The number of turns in the primary winding is 400.

13. The number of turns in the secondary winding is **(A)** 16   **(B)** 30   **(C)** 1000   **(D)** 2000   **(E)** 10,000

14. The efficiency of the transformer is **(A)** 75%   **(B)** 80%   **(C)** 85%   **(D)** 90%   **(E)** 95%

EXPLANATIONS TO QUESTIONS Chapter 12

Answers

1. **(A)**	4. **(D)**	7. **(D)**	10. **(B)**	13. **(E)**
2. **(C)**	5. **(E)**	8. **(C)**	11. **(B)**	14. **(A)**
3. **(C)**	6. **(E)**	9. **(C)**	12. **(B)**	

Explanations

1. **(A)** Heating increases the random motion of the particles in the magnet. This leads to a less orderly arrangement of molecular magnets (or domains) in the magnet, making the magnet weaker.

2. **(C)** The emf induced in a wire depends on the length of the wire cutting the magnetic field, on the strength of the magnetic field being cut, and on the speed with which the field is being cut at right angles. In the practical design of the generator, the thickness of the wire used is important but does not affect directly the emf produced because it does not affect the three factors mentioned. Once the generator reaches constant speed, the length of time the generator operates does not affect the above three factors.

3. **(C)** Four kilometers of wire are used to connect the generator to the factory terminals. Since the wire has a resistance of 0.03 Ω/km, 4 km will have a resistance of 0.12 Ω. This resistance is in series with the factory load, which gets 50 A. The IR-drop in the connecting wires = (50 A) $\times$ (0.12 Ω) = 6 V. Since the generator supplies 120 V to the circuit and the drop in the connecting wires is 6 V, 114 V will be left for the factory load (In a series circuit, $V_T = V_1 + V_2$). A voltmeter should measure this voltage at the factory terminals.

R_1 15 Ω
30 Ω
90 V

4. **(D)** When S_1 is open and S_2 is closed, S_1 has no effect. We then have a series-parallel circuit: R_2 and R_3 are in parallel; their combination is in series with R_1 and the generator supplying 90 V. Since R_2 and R_3 have the same resistance, 30 ohms, their combined value is 30/2 ohms, or 15 ohms. The equivalent circuit is then as shown. The total resistance of the circuit then is 45 ohms. (In a series circuit, $R_T = R_1 + R_2$.)

$$I_T = V_T/R_T = 90 \text{ V}/45 \ \Omega = 2 \text{ A}$$
$$V_1 = I_1 R_1 = 2 \text{ A} \times 30 \ \Omega = 60 \text{ V}; \quad I_T = I_1$$

5. **(E)** When switch S_1 is closed, we have a short-circuit across R_2 and R_3. Their combined resistance is zero ohms, because the switch, in parallel with them, is assumed to have zero resistance. The circuit is then the equivalent of having the generator connected directly to R_1. The potential difference across R_1 is then the same as the voltage supplied by the generator.

6. **(E)** When switch S_2 is open, there is a break in the whole circuit and no current flows in any part. We can find the answer to the problem in different ways. One way is to realize that, when no current flows through a resistor, there is no voltage drop across it. Therefore the voltage supplied by the

generator will be available at the break, and this is what the voltmeter should measure. Another way is to think of the voltmeter as completing the circuit; the voltmeter then acts as a resistor as well as a meter. The resistance of the voltmeter is high: several thousand ohms. The current through it and the other resistors in the circuit will be small. The IR-drop across the other resistors in the circuit (having small resistance) will be negligibly small. Practically the full generator voltage will be across the voltmeter, and the voltmeter will record that voltage.

7. **(D)** When the magnet approaches the coil, electrons will flow through the coil and from Z to Y. This follows from Lenz's law. An emf is induced in the coil (because the magnetic field moves with respect to the coil); the direction of the induced current must be such as to oppose the approach of the magnet by producing poles in the coil, as shown. The left-hand rule applied to the coil (thumb pointing in direction of N-pole) then gives the direction of electron flow indicated. When the magnet has moved through the coil and is moving away from it, the direction of the induced current must be reversed: In that case the poles of the coil will be reversed, which is needed to oppose the motion.

8. **(C)** The soft-iron armature X is magnetized by induction: the part on the left becomes an S-pole; the part on the right an N-pole. The falling of X is then equivalent to a magnet moving near a coil and a current will be induced in the coil. According to Lenz's law, the direction of the current should be such as to oppose the falling of X. This will be so if the top of the coil becomes a north pole, opposing the falling N-pole. The left-hand rule for the coil indicates that electron flow is from Z to Y.

9. **(C)** There will be a change of current in coil 1; the resulting change in the magnetic field in the iron core affects coil 2 in spite of any insulation. The current is momentary, because an emf is induced only while there is a change in the magnetic field. We can't tell whether the needle moves to the left or right because we don't have enough information about the connection to the galvanometer.

10. **(B)** The closing of the switch results in electron flow through W from right to left. The left-hand rule for a wire tells us the direction of the resulting magnetic field around the wire: in front of the wire downward, behind the wire upward. The magnetic field due to the two poles is thus reinforced in front, weakened in back of the wire. The resulting force is toward the back.

11. **(B)** $V = Blv$
    $= (5 \text{ teslas}) (0.03 \text{ m}) (2 \text{ m/s})$
    $= 0.3 \text{ volt}$

12. **(B)** Efficiency = (work or power output)/(work or power input). In order for this ratio to be equal to 1 (or 100%), the numerator and denominator must be equal; i.e., the power supplied to the primary of the transformer equals the power supplied by the secondary to the device connected to it.

13. **(E)** In such a transformer,

$$\frac{\text{number of turns on the secondary}}{\text{number of turns on the primary}} = \frac{\text{secondary emf}}{\text{primary emf}}$$

$$\frac{N_s}{400} = \frac{3000 \text{ V}}{120 \text{ V}}; \; N_s = 10,000$$

14. **(A)**

$$\text{efficiency} = \frac{V_s I_s}{V_p I_p} = \frac{3000 \text{ V} \times 0.06 \text{ A}}{120 \text{ V} \times 2 \text{ A}} = 0.75 = 75\%$$

13

Elements of Electronics

Stereos, computers, and other "miracles" of modern electronics are created from devices based firmly in physics. Some of the devices are included in some high school physics courses. However, reread the Introduction (p. 2) to help you plan your study.

CAPACITORS AND CAPACITANCE

A *capacitor* consists of two conductors separated by an insulator or *dielectric*. The capacitor was formerly called a condenser. Common dielectrics are paper, mica, air, ceramic. Capacitors are often named by the dielectric used; e.g., paper capacitors. In some capacitors the the relative positions of the two conductors can be changed; these capacitors are known as *variable capacitors;* the others are known as *fixed capacitors*. The *Leyden jar* is an old type of capacitor in which the insulator is a glass jar. The *function* of a capacitor is to store an electric charge. Capacitors are used in tuning a radio, in reducing hum in a radio by smoothing the rectified output of the power supply (see also p. 124), and reducing sparks at electrical contacts.

How does a capacitor store a charge? *Let us first imagine a capacitor in a dc circuit*—connect a capacitor to a battery. On the negative terminal of the battery is an excess of electrons. These elec-

trons repel each other and we have provided a path for these electrons. They start moving along the connecting wire A to B, the right plate of the capacitor. At the same time, electrons are attracted from wire D and plate C of the capacitor to the positive terminal of the battery, where there is a deficiency of electrons. As a result there is a difference of potential between the plates of the capacitor. For every electron that gets to plate B there is another electron that leaves plate C. Notice that no electrons move through the dielectric. There is a motion of charge through the wires until the potential difference between the plates of the capaci-

tor is equal to the emf of the battery. It usually takes only a fraction of a second for this to happen; the capacitor is charged almost immediately.* For a given capacitor the amount of charge that is stored depends on the voltage; if we double the emf of the battery, we double the charge on the capacitor and we double the voltage across the capacitor. If we disconnect the capacitor from the battery, the capacitor can stay charged indefinitely and have a difference of potential between its plates.

$$Q = CV$$

where Q is the charge on either plate of the capacitor, C is the capacitance of the capacitor, and V is

---

*If a resistor is connected in series with the capacitor, the charging current is reduced, so the capacitor gets charged more slowly. The greater the resistance, the slower is the rate of charging.

the voltage or potential difference of the capacitor. If the voltage is expressed in volts and the charge in coulombs, then the capacitance is given in *farads* (F). The farad is a rather large unit. Capacitance is usually expressed in microfarads (μF).

$$\boxed{\textbf{1 farad} = \textbf{10}^6 \textbf{ microfarads}}$$

The capacitance of a capacitor is proportional to the area of its plates. If we double the area of the plates, we provide twice as much space for storing electrons. The capacitance of a capacitor is inversely proportional to the distance between the plates; if we double the distance between the plates, we reduce the capacitance to one-half of its original value. The capacitance also depends on the nature of the dielectric. Since capacitors store charge at some potential difference (energy per charge), it is appropriate to think of capacitors as storing energy. Indeed, that is one of their functions in photographic strobe lights and other electronic equipment. The actual value of the electric potential energy stored in a capacitor is given by

$$\text{potential energy}_{\text{(capacitor)}} = \frac{1}{2} CV^2$$

From the above discussion and formulas, you will have no trouble seeing that

$$P.E._{\text{(capacitor)}} = \frac{1}{2} CV^2 = \frac{1}{2} QV = \frac{1}{2} \frac{Q^2}{C}$$

CATHODE RAY TUBES

Edison Effect

Thomas A. Edison discovered that electric current will flow in a vacuum between a heated filament and a cold metal plate if the positive terminal of a battery is connected to the plate and the negative terminal to the filament.

Thermionic Emission

Thermionic emission is the giving off of electrons by a heated metal. The higher the temperature of the metal, the greater is the electron emission. The TV picture tube is an example of vacuum tubes which depend on this principle. They are sometimes called *thermionic* tubes. In these tubes, the part that is heated so that it will give off electrons is called the *cathode*. The *directly heated* cathode is heated because it is connected directly to a source of emf. The *indirectly heated* cathode is a sleeve slipped over a filament from which it is insulated. The filament is connected to a source of emf; the hot filament heats the cathode by radiation.

Electron Beams

Once a cathode has released electrons by thermionic emission, the electrons can be accelerated to high energies. This is done by an electric field, established between the negative cathode and positive anode (plate). In a cathode ray tube (CRT), when the electrons reach the anode, those moving along the axis find a hole. With their now considerable momentum, they continue on to the face of the tube. No particles inhibit their motion, as the air has been evacuated. Such a tube is called a "vacuum tube." When the beam's energy is released, the phosphor glows. This is the dot seen when many television sets are turned off.

Television

The control circuitry provides for horizontal and vertical movement of the beam. The diagram that follows shows a tube utilizing electrostatic deflection. If the upper vertical deflection plate is charged positively and the lower one negatively, the beam will be deflected upwards. Similar control can be exerted horizontally, giving the beam access to the entire portion of the tube on which a picture must be drawn. Instead of deflecting plates, many television sets utlize perpendicular coils, which exert a magnetic force according to $F = qvB$.

But so far we have only a beam drawing horizontal lines from top to bottom; the result would be a white screen. The part of a television set controlled by the television signal is the grid. When the grid is charged highly negative, most electrons are repelled back to the cathode, and the screen is black. By varying the negativity of the grid, white, black, and shades of gray may be produced. Color television has a similar basis in theory, but the tubes are much more difficult (and expensive!) to manufacture.

Cathode Ray Tube

In the United States, television pictures consist of 525 horizontal lines drawn every 1/30 of a second. That is, thirty complete pictures are drawn every second. Note that the diagram below is recognizable even though it is drawn with only eleven lines. Television pictures are much sharper! High Definition Television (HDTV) is currently under development. With more than twice as many lines as the current standard, the images are of nearly photographic quality.

Scanned Image

SEMICONDUCTOR DEVICES

A *semiconductor* is a material whose conductivity is very low in comparison with conductors like copper, but greater than that of insulators like glass. Common semiconductors are germanium and silicon. In practice a small, precise amount of a selected impurity is added to the pure semiconductor to give it the desired characteristics. For example, one part per million of arsenic might be added to a germanium crystal to provide it with free or loosely held electrons. Such a substance is called "donor" or N-type material. (The crystal as a whole remains electrically neutral.) If we use gallium instead of arsenic as the impurity, the germanium has an insufficiency of electrons, referred to as holes, in its crystal structure. Such a substance is called "acceptor" or P-type material. (This crystal, too, as a whole is neutral.)

Semiconductor Diodes

When a piece of N-type crystal is in contact with a piece of P-type crystal, the contact surface is called a *P-N junction*. At this junction electrons can go readily in only one direction, from the N-type crystal to the P-type crystal. The conductivity is poor in the opposite direction.

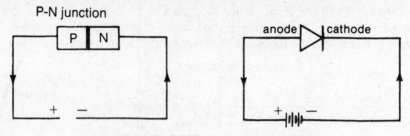

Conducting Arrangement of Crystal Diode

One of the chief uses of a diode is to *rectify*—that is, to change ac to dc. The diagram shows the circuit for a *half wave rectifier*, with the output as seen on a cathode ray oscilloscope.

Half-Wave Rectifier Circuit   *Half-Wave Rectified D.C. Output*

Transistors

A *transistor* has two junctions, which may be formed by a P-type wafer between two sections of N-type, giving an N-P-N transistor. There can also be a P-N-P type transistor, in which an N-type wafer is between two P-types.

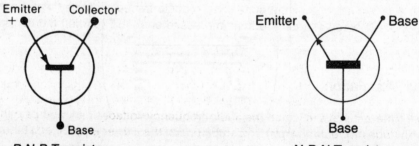

P-N-P Transistor   *N-P-N Transistor*

The miniaturization of radios, calculators, and computers has become widespread due to many factors; the semiconductor diode and transistor require no heat, they can be made very small on a mass-production basis, they require little power, and they can be readily combined in useful combinations in *integrated circuits*.

The diagram that follows shows a transistor in one of its primary applications: an *amplifier* circuit. An amplifier takes a weak input signal (from a microphone for example), adds energy from some external source (battery or power line), and delivers an output signal that is a faithful reproduction of the input signal in frequency, but at a much greater amplitude (sufficient to drive a loudspeaker, for example.)

N-P-N-Common Emitter Amplifier Circuit

TRANSMITTER-RECEIVER

A radio frequency system consists of a *transmitter*, which sends out information such as speech, music, or video, and a *receiver*, which translates the message sent by the transmitter. It has been found that, in order to radiate waves over significant distances through space, we must use electromagnetic waves of frequencies higher than the audio range. Those that are suitable for radio transmission are called *radio* frequencies (RF). These radio frequencies are used as the carriers for the audio frequencies (AF) that compose the speech or music and video frequencies (VF) that compose pictures. The longitudinal waves of speech or music are converted to electrical currents of the same frequencies with the aid of a mircophone. These audio frequencies may then be amplified with the aid of transistors. These voltages are then impressed on the RF carrier; the AF is said to *modulate* the carrier.

Amplitude Modulation

There are different ways in which the audio frequency voltages can modulate the carrier. One of these is *amplitude modulation (AM)*: the amplitude of the carrier is changed at the frequency of the

RF $+$ AF $=$ Mod. RF [AM]

AF. The greater the amplitude change of the AF, the greater is the amplitude change of the RF. Notice that both the top and the bottom of the RF are changed in amplitude to the same degree, and that the outline of both top and bottom of the modulated RF is the shape of the AF. The carrier frequencies used for commercial AM broadcasting are 550 to 1650 kilohertz (kHz).

Frequency Modulation

In *frequency modulation* (*FM*) the frequency of the carrier is changed at the frequency of the AF. The greater the amplitude of the AF, the greater is the frequency change of the carrier; that is, the amplitude of the AF determines how much the frequency changes, while the frequency of the AF

RF + AF = FM

determines the rate at which this change takes place. The FM band of frequencies is about 88 to 108 MHz. (One mega- is equal to one million.) An FM system can be designed readily to be relatively static-free as compared with AM.

The *antenna* at the transmitter is used to radiate electromagnetic waves whose frequency and variation are the same as those of the modulated RF described before. These electromagnetic radio waves travel through space with the same speed as other electromagnetic waves such as light: about 3×10^{10} cm/s, or 3×10^8 m/s, or 186,000 mi/sec. The length of the antenna at the transmitter is often made about one-half that of a wavelength. This is easily calculated. For example, if we want to transmit a frequency of 100 megahertz

$$\text{wavelength } (\lambda) = \frac{\text{speed of wave}}{\text{frequency}} = \frac{3 \times 10^8 \text{ m/s}}{100 \times 10^6 \text{ hertz}}$$
$$\lambda = 3 \text{ meters}$$
$$\tfrac{1}{2}\lambda = 1.5 \text{ meter}$$

The antenna would be about 1.5 meters long.

At the *receiver*, electromagnetic waves of many frequencies pass the antenna and induce electric currents in it of the same frequency as the carrier. When we tune the receiver, we usually vary a capacitor to establish resonance for the desired carrier frequency. In the receiver we need a *detector* circuit in which a semiconductor diode may be used in a circuit similar to the half-wave rectifier described before. In the detector, however, after rectifying the modulated RF, we use a filter circuit to recover the AF which was used to modulate the RF. The detector is said to *demodulate* or detect. The AF electrical currents are used to operate a *reproducer* which converts the electrical currents to longitudinal sound waves in the surrounding medium. The reproducers may be loudspeakers or earphones.

Television transmission consists of the sending of two messages: sound and picture. FM is used for sound transmission, AM for picture transmission. At the transmitter a camera is used to translate information about the picture into electrical signals whose frequency range is up to about 4 MHz (video frequencies). This is done by a scanning process which is repeated in a somewhat different way in the picture tube of the TV receiver.

In the television cameras, and elsewhere, an important principle is the photoelectric effect; when light shines on some metals at room temperatures electrons are emitted. A *photoelectric cell* is a vacuum tube in which the cathode is made of such metal; another metal is used for the plate or collector to which the electrons go when an external voltage is used to keep the collector positive with respect to the cathode. In a photovoltaic cell a somewhat similar process takes place when light falls on two specially selected materials which are in contact with each other; no external voltage is required.

The photoelectric effect will be discussed further in the next chapter.

QUESTIONS Chapter 13

Select the choice that best completes the statement.

For 1–4. A certain capacitor consists of two metal plates in air placed parallel and close to each other but not touching. The capacitor is connected briefly to a dc generator so that the difference in potential between the two plates becomes 12,000 V. The capacitance of the capacitor is 1×10^{-6} microfarad.

1. The charge on either plate is, in coulombs, **(A)** 1.2×10^{-8} **(B)** 1.2×10^{-6} **(C)** 1.2×10^{-4} **(D)** 1.2×10^{-2} **(E)** 1.2

2. If a thin uncharged glass plate is then slipped between the two metal plates without touching them, the charge on each plate **(A)** will increase by an amount depending on the thickness of the glass **(B)** will decrease by an amount depending on the thickness of the glass **(C)** will increase by an amount depending on the distance the glass plate was inserted **(D)** will decrease by an amount depending on the distance the glass plate was inserted **(E)** will not change

3. As a result of the insertion of the glass plate, the potential difference between the plates **(A)** increases by an amount depending on the thickness of the glass **(B)** increases by an amount depending on the distance the glass is inserted **(C)** decreases somewhat **(D)** decreases to zero **(E)** does not change

4. How much energy, in joules, is stored on the plates? **(A)** 6.0×10^{-21} **(B)** 6.0×10^{-9} **(C)** 1.2×10^{-8} **(D)** 7.2×10^{-5} **(E)** 1.44×10^{-4}

5. When a metal is heated sufficiently, electrons are given off by the metal. This phenomenon is known as **(A)** thermionic emission **(B)** photoelectric effect **(C)** piezoelectric effect **(D)** secondary emission **(E)** canal ray emission

6. When a radio station is broadcasting a musical program, the antenna of its transmitter **(A)** radiates RF electromagnetic waves **(B)** radiates AF electromagnetic waves **(C)** radiates RF longitudinal waves **(D)** radiates AF longitudinal waves **(E)** none of the above

7. Cathode rays are **(A)** sharp projections on the cathodes of diodes **(B)** sharp projections on the cathodes of triodes **(C)** striations in a gas discharge tube **(D)** proton beams **(E)** electron beams

8. A cathode ray oscilloscope has two pairs of deflection plates. If no voltage is applied to one pair, while the voltage applied to the other pair is ac of the type used for power in most homes, the pattern on the face of the oscilloscope will be most like **(A)** a square wave **(B)** a sine wave **(C)** a saw-tooth wave **(D)** an ellipse **(E)** a straight line

9. Two good students, X and Y, connect a diode in series with a battery and a milliammeter. When X performs the experiment, he gets a zero reading on his milliammeter. Y gets the desired half-scale deflection on her meter. If both use identical equipment, the most probable reason for the difference is **(A)** X has reversed connections to the milliammeter **(B)** Y has reversed connections to the milliammeter **(C)** Y has reversed connections to the battery **(D)** X has reversed connections to the battery **(E)** X has used the wrong color wire

10. In a cathode ray tube, **(A)** electrons go from cathode to plate and then from plate to cathode **(B)** electrons go from cathode to plate only **(C)** electrons go from plate to cathode only **(D)** electrons go from cathode to plate and protons go from plate to cathode **(E)** protons go from cathode to plate and electrons go from plate to cathode

11. In a cathode ray tube, electrons for the electron current come chiefly from **(A)** the grid **(B)** the plate **(C)** the cathode **(D)** the getter **(E)** ionization of residual gases in the tube

12.   A N-P-N transistor is connected in a common emitter amplifier circuit. A milliammeter is inserted between the collector and emitter. The base current (current between base and emitter) is 30 microamps and the milliammeter reads 10 mA. When the base current is changed to 60 microamps, the milliammeter reading will **(A)** not change   **(B)** become 20 mA   **(C)** become 5 mA **(D)** decrease to some value between 5 and 10 mA   **(E)** decreases, possibly even to zero

13.   The operation of a transistor requires **(A)** that the emitter be heated   **(B)** that the base be heated   **(C)** that the collector be heated   **(D)** that the collector be enclosed in a vacuum   **(E)** none of the above

EXPLANATIONS TO QUESTIONS Chapter 13

Answers

1. **(A)**	4. **(D)**	7. **(E)**	10. **(B)**	13. **(E)**
2. **(E)**	5. **(A)**	8. **(E)**	11. **(C)**	
3. **(C)**	6. **(A)**	9. **(D)**	12. **(B)**	

Explanations

1. **(A)** The capacitance equals the charge on either plate divided by the resulting difference of potential: $C = \dfrac{Q}{V}$; $Q = CV = (1 \times 10^{-6} \times 10^{-6}$ farad$) \times (1.2 \times 10^4$ V$)$; $Q = 1.2 \times 10^{-8}$ coulomb.

2. **(E)** Since the glass is an insulator, and the air is an insulator, no path is provided for electrons to go to or from the metal plates. Even accidental touching of the metal by the glass will not result in a significant transfer of electrons.

3. **(C)** Since $C = Q/V$, $V = Q/C$. In question 3 we saw that the charge Q did not change. What happened to the capacitance C? By inserting the glass we replaced some of the air by a solid dielectric. Ths increased the capacitance. Since the denominator (C) increased, while the numerator (Q) remained the same, the value of the fraction (V) decreased.

4. **(D)** $P.E._{\text{(capacitor)}} = \dfrac{1}{2} CV^2$

$$= \dfrac{1}{2} \times 1 \times 10^{-6} \times 10^{-6} \text{ farad} \times (1.2 \times 10^4 \text{ volts})^2$$

$$= 7.2 \times 10^{-5} \text{ joules}$$

5. **(A)** Thermionic emission is the giving off of electrons by a metal when it is heated. Secondary emission may occur in vacuum tubes: this is the emission of electrons from a cold electrode, such as the plate, when it is bombarded by fast electrons.

6. **(A)** All the waves radiated by an antenna are electromagnetic waves; these are transverse. It is not practical to radiate and transmit AF electromagnetic waves over long distances. When a radio station is On The Air, it radiates an RF electromagnetic wave. This wave may be modulated or not, but it is RF.

7. **(E)** The term *cathode ray* came into use before its actual nature was known. Further study showed that the rays are fast-moving electrons.

8. **(E)** In the cathode ray oscilloscope a fine beam of fast-moving electrons is accelerated towards a fluorescent screen, as in a TV picture tube. Where the electrons hit the screen there is a bright spot of light. One pair of deflection plates deflects the electrons horizontally, the other pair vertically, when a difference of potential is applied to the plates. The amount of deflection depends on the magnitude of the applied voltage. When an ac voltage is applied to one pair of plates, the fast-moving electrons will be deflected varying amounts depending on the instantaneous voltage. Therefore, on the screen there will be a succession of bright spots of light which will appear as a line. If no volt-

age is applied to the other pair of plates, the deflection is along one straight line, and the pattern on the fluorescent screen will be a straight line.

9. **(D)** Study the diagram of the half-wave rectifier. You will see that reversing the connections to the meter would result in a negative reading. However, no current can go from donor to acceptor unless the donor is connected to the negative terminal of the battery (through the milliammeter). If the battery connections were reversed, the acceptor would be negative with respect to the donor and repel electrons.

10. **(B)** A cathode ray tube is like a check valve; electrons can go only one way through it, from cathode to plate. Ordinarily there are no protons in motion in a vacuum tube.

11. **(C)** In the cathode ray tube we depend on thermionic emission to yield the electrons that move through the space in the tube. The cathode is the only element that can act as the emitter of electrons in the vacuum tube. The *getter* is a piece of metal used inside the vacuum tube during manufacturing to help achieve a good vacuum.

12. **(B)** The common emitter amplifier is a *proportional* amplifier. That is, small changes in the base-emitter circuit are reproduced proportionally in the collector-base circuit.

13. **(E)** One of the advantages of a transistor is that no heated cathode is used to supply electrons. Electrons are made available by using semiconductors, which have free electrons. The transistor is a solid-state device; the motion of electrons in it takes place within a solid and no vacuum is needed.

14

Photons, Atoms, Nuclei

In geometrical optics, we were concerned only with effects that could be explained by light travelling in straight lines. In physical optics, we discovered that light could diffract around obstacles, which implied that light had wave characteristics. In 1905, Albert Einstein gave a surprising explanation of an effect that implies that light can exhibit particle characteristics.

PHOTOELECTRIC EFFECT

When visible light hits most metals, electrons remain bound to the atoms. However, when high frequency electromagnetic radiation hits metals, electrons are emitted. This is called the *photoelectric effect*, and the electrons emitted are called *photoelectrons*.

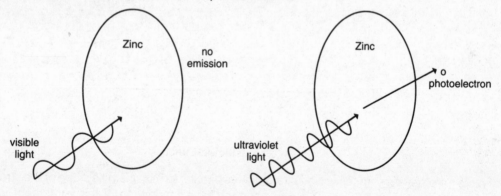

Photoelectric Effect

Einstein's theory invokes the *quantum theory* of light, which states that light is emitted and absorbed in little bundles of energy. Historically, the notion of the quantum of energy was introduced by Planck in 1900 to explain the continuous spectrum produced by a hot blackbody. This ideal object is also a perfect absorber of light (page 84).

The photoelectric effect has some surprising features. If careful measurements are made with monochromatic light, the following observations can be made:

1. If the intensity of the light is increased, the *number* of emitted electrons increases.
2. If the intensity of the light is increased, the *speed* of the emitted electrons does not increase.
3. If we decrease the frequency of the light gradually, we reach a frequency below which no electrons come off. This is known as the *threshold frequency*. No matter how much we increase the intensity of the radiation, if it is below the threshold frequency, no electrons will be emitted by the substance.

4. For each substance, the speed of the emitted electrons is not the same for all electrons. The maximum speed and kinetic energy increase with the frequency of the incident radiation.
5. Different substances have different threshold frequencies.
6. If the frequency which is used is above the threshold frequency, even the weakest radiation will result in the emission of electrons, and their maximum speed will be the same as when very intense radiation of the frequency is used.

Only the first of these observations can be easily explained by the wave theory. Albert Einstein explained them all simply by using an expanded concept of the quantum. He suggested that we think of electromagnetic energy as being granular, traveling through space as little "grains," and being emitted and absorbed this way. The amount of energy, or quantum, in each grain is given by Planck's formula, $E = hf$, where f is the frequency of the radiation. (The term *photon* is often used to refer to the "grain," and *quantum* to the amount of energy in it; sometimes the terms are used interchangeably.) All photons in a monochromatic radiation of a given frequency are the same, but they are different from the photons in radiation of a different frequency. The higher the frequency, the greater the energy of the photon. All photons travel with the same speed, the speed of light.

Energy has to be used to remove an electron from a material. Some electrons are removed more readily than others. The *work function (W)* of a material is the minimum amount of energy needed to remove an electron from the material. Different materials have different work functions. If light shines on a material and a photon has energy greater than the work function, the photon may be absorbed by an electron, and the electron comes off with a kinetic energy equal to the difference between the quantum of energy and the work function of the material:

$$E_k = hf - W$$

For a given material, if we increase the frequency of the monochromatic radiation, the kinetic energy of the fastest photoelectron will increase. If we plot a graph of the kinetic energy of the fastest electrons against frequency of radiation used, we get a straight line:

Photoelectric Effect

The plots for other substances will be straight lines parallel to this one. The slope of the straight line is Planck's constant, $h = 6.63 \times 10^{-34}$ joule-second. The magnitude of the y-intercept is the work function of the material. The photon which has that amount of energy is just barely able to remove an electron from this material and has a frequency equal to the threshold frequency:

$$W = hf_0$$

For example, suppose that we have a material whose work function is 3.0×10^{-19} joule, and light with a wavelength of 4000 angstrom units is shining on it. Let's calculate a few relevant quantities. What is the energy of each photon? $E = hf = hc/\lambda$

$$E = (6.63 \times 10^{-34} \text{ J} \cdot \text{s}) (3 \times 10^8 \text{ m/s})/(4000 \times 10^{-10} \text{ m})$$
$$= 5.0 \times 10^{-19} \text{ joule}$$

What is the speed of the fastest photoelectron?

$$E_k = hf - W$$
$$= 5.0 \times 10^{-19} \text{ joule} - 3.0 \times 10^{-19} \text{ joule}$$
$$= 2.0 \times 10^{-19} \text{ joule}$$
$$E_k = \frac{1}{2} mv^2$$
$$2.0 \times 10^{-19} \text{ joule} = \frac{1}{2} (9.1 \times 10^{-31} \text{ kg}) \, v^2$$
$$v = 6.6 \times 10^5 \text{ m/s}$$

When dealing with small energies such as those possessed by electrons and photons, we often find it convenient to introduce another unit of energy. The *electron volt (eV)* is the energy one electron acquires when it is accelerated through a difference of potential of one volt.

$$1 \text{ eV} = 1.6 \times 10^{-19} \text{ joule}$$

With the quantum theory verified and expanded by Einstein's explanation of the photoelectric effect, more discoveries came rapidly.

ATOMIC MODELS

The existence of atoms was first theorized by the ancient Greeks. They proposed a unit of matter so small as to be indivisible. When he discovered the electron, J.J. Thompson proved that the "atom" discussed in laboratories was in fact divisible. He proposed an atomic model wherein electrons were scattered through a medium of positive charge like raisins in a pudding.

Ernest Rutherford performed a number of experiments in which alpha particles given off by radioactive materials were shot at thin gold foil. On the basis of observations and theoretical calculations he decided (1910) that (1) atoms are mostly empty space; (2) practically all of the atom's mass is concentrated in a very small nucleus; (3) the nucleus is postively charged because of its protons; and (4) the neutral atom has as many electrons outside the nucleus as there are excess protons in the nucleus. (Neutrons were not discovered until 1932. Rutherford assumed that there were enough other protons and an equal number of electrons in the nucleus to provide the rest of the mass which the atom has.) The electrons are relatively far from the nucleus. Alpha particles shot into the atom are scattered at various angles because of the coulomb force of repulsion between its positive charge and the positive charge of the nucleus. The closer its path is to the nucleus, the greater is the angle of scattering. Unfortunately, the Rutherford model of the atom was unstable. If atoms were so constructed, the universe would collapse in a small fraction of a second as electrons spiralled into positive nuclei, radiating energy as they went.

Niels Bohr (1913) used the Rutherford model of the atom and quantum theory to develop a stable atomic model. He specifically considered hydrogen, because it consisted of only two objects (an electron and a proton), and because the known spectrum of hydrogen at that time consisted of a few lines in the visible and infrared whose wavelengths were well known. Bohr postulated:

1. The electron of the hydrogen atom revolves around its nucleus (a proton) in only definite, allowed orbits. No energy is radiated by the atom while the electron is in these orbits.
2. The most stable orbit is the one closest to the nucleus. In this condition the atom (or the electron) is said to be in the *ground state*. The electron then has the least amount of energy with respect to the nucleus.
3. The atom can be raised to higher or excited energy states which are fairly stable. Only definite quantized amounts of energy can be absorbed for the change to higher energy states or levels. (Bohr thought of the energy in terms of the amount of work required to pull the negative electron away from the positive nucleus.) For example, 10.2 eV are needed to raise it to the second energy level, and 12.08 eV to the third level from the ground state.
4. When the atom returns to a lower energy state, it can only jump back to one of the allowed energy states, and the difference in energy is given off as a photon. The jump may be to the ground state or an intermediate one. The hydrogen lines in the visible spectrum had been observed by Balmer; they involve electrons falling to the n = 2 state.

5. Only specified orbits are permitted. For all orbits of the electron: $mvr = \dfrac{nh}{2\pi}$, where m is the mass

of the electron, v its orbital speed, r the radius of the orbit, h Planck's constant. The product mvr is *known as the angular momentum* of the electron due to its orbit around the nucleus.

The diagram shows some of the energy levels of hydrogen. On the left, under n, the allowed levels are numbered, starting with the ground state as number 1. They are known as the *principal quantum*

Hydrogen

numbers. On the right, under *eV*, are two columns of numbers. Both give the energy of each level in electron volts. One uses the ground state as the reference level and labels it the *zero level*. Since it is the lowest energy level, the other levels are positive with respect to it. Frequently the ionization state is taken as the reference and is assigned the zero value. The other levels are lower in energy than the ionization state, and therefore the numbers are negative. The difference between any two energy levels is, of course, the same (allowing for significant figures) in both columns. Notice, for example, that both columns tell us that 13.6 eV are needed to ionize the hydrogen atom from the ground state. If the atom is in the $n = 3$ state, only 1.5 eV is needed to ionize the atom, but if a photon whose energy is 1.5 eV hits a hydrogen atom in the ground state, it will not be absorbed. The collision is elastic.

Slow Collisions

When a stream of electrons passes through a gas, the electrons may lose energy as they collide with the atoms of the gas. In some collisions practically no energy is lost; in some collisions practically all the energy may be lost by the electron. For example, an electron having energy of 7 eV may lose nearly all of it when hitting the same atom. Careful experiments show that during such collisions atoms can absorb only definite bundles of energy—quanta.

Compton Effect

In the description of the photoelectric effect we stressed a very important characteristic. In order to raise the hydrogen atom to a higher energy state, such as from the ground state to $n = 2$, the photon which arrives must have the exact quantum of energy, 10.2 eV. If it has 11.5 eV it will not raise the electron to a higher level. In 1923, A.H. Compton discovered that if very high energy photons hit a material like carbon, a different effect is observed. When he used high-energy X rays, he found that some of the scattered X rays had a lower frequency than the original X rays. He was able to explain this effect quantitatively by reasoning that each photon has a momentum of hf/c ($= h/\lambda$); the photon collides with an electron in the carbon atom and loses some of its energy and momentum to the electron; energy and momentum are conserved. the photon behaves like a particle.

$$\text{momentum of the photon} = \frac{\text{Planck's constant}}{\text{wavelength}}$$

$$p = \frac{h}{\lambda}$$

DeBroglie Wavelength

In 1924, a young Ph.D. candidate named Louis deBroglie reasoned that if photons could display momentum, particles should be able to display wave characteristics. If momentum of photon = hf/c, then

$$\lambda = \frac{h}{mv}$$

Sometimes called a *matter wave*, it is indeed possible to calculate the wavelength for any known mass whose velocity is specified.

Davisson and Germer

DeBroglie wavelengths were soon verified in electron diffraction experiments by Davisson and Germer in the United States, and Thompson in England.

ATOMS AND RADIOACTIVITY

There are over 100 different chemical elements. One way in which they differ from each other is in the charge of the nucleus of the individual atom. The *atomic number* (Z) of an element is the number of protons in the nucleus of the atom; since the neutral atom is electrically uncharged, the atomic number is also the number of electrons surrounding the nucleus. (Hydrogen has an atomic number of 1; oxygen an atomic number of 8; uranium an atomic number of 92.) All elements whose atomic numbers are greater than 92 are man-made; they are known as the *transuranic* elements. Many of these were first made in the U.S. One of these is nobelium ($Z = 102$). Lawrencium has an atomic number of 103. All atoms, except those of common hydrogen, contain neutrons in the nucleus in addition to protons. The *mass number* is the total number of protons and neutrons in the nucleus. Most chemically pure elements contain atoms that are identical in atomic number but different in mass number because they differ in the number of neutrons; these are called *isotopes* of the element. The actual mass of the proton is extremely small; the mass of the neutron is slightly greater. Each of these is about 1840 times as massive as the electron.

The mass of the nucleus is less than the sum of the masses of the *nucleons* (protons and neutrons) which compose it. Einstein had predicted that mass and energy might be converted into one another.

$$E = mc^2$$

The equivalent amounts are given by the relation in which m is the mass converted, c the speed of light, and E the equivalent amount of energy. If m is in kilograms, and c in meters per second, E is in joules. The *binding energy* of a nucleus is the energy equivalence of the difference in mass between the nucleus and the sum of the masses of the nucleons; it is the energy which would have to be supplied to break the nucleus into its component protons and neutrons. The nature of the nuclear force which holds the nucleus together is not fully understood. It is greater than electromagnetic and gravitational forces, but acts over short distances only.

Henri Becquerel discovered nuclei that broke up spontaneously, and in this process were found to give off some "radiation" that ionized the chemicals in a photographic emulsion. Such nuclei are said to be *radioactive*. This radioactivity is not affected by temperature or any other treatment we can give.

Natural radiation was found to consist of three different types of particles; they were called alpha, beta, and gamma. *Alpha particles* are helium nuclei; *beta particles* are electrons; *gamma rays* are electromagnetic waves similar to X rays, but of higher frequency. An element can change into a different element; this is known as *transmutation*, a process in which a charged particle is emitted or absorbed by a nucleus. The *half-life* of a radioactive element is the length of time it takes for one-half of a given mass of an element to transmute into a different element. For example, an ejected particle may be a proton, an alpha particle, or an electron. Although not normally present in the nucleus, electrons may be ejected, since a neutron can change into a proton and an electron upon disintegration.

NUCLEAR CHANGES

Atomic Mass Unit

When dealing with nuclear changes we often find it convenient to use a small mass unit. The *atomic mass unit* (*amu* or *u*) is defined as one-twelfth of the mass of an atom of carbon-12, that is, of the isotope of carbon which has a mass number of 12. One atomic mass unit then turns out to be approximately equal to 1.66×10^{-27} kg. Often conventional energy units are used instead of mass units:

$$E = mc^2$$
$$= (1.66 \times 10^{-27} \text{ kg}) (3 \times 10^8 \text{ m/s})^2$$
$$= 1.49 \times 10^{-10} \text{ J} \quad = \frac{1.49 \times 10^{-10}}{1.6 \times 10^{-19}} \text{ eV}$$
$$= 0.931 \times 10^9 \text{ eV}$$

In other words, 1 amu is approximately equal to 931 MeV.

SOME NUCLEAR REACTIONS

We mentioned above that there are naturally radioactive elements and that their nuclei break up. Changes in nuclei also occur in the laboratory as a result of bombardment with fast-moving particles. Rutherford did this with alpha particles obtained from radioactive substances. Now it is frequently done by using particles speeded up with particle accelerators. Now let us look at some equations that represent the reactions.

In all of these nuclear reactions, atomic number and mass number are conserved; that is, the algebraic sum of the atomic numbers on the left side of the equation must equal the sum on the right; and the sum of the mass numbers on the left side must equal the sum on the right. Atomic number is written as a subscript of the chemical symbol of the element and mass number as the superscript.

Natural Radioactivity—Alpha Decay

$$^{226}_{88}\text{Ra} \rightarrow {}^{222}_{86}\text{Rn} + {}^{4}_{2}\text{He}$$

Note that the atomic numbers on each side add up to 88 and the mass numbers to 226. You will recall that the alpha particle is the nucleus of the common helium atom, which escapes this reaction with great speed. This is an example of *alpha decay*.

Natural Radioactivity—Beta Decay

$$^{24}_{11}\text{Na} \rightarrow {}^{24}_{12}\text{Mg} + {}^{0}_{-1}\text{e}$$

In beta decay an electron (the negative beta particle) is given off. Note that its mass number is zero and its charge is −1. For the electron and neutron, atomic number is replaced by charge. Algebraically the subscripts on the right add up to 11, which is what we started with on the left side. In beta decay neutrinos are also given off, a fact not always shown. The charge and mass of the neutrino are zero. (Recently some scientists expressed the belief that the rest mass is not exactly zero.) Here we do not distinguish between neutrino and antineutrino.

Natural Radioactivity—Gamma Radiation

Gamma radiation occurs during a reorganization of nuclear energies. Atomic numbers are unaffected (that is, the element stays the same).

$$_{43}^{99}\text{Tc} \rightarrow {}_{43}^{99}\text{Tc} + \gamma$$

First Artificial Transmutation

$$_{7}^{14}\text{N} + {}_{2}^{4}\text{He} \rightarrow {}_{8}^{17}\text{O} + {}_{1}^{1}\text{H}$$

Bombarding nitrogen with alpha particles in 1919, Rutherford became the first person to convert one element into another in a laboratory.

Discovery of the Neutron

$$_{4}^{9}\text{Be} + {}_{2}^{4}\text{He} \rightarrow {}_{6}^{12}\text{C} + {}_{0}^{1}\text{n}$$

In 1932, Chadwick noted that when beryllium is bombarded with alpha particles, a free neutron is emitted along with the production of an isotope of carbon. Note that the mass number of the neutron (like that of the proton) is 1, but its charge is zero.

Note that both the above artificial transmutations require only the input energies of alpha particles resulting from natural radioactivity. Now we shall consider some machines used in physics for higher energy experimentation.

PARTICLES AND PARTICLE ACCELERATORS

As indicated above, it is believed that the nuclei of all atoms except common hydrogen contain protons and neutrons (the *nucleons*). The nucleus is surrounded by electrons. In the neutral atom, the number of these electrons is equal to the number of protons in the nucleus (the atomic number). Other particles have been discovered, some after their existence was predicted by theory. Many more than 100 of these particles, referred to as *elementary particles*, are now known. Some appear to fit the ancient Greek idea of indivisible matter. There is no theory available yet that completely accounts for the existence, characteristics, and behavior of these particles. Most of these are now believed to be composed of a small number of *quarks,* whose charge is believed to be only one-third of an electron's. For example, it is believed that the proton and neutron contain three quarks each. Particle accelerators have been built to obtain more facts and examine theories on the nature of matter.

In 1934 Yukawa predicted the existence of a particle with mass intermediate between that of the electron and that of the proton. Later several different ones were actually found and are called *mesons*. Neutral mesons as well as positive and negative mesons have been found. The negative pi-meson fits Yukawa's description. The pi-mesons (also known as *pions*) have a mass about 270 times that of the electron. The mesons are unstable. The breakdown of the pi-meson results in the production of a lighter particle, the *muon.*

Particles heavier than the neutron have been found. An example is the upsilon particle, which has a mass about 10 times that of the proton.

Antiparticles have been found. The antiparticles of the charged particles have the same mass as the corresponding particle but an opposite charge. The *positron* is the antiparticle of the electron.

These various particles are often referred to as elementary particles; but this no longer implies that they are indivisible. For example, the neutron can last indefinitely inside the nucleus, but outside the nucleus it is unstable and decays into a proton and electron. In this and similar reactions conservation of energy and conservation of momentum suggested the existence of the *neutrino*–a neutral particle with practically zero rest mass. The concept of such a particle was introduced by

Pauli in 1931 and carried further by Fermi, who suggested the name. The neutrino was detected experimentally in 1956. (See page 143.)

The list of elementary particles usually includes the *photon*. It always moves with the speed of light, has zero rest mass, and has an amount of energy depending on the frequency of the electromagnetic wave it represents.

Like the electron, the muon has a neutrino associated with it. The *tau* particle, still heavier than the muon, also has a neutrino associated with it. All have antiparticles.

Particle Accelerators

Particle accelerators are helpful for examination of the nucleus. The greater the energy of the particles used to bombard or "smash" the nucleus, the more detail the physicist expects to find about the structure of the nucleus and its particles. This bombardment has led to the discovery of some of the particles mentioned above.

The energy possessed by the bombarding particles is usually described in terms of million electron volts (*MeV*) or billion electron volts (*GeV: G* is for *giga-*; it equals 10^9). One *electron volt* is the energy one electron acquires on being accelerated through a difference of potential of one volt. Electrons or protons are frequently used as the particles or bullets of these atom smashers. These, like other charged particles, can be accelerated by being placed in an electric field. In the *Van de Graaff* machine and in the *linear accelerator* the particle gains speed along a straight path. In the linear accelerator a series of cylindrical electrodes is used and the particles acquire more and more energy as they pass between successive pairs of electrodes. To achieve high energies a very long evacuated pipe is required.

In order to avoid the need for such long pipes, circular particle accelerators have been constructed. The equivalent length of path is achieved by having the particles go around the circular path many times. The charged particles are forced to go in a circular path by a magnetic field directed at right angles to the path of the particles. The first of these was the *cyclotron* invented by E. O. Lawrence in 1932. In the cyclotron a flat, evacuated cylindrical box is placed between the poles of a strong electromagnet. Inside the box are two hollow, **D**-shaped electrodes called *dees*. The protons or deuterons to be accelerated are fed into the space between the electrodes. An ac voltage of high frequency (about 10^7 hertz) is applied to the dees, and the particles are accelerated across the gap.

Top View of Dees

The magnetic field bends the moving particles into a circular path. The voltage reverses in time to accelerate the particles emerging from the dee. After 100 trips around the cyclotron the particles may acquire an energy of several million electron volts. Successive semicircular paths in the dees are of larger radius, but each of these is covered in equal lengths of time because the greater speed of the particles just compensates for the increased length of path.

Subatomic particles can move fast enough to display effects predicted by Einstein's special theory of relativity. As can be seen from the following equations, objects at normal speeds behave as expected (v^2/c^2 is essentially 1), but at speeds near the speed of light, masses increase and lengths decrease.

$$mass_{relativistic} = \frac{mass_{rest}}{\sqrt{1-(v^2/c^2)}}$$

$$length_{relativistic} = length_{rest}\sqrt{1-(v^2/c^2)}$$

When a proton has acquired a speed corresponding to an energy of about 10 MeV a relativity effect sets in: its mass starts to increase noticeably with further increases in energy. It therefore takes the particle longer to cover each successive semicircle. The frequency of the ac voltage applied to the dees must therefore change to compensate for this increase in mass. This is done in the *synchrocyclotron*, which uses a constant magnetic field but an electric field of changing frequency. (It uses a frequency modulated oscillator.) In the *synchrotron* both the magnetic field and the frequency of the electric field are changed. This results in a circular path of almost constant radius for the particles and also in a saving of material for the magnet. The largest accelerator currently operational in the United States is at Fermilab in Batavia, Illinois.

FISSION AND FUSION

Fission

Fission is the splitting of a massive nucleus into two large fragments with the simultaneous release of energy and some particles which can also produce fission. For example, the massive uranium nucleus (mass number 235) fissions on capture of a neutron and releases a large amount of energy and two or more neutrons. The total mass of all the particles produced is less than the mass of the original uranium atom plus neutron. The difference in mass accounts for the energy produced in the form of kinetic energy (fast-moving particles) and gamma rays. If the uranium is arranged so that the released neutrons will, in turn, fission other uranium nuclei, we have a *chain reaction*. This is done in a *nuclear reactor* or pile, in which the fissionable material is arranged so that the release of energy can be controlled. Boron rods are used as *control rods*: boron absorbs neutrons readily, and if the pile gets too active, the rods are inserted to cut down on the rate. Cadmium may also be used in the control rod. Fission of uranium-235 is most likely to proceed with slow-moving neutrons; *moderators* are used to slow down the neutrons. Moderator materials are graphite and deuterium (used in heavy water). In the so-called A-bomb or fission bomb relatively large amounts of fissionable material are split in a short time with the consequent release of tremendous amounts of energy and radioactive material. Radiation hazards in case of a nuclear reactor breakdown and in disposal of nuclear wastes are a serious concern.

Fusion

In *fusion* the nuclei of some light elements like lithium and hydrogen combine; again there is a loss of some mass with the consequent release of energy. The fusion reaction requires a temperature of millions of degrees. This is therefore called a *thermonuclear reaction* and has been achieved in an uncontrollable way in the H-bomb; here an A-bomb is first used to produce the required high temperature. Scientists are working towards achieving a controllable fusion reaction. This will make available tremendous amounts of energy everywhere by the use of the hydrogen in water.

QUESTIONS Chapter 14

Select the choice that best answers the question or completes the statement.

1. Of the following, the particle whose mass is closest to that of the electron is the (A) positron (B) proton (C) neutron (D) neutrino (E) deuteron

2. When a beta particle is emitted from the nucleus of an atom, the effect is to (A) decrease the atomic number by 1 (B) decrease the mass number by 1 (C) increase the atomic number by 1 (D) increase the mass number by 1 (E) decrease the atomic number by 2

3. Gamma rays consists of (A) helium nuclei (B) hydrogen nuclei (C) neutrons (D) high-speed neutrinos (E) radiation similar to X rays

4. Neutrons penetrate matter readily chiefly because they (A) occupy no more than one-tenth of the volume of electrons (B) occupy no more than one-tenth of the volume of protons (C) have a smaller mass than protons (D) are electrically neutral (E) are needlelike in shape

5. It is characteristic of alpha particles emitted from radioactive nuclei that they **(A)** are sometimes negatively charged   **(B)** usually consist of electrons   **(C)** are helium nuclei   **(D)** are hydrogen nuclei   **(E)** are the ultimate unit of positive electricity

Lead

For 6-7. R is a natural radioactive material. F is a fluorescent screen. A magnetic field is to be imagined perpendicular down into the paper. Bright spots appear on the screen at T, S, and P. The space between R and the screen is evacuated.

6. The emanation from R which produced spot P is   **(A)** electrons   **(B)** protons   **(C)** alpha particles   **(D)** N-poles   **(E)** S-poles

7. If paper is inserted at X, which of the following is (are) most likely to be blocked by the paper? **(A)** N-pole   **(B)** S-pole   **(C)** electrons   **(D)** alpha particles   **(E)** gamma rays

8. When describing isotopes of the same element, the most accurate statement is that they have **(A)** the same spin as a top   **(B)** the same atomic mass but different atomic numbers   **(C)** the same atomic number but different atomic masses   **(D)** the same chemical properties and therefore cannot be separated   **(E)** a coexistence limit; that is, no element can have more than three isotopes

9. A metal plate is illuminated with monochromatic light, and photoelectrons are observed to come off. If the intensity of this light is reduced to one-fourth of its original value, then the maximum kinetic energy of the photoelectrons will be   **(A)** zero   **(B)** unchanged   **(C)** reduced to one-fourth of the original value   **(D)** reduced to one-half of the original value   **(E)** reduced to one-sixteenth of the original value

10. A photon whose energy is E_p joules strikes a photosensitive surface whose work function is W joules. The maximum energy of the ejected photoelectron is equal to   **(A)** E_p **(B)** W   **(C)** $W + E_p$ **(D)** $W - E_p$ **(E)** $E_p - W$

11. In the nuclear reaction $_1^2 H + _1^3 H \rightarrow _2^4 He + _0^1 n + Q$
Q represents the energy released. The masses of the nuclei are: $_1^2 H = 2.01472$ amu; $_1^3 H = 3.01697$ amu; $_2^4 He = 4.00391$ amu; $_0^1 n = 1.00897$ amu. This reaction is primarily an example of   **(A)** fission   **(B)** fusion   **(C)** ionization   **(D)** alpha decay   **(E)** neutralization

12. In the reaction shown in question 11, the value of Q, in amu, is closest to   **(A)** 5.03169   **(B)** 5.01288   **(C)** 0.01881   **(D)** 5.01288   **(E)** 2.01472

13. In the nuclear reaction shown below, what is the value of the coefficient y?
$$_{92}^{235} U + _0^1 n \rightarrow _{56}^{144} Ba + _{36}^{89} Kr + y _0^1 n$$
(A) 0   **(B)** 1   **(C)** 2   **(D)** 3   **(E)** 4

EXPLANATIONS TO QUESTIONS Chapter 14

Answers

1. **(A)**	4. **(D)**	7. **(D)**	10. **(E)**	12. **(C)**
2. **(C)**	5. **(C)**	8. **(C)**	11. **(B)**	13. **(D)**
3. **(E)**	6. **(A)**	9. **(B)**		

Explanations

1. **(A)** The positron is sometimes referred to as a positive electron to suggest that it is similar to the negative electron in all respects except electric charge. The mass of the neutrino is zero or practically

zero; that of the proton and neutron is more than 1800 times as great as that of the electron. The deuteron is a combination of a proton and neutron and forms the nucleus of an isotope of hydrogen. The triton is the nucleus of the heavy hydrogen isotope containing one proton and two neutrons.

2. **(C)** The emission of an electron from the nucleus is the result of the break-up of a neutron in the nucleus into an electron and a proton. The electron is emitted, leaving the proton in the nucleus and thus raising the positive charge in the nucleus by 1. Since atomic number is defined as the number of protons in the nucleus, the atomic number went up by 1.

3. **(E)** Gamma rays and X rays are electromagnetic waves. Their wavelength depends on the method of production, but is roughly about 1 angstrom unit or 10^{-8} cm.

4. **(D)** Neutrons are electrically neutral. Their volume is about the same as that of electrons and protons. The mass of a neutron is slightly greater than that of a proton. There is a great deal of empty space in all atoms; because neutrons are electrically neutral, they can go through this space near electrons and nuclei without experiencing electric forces.

5. **(C)** Alpha particles emitted from radioactive sources are helium nuclei; i.e., they have a positive charge and consist of two protons and two neutrons. Hydrogen nuclei are protons. Both protons and positrons are smaller units of positive charge, each having ½ of the charge of the alpha particle.

6. **(A)** The magnetic field at right angles to the path of the emanation from the radioactive material deflects positive charges in one direction, negative charges in the opposite direction. Gamma rays are not deflected at all and produce a spot at S. Electrons are usually deflected more than alpha particles because they have a much smaller mass than the alpha particles. The speed of the emitted particles is quite high.

7. **(D)** There are no N-poles or S-poles emitted. (Furthermore, they only occur in pairs.) In natural radio-activity gamma rays are most penetrating. Beta particles are next, and then come alpha particles.

8. **(C)** Isotopes of the same element have the same atomic number but differ in atomic mass because their nuclei differ in the number of neutrons. They are similar in chemical properties, but many methods have been devised for their separation. One of these is roughly similar to the set-up in question 6. Ions of the element are produced. They are projected into a magnetic field. The ions of the isotopes have the same charge and are deflected in the same direction, but because they differ in mass, the amount of deflection will be different for the different isotopes.

9. **(B)** Reducing the intensity of monochromatic light merely reduces the number of photons in the light; its frequency is not changed. Therefore each photon which interacts with an electron in the metal has the same amount of energy as before. Therefore each electron that is emitted can have the same maximum kinetic energy as before, $hf - W$. (However, the number of photoelectrons will be reduced.)

10. **(E)** In the photoelectric effect, the energy which the photon has is used for two things when it interacts with an electron in the metal: part is used to do the necessary work to overcome the force which holds the electron in the metal; the rest is used to give the electron kinetic energy: $E_p = W + E_k$. This, of course, is equivalent to $E_k = E_p - W$.

11. **(B)** Fusion is the combining of two nuclei to produce a more massive nucleus. Here the nuclei of two isotopes of hydrogen combine to produce helium. It is true that the alpha particle is a helium nucleus, but in alpha decay the alpha particle is emitted from a single unstable heavy nucleus.

12. **(C)** You can save time if you recognize that this is a mental problem. The value of Q is the difference between the sum of the amu's on the left side of the equation and the sum of the amu's on the right side. The sum on the left side is a little over 5, and the sum on the right side is also a little over 5. The difference, therefore, has to be less than one. The only possible choice is (C).

13. **(D)** The sum of the mass numbers (superscripts) on the left side is 236. The sum on the right side has to be the same. For the first two products, Ba and Kr, the sum is only 233. We need 3 neutrons to provide the additional 3.

15

Triangles, Graphs, and Calculators

Formulas describe relationships among variables. In elementary physics the relationships described are simple. Fundamental to an understanding of vectors is the triangle, usually a right triangle in elementary courses. Graphs are drawn to give visual representation of relationships, many of which are similar. Calculators provide a timesaving way of working through arithmetic, even if they are not allowed in an examination.

RIGHT TRIANGLES

The Pythagorean theorem may be applied to any right triangle. If c is the hypotenuse, then $a^2 + b^2 = c^2$.

  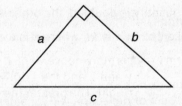

Certain Pythagorean triangles have simply valued sides. These are often used in physics to teach and test concepts when there isn't excess time for arithmetic. Since they are used so frequently, you should commit them to memory.

$(1 + 1 = 2)$

$(3 + 1 = 4)$

149

(9 + 16 = 25)   (25 + 144 = 169)

The trigonometric relationships in a right triangle are also important, and are given in terms of one of the acute angles.

$$\text{sine } \theta \text{ or sine } \theta = \frac{\text{opposite}}{\text{hypotenuse}}$$

$$\text{cosine } \theta \text{ or cos } \theta = \frac{\text{adjacent}}{\text{hypotenuse}}$$

$$\text{tangent } \theta \text{ or tan } \theta = \frac{\text{opposite}}{\text{hypotenuse}}$$

GRAPHS

One Quantity Is Proportional to Another Quantity

When one quantity is doubled, the other is doubled; when one is tripled, the other is tripled. This can be represented by $v = kt$, where k is a constant, or by a proportion: $\frac{v_1}{v_2} = \frac{t_1}{t_2}$. For plotting the graph, the form $v = kt$, is more convenient. If we know the value of k, we can make a table of values of

v and t, and then draw the graph. We get a straight line passing through the origin. The greater the value of k, the steeper is the straight line. The steepness is called *slope*. What is the physical significance of such a graph? For example, it may represent the speed of an object starting from rest and moving with constant accleration. We gave this relationship as $v = at$. Graph 2 represents greater acceleration than graph 1. Thus v would represent the speed of the object; t the time elapsed since the start of the motion. The graph can also represent Ohm's law, $V = IR$, showing the relationship between voltage and current for a given resistor. Then v would represent the voltage across the resistor; t the current through the resistor. Graph 2 would be for a greater resistance than graph 1.

One Quantity Varies Inversely With Another Quantity

When one quantity is doubled, the other is divided by two; when one quantity is tripled, the other is divided by three. This can be represented by $pV = k$, or by $p = k/V$, where the variable quantities are p and V, and k is a constant. The graph for this is a hyperbola.

Boyle's law is represented by such a graph. The p would represent the pressure of the gas and V its volume. At point X would be a condition of large pressure but small volume; at Y the pressure is small but the volume is large.

One Quantity Varies as the Square of Another Quantity

When one quantity is doubled, the other is quadrupled. The formula for such a relationship is $S = kt^2$, where the variable quantities are S and t; k is constant. The graph for such a variation is a parabola. This could represent the distance covered by a freely falling object, or any object with constant acceleration, in time t.

One Quantity Varies Linearly with Another Quantity

The graph for such a variation is a straight line. The proportional relationship given at the beginning of this chapter is a special case of this variation. A formula for this linear variation is $v = v_0 + at$. It describes the relationship between v and t, with v_0 and a as constants. Then v_0 is the value which v has when $t = 0$. The equation could represent the speed v of an object moving with constant acceleration a. The speed of the object when the timing started is v_0, and t represents the elapsed time. Graphs 1 and 2 represent motions with the same initial speed; graph 2 represents the one with the greater acceleration. Graph 3 is the special case mentioned in which the initial velocity is zero. The acceleration for the motion described by graph 3 is the same as for graph 1 since the slopes of the two graphs are the same.

Empirical Graphs

These are graphs based on experimental data. All measurements in the laboratory except counting involve some error. Some errors result from the fact that no perfect instruments can be made; no one can avoid these errors. Some errors result from carelessness; everyone can try to avoid these errors. Suppose we measure the voltage across a resistor as we send various currents through the resistor. Let us plot the voltage against the current. The experimental points will not fall along a straight line. What graph shall we draw? When we had the mathematical formula first, we obtained the points for the graph by substitution in the formula. The construction of the graph then consisted

of drawing a smooth curve through all the plotted points. In the experimental graph we know that each plotted point includes a representation of error. This error may make some measured quantities too large, some too small. We try to take this into account when drawing the empirical graph. We usually draw a smooth curve that has approximately as many plotted points on one side of the curve as on the other. In this case, a straight line seems to do this well. If the straight line goes through the origin, the graph suggests a proportional relationship between voltage and current. This doesn't surprise us if we recall Ohm's law. Suppose the graph looks more like a parabola. We may have introduced a systematic error; we may have overlooked something; or, rarely, we may have discovered something new. In this case, perhaps, the resistance did not remain constant as the current increased. Unexpected results require further investigation.

CALCULATOR CAUTIONS

As of this writing, calculators are not allowed on the SAT II physics test. However, an inexpensive scientific calculator will save you much time in your coursework and review. Here are a few items to assist you in using your calculator to get correct answers.
1. Be careful that the mode is set to "degrees" if that is what you want. More advanced rotational motion problems are usually done in radians.
2. The (+/−) button is only for changing the sign of the displayed numerals—NOT for performing the operations of addition or subtraction.

3. Make sure you know how *your* calculator handles powers of ten. In most cases there is an "EXP" or "EE" or similar key that means "times 10 to the." If so, to enter 67 million you will probably press "6" "." "7" "EXP" "7". If this does not register as 6.7 07 or 6.7E7 or the equivalent, you may have made a keying error. If not, your calculator uses a different format. Read its manual!

4. 10^6 is usually entered as "1" "EXP" "6" (one-times-ten-to-the-sixth).

5. If your calculator has a function key (which allows some keys to do double duty), make sure you press it before calling on a key's second function.

6. Different calculators have different ways of handling inverse trigonometric functions. If you want "the angle whose sine is .5", you might need to press

$$\text{".5" "arc" "sin"}$$
$$or \qquad \text{"2nd" "sin}^{-1}\text{" ".5"}$$
$$or \qquad \text{"sin" "}x^{-1}\text{" ".5"}$$

or some other combination. Read the manual!

7. Some calculators require a multiplication sign between parentheses. Others take multiplication as the default, as you would in written algebraic form.

8. Exponents (as in y^x) may display only after the y value disappears, or may show a ↑.

9. Calculators follow the rules of arithmetic, and thus may display a physically absurd number of figures. For example, if you divide 3 meter^2 by 9 meters, you might get 0.333333333 meter as a result. But you certainly know that your work was not precise to 9 significant figures! Most physics textbooks have simple rules for dealing with significant figures.

10. If you need to divide a new number by a number already in the calculator, it is easiest to multiply by the inverse. Press the inverse key (usually "$1/x$"), the "times" key, and then the new number.

QUESTIONS Chapter 15

Select the choice that best completes the statement.

1. If a right triangle has sides of 2.5 meters and 2.5 meters, what is its hypotenuse in meters? **(A)** 2.5 **(B)** 3.54 **(C)** 5 **(D)** 6.25 **(E)** 12.5

For 2–4. If in the set of graphs shown, the ordinate represents distance and the abscissa represents time,

2. the graph which could well represent no motion is **(A)** 1 **(B)** 2 **(C)** 3 **(D)** 4 **(E)** none of these

3. the graph which could well represent uniformly accelerated motion starting from rest is **(A)** 1 **(B)** 2 **(C)** 3 **(D)** 4 **(E)** none of these

4. the graph which represents motion with the smallest constant speed is **(A)** 1 **(B)** 2 **(C)** 3 **(D)** 4 **(E)** none of these

For 5–6. If, in the graphs shown, the ordinate represents velocity and the abscissa represents time,

5. the graph which represents motion with the greatest acceleration is **(A)** 1 **(B)** 2 **(C)** 3 **(D)** 4 **(E)** none of these

6. the graph which could refer to an object in equilibrium is **(A)** 1 **(B)** 2 **(C)** 3 **(D)** 4 **(E)** none of these

EXPLANATIONS TO QUESTIONS Chapter 15

Answers

1. **(B)**   4. **(C)**
2. **(D)**   5. **(B)**
3. **(E)**   6. **(D)**

Explanations

1. **(B)** $a^2 + b^2 = c^2$

    $6.25 m^2 + 6.25 m^2 = 12.5 m^2$

    $c = \sqrt{12.5 m^2} = 3.54 m$

A much faster solution is to recognize that this is an equilateral (45°) right triangle, so its hypotenuse must be equal to the value of one side x $\sqrt{2}$ (look back at the diagrams at the beginning of this chapter).

2. **(D)** The horizontal line of graph 4 indicates that the distance remains the same as time goes on. This could represent the state of rest with the distance, measured from some arbitrary point to the object, remaining constant. (Graph 4 could also represent circular motion, the unchanging distance being measured from the object to the center of its circular orbit.)

3. **(E)** For uniformly accelerated motion, distance covered is proportional to the square of the elapsed time ($s = \frac{1}{2}at^2$). The graph of distance against time is a parabola with the axis of symmetry parallel to the Y-axis. If graph 1 were rotated 90° counterclockwise, it would have approximately the right shape.

4. **(C)** For motion with constant speed, the distance covered is proportional to time ($s = vt$). Graphs 2 and 3 represent such motion. The slope of graph 3 is smaller than that of graph 2: the object whose motion is described by graph 3 covers less distance in unit time than the object described by graph 2; its speed is less. Graph 1 does not describe motion with constant speed.

5. **(B)** When acceleration is positive, velocity increases with time. This is represented by graphs 2 and 3. For the same change in time, the velocity increases more rapidly in graph 2 than in graph 3. This means that the acceleration in graph 2 is greater.

6. **(D)** If an object is in equilibrium, the unbalanced force acting on it is zero; therefore, according to Newton's second law, its acceleration is zero. If an object's acceleration is zero, its speed and direction of motion do not change. Graph 4 represents motions with constant speed; it could describe the motion of an object in equilibrium.

PRACTICE TEST 1

Answer Sheet

1. (A) (B) (C) (D) (E)	26. (A) (B) (C) (D) (E)	51. (A) (B) (C) (D) (E)
2. (A) (B) (C) (D) (E)	27. (A) (B) (C) (D) (E)	52. (A) (B) (C) (D) (E)
3. (A) (B) (C) (D) (E)	28. (A) (B) (C) (D) (E)	53. (A) (B) (C) (D) (E)
4. (A) (B) (C) (D) (E)	29. (A) (B) (C) (D) (E)	54. (A) (B) (C) (D) (E)
5. (A) (B) (C) (D) (E)	30. (A) (B) (C) (D) (E)	55. (A) (B) (C) (D) (E)
6. (A) (B) (C) (D) (E)	31. (A) (B) (C) (D) (E)	56. (A) (B) (C) (D) (E)
7. (A) (B) (C) (D) (E)	32. (A) (B) (C) (D) (E)	57. (A) (B) (C) (D) (E)
8. (A) (B) (C) (D) (E)	33. (A) (B) (C) (D) (E)	58. (A) (B) (C) (D) (E)
9. (A) (B) (C) (D) (E)	34. (A) (B) (C) (D) (E)	59. (A) (B) (C) (D) (E)
10. (A) (B) (C) (D) (E)	35. (A) (B) (C) (D) (E)	60. (A) (B) (C) (D) (E)
11. (A) (B) (C) (D) (E)	36. (A) (B) (C) (D) (E)	61. (A) (B) (C) (D) (E)
12. (A) (B) (C) (D) (E)	37. (A) (B) (C) (D) (E)	62. (A) (B) (C) (D) (E)
13. (A) (B) (C) (D) (E)	38. (A) (B) (C) (D) (E)	63. (A) (B) (C) (D) (E)
14. (A) (B) (C) (D) (E)	39. (A) (B) (C) (D) (E)	64. (A) (B) (C) (D) (E)
15. (A) (B) (C) (D) (E)	40. (A) (B) (C) (D) (E)	65. (A) (B) (C) (D) (E)
16. (A) (B) (C) (D) (E)	41. (A) (B) (C) (D) (E)	66. (A) (B) (C) (D) (E)
17. (A) (B) (C) (D) (E)	42. (A) (B) (C) (D) (E)	67. (A) (B) (C) (D) (E)
18. (A) (B) (C) (D) (E)	43. (A) (B) (C) (D) (E)	68. (A) (B) (C) (D) (E)
19. (A) (B) (C) (D) (E)	44. (A) (B) (C) (D) (E)	69. (A) (B) (C) (D) (E)
20. (A) (B) (C) (D) (E)	45. (A) (B) (C) (D) (E)	70. (A) (B) (C) (D) (E)
21. (A) (B) (C) (D) (E)	46. (A) (B) (C) (D) (E)	71. (A) (B) (C) (D) (E)
22. (A) (B) (C) (D) (E)	47. (A) (B) (C) (D) (E)	72. (A) (B) (C) (D) (E)
23. (A) (B) (C) (D) (E)	48. (A) (B) (C) (D) (E)	73. (A) (B) (C) (D) (E)
24. (A) (B) (C) (D) (E)	49. (A) (B) (C) (D) (E)	74. (A) (B) (C) (D) (E)
25. (A) (B) (C) (D) (E)	50. (A) (B) (C) (D) (E)	75. (A) (B) (C) (D) (E)

PRACTICE TEST 2

Answer Sheet

1. Ⓐ Ⓑ Ⓒ Ⓓ Ⓔ   26. Ⓐ Ⓑ Ⓒ Ⓓ Ⓔ   51. Ⓐ Ⓑ Ⓒ Ⓓ Ⓔ
2. Ⓐ Ⓑ Ⓒ Ⓓ Ⓔ   27. Ⓐ Ⓑ Ⓒ Ⓓ Ⓔ   52. Ⓐ Ⓑ Ⓒ Ⓓ Ⓔ
3. Ⓐ Ⓑ Ⓒ Ⓓ Ⓔ   28. Ⓐ Ⓑ Ⓒ Ⓓ Ⓔ   53. Ⓐ Ⓑ Ⓒ Ⓓ Ⓔ
4. Ⓐ Ⓑ Ⓒ Ⓓ Ⓔ   29. Ⓐ Ⓑ Ⓒ Ⓓ Ⓔ   54. Ⓐ Ⓑ Ⓒ Ⓓ Ⓔ
5. Ⓐ Ⓑ Ⓒ Ⓓ Ⓔ   30. Ⓐ Ⓑ Ⓒ Ⓓ Ⓔ   55. Ⓐ Ⓑ Ⓒ Ⓓ Ⓔ
6. Ⓐ Ⓑ Ⓒ Ⓓ Ⓔ   31. Ⓐ Ⓑ Ⓒ Ⓓ Ⓔ   56. Ⓐ Ⓑ Ⓒ Ⓓ Ⓔ
7. Ⓐ Ⓑ Ⓒ Ⓓ Ⓔ   32. Ⓐ Ⓑ Ⓒ Ⓓ Ⓔ   57. Ⓐ Ⓑ Ⓒ Ⓓ Ⓔ
8. Ⓐ Ⓑ Ⓒ Ⓓ Ⓔ   33. Ⓐ Ⓑ Ⓒ Ⓓ Ⓔ   58. Ⓐ Ⓑ Ⓒ Ⓓ Ⓔ
9. Ⓐ Ⓑ Ⓒ Ⓓ Ⓔ   34. Ⓐ Ⓑ Ⓒ Ⓓ Ⓔ   59. Ⓐ Ⓑ Ⓒ Ⓓ Ⓔ
10. Ⓐ Ⓑ Ⓒ Ⓓ Ⓔ   35. Ⓐ Ⓑ Ⓒ Ⓓ Ⓔ   60. Ⓐ Ⓑ Ⓒ Ⓓ Ⓔ
11. Ⓐ Ⓑ Ⓒ Ⓓ Ⓔ   36. Ⓐ Ⓑ Ⓒ Ⓓ Ⓔ   61. Ⓐ Ⓑ Ⓒ Ⓓ Ⓔ
12. Ⓐ Ⓑ Ⓒ Ⓓ Ⓔ   37. Ⓐ Ⓑ Ⓒ Ⓓ Ⓔ   62. Ⓐ Ⓑ Ⓒ Ⓓ Ⓔ
13. Ⓐ Ⓑ Ⓒ Ⓓ Ⓔ   38. Ⓐ Ⓑ Ⓒ Ⓓ Ⓔ   63. Ⓐ Ⓑ Ⓒ Ⓓ Ⓔ
14. Ⓐ Ⓑ Ⓒ Ⓓ Ⓔ   39. Ⓐ Ⓑ Ⓒ Ⓓ Ⓔ   64. Ⓐ Ⓑ Ⓒ Ⓓ Ⓔ
15. Ⓐ Ⓑ Ⓒ Ⓓ Ⓔ   40. Ⓐ Ⓑ Ⓒ Ⓓ Ⓔ   65. Ⓐ Ⓑ Ⓒ Ⓓ Ⓔ
16. Ⓐ Ⓑ Ⓒ Ⓓ Ⓔ   41. Ⓐ Ⓑ Ⓒ Ⓓ Ⓔ   66. Ⓐ Ⓑ Ⓒ Ⓓ Ⓔ
17. Ⓐ Ⓑ Ⓒ Ⓓ Ⓔ   42. Ⓐ Ⓑ Ⓒ Ⓓ Ⓔ   67. Ⓐ Ⓑ Ⓒ Ⓓ Ⓔ
18. Ⓐ Ⓑ Ⓒ Ⓓ Ⓔ   43. Ⓐ Ⓑ Ⓒ Ⓓ Ⓔ   68. Ⓐ Ⓑ Ⓒ Ⓓ Ⓔ
19. Ⓐ Ⓑ Ⓒ Ⓓ Ⓔ   44. Ⓐ Ⓑ Ⓒ Ⓓ Ⓔ   69. Ⓐ Ⓑ Ⓒ Ⓓ Ⓔ
20. Ⓐ Ⓑ Ⓒ Ⓓ Ⓔ   45. Ⓐ Ⓑ Ⓒ Ⓓ Ⓔ   70. Ⓐ Ⓑ Ⓒ Ⓓ Ⓔ
21. Ⓐ Ⓑ Ⓒ Ⓓ Ⓔ   46. Ⓐ Ⓑ Ⓒ Ⓓ Ⓔ   71. Ⓐ Ⓑ Ⓒ Ⓓ Ⓔ
22. Ⓐ Ⓑ Ⓒ Ⓓ Ⓔ   47. Ⓐ Ⓑ Ⓒ Ⓓ Ⓔ   72. Ⓐ Ⓑ Ⓒ Ⓓ Ⓔ
23. Ⓐ Ⓑ Ⓒ Ⓓ Ⓔ   48. Ⓐ Ⓑ Ⓒ Ⓓ Ⓔ   73. Ⓐ Ⓑ Ⓒ Ⓓ Ⓔ
24. Ⓐ Ⓑ Ⓒ Ⓓ Ⓔ   49. Ⓐ Ⓑ Ⓒ Ⓓ Ⓔ   74. Ⓐ Ⓑ Ⓒ Ⓓ Ⓔ
25. Ⓐ Ⓑ Ⓒ Ⓓ Ⓔ   50. Ⓐ Ⓑ Ⓒ Ⓓ Ⓔ   75. Ⓐ Ⓑ Ⓒ Ⓓ Ⓔ

PRACTICE TEST 3

Answer Sheet

1. Ⓐ Ⓑ Ⓒ Ⓓ Ⓔ	26. Ⓐ Ⓑ Ⓒ Ⓓ Ⓔ	51. Ⓐ Ⓑ Ⓒ Ⓓ Ⓔ
2. Ⓐ Ⓑ Ⓒ Ⓓ Ⓔ	27. Ⓐ Ⓑ Ⓒ Ⓓ Ⓔ	52. Ⓐ Ⓑ Ⓒ Ⓓ Ⓔ
3. Ⓐ Ⓑ Ⓒ Ⓓ Ⓔ	28. Ⓐ Ⓑ Ⓒ Ⓓ Ⓔ	53. Ⓐ Ⓑ Ⓒ Ⓓ Ⓔ
4. Ⓐ Ⓑ Ⓒ Ⓓ Ⓔ	29. Ⓐ Ⓑ Ⓒ Ⓓ Ⓔ	54. Ⓐ Ⓑ Ⓒ Ⓓ Ⓔ
5. Ⓐ Ⓑ Ⓒ Ⓓ Ⓔ	30. Ⓐ Ⓑ Ⓒ Ⓓ Ⓔ	55. Ⓐ Ⓑ Ⓒ Ⓓ Ⓔ
6. Ⓐ Ⓑ Ⓒ Ⓓ Ⓔ	31. Ⓐ Ⓑ Ⓒ Ⓓ Ⓔ	56. Ⓐ Ⓑ Ⓒ Ⓓ Ⓔ
7. Ⓐ Ⓑ Ⓒ Ⓓ Ⓔ	32. Ⓐ Ⓑ Ⓒ Ⓓ Ⓔ	57. Ⓐ Ⓑ Ⓒ Ⓓ Ⓔ
8. Ⓐ Ⓑ Ⓒ Ⓓ Ⓔ	33. Ⓐ Ⓑ Ⓒ Ⓓ Ⓔ	58. Ⓐ Ⓑ Ⓒ Ⓓ Ⓔ
9. Ⓐ Ⓑ Ⓒ Ⓓ Ⓔ	34. Ⓐ Ⓑ Ⓒ Ⓓ Ⓔ	59. Ⓐ Ⓑ Ⓒ Ⓓ Ⓔ
10. Ⓐ Ⓑ Ⓒ Ⓓ Ⓔ	35. Ⓐ Ⓑ Ⓒ Ⓓ Ⓔ	60. Ⓐ Ⓑ Ⓒ Ⓓ Ⓔ
11. Ⓐ Ⓑ Ⓒ Ⓓ Ⓔ	36. Ⓐ Ⓑ Ⓒ Ⓓ Ⓔ	61. Ⓐ Ⓑ Ⓒ Ⓓ Ⓔ
12. Ⓐ Ⓑ Ⓒ Ⓓ Ⓔ	37. Ⓐ Ⓑ Ⓒ Ⓓ Ⓔ	62. Ⓐ Ⓑ Ⓒ Ⓓ Ⓔ
13. Ⓐ Ⓑ Ⓒ Ⓓ Ⓔ	38. Ⓐ Ⓑ Ⓒ Ⓓ Ⓔ	63. Ⓐ Ⓑ Ⓒ Ⓓ Ⓔ
14. Ⓐ Ⓑ Ⓒ Ⓓ Ⓔ	39. Ⓐ Ⓑ Ⓒ Ⓓ Ⓔ	64. Ⓐ Ⓑ Ⓒ Ⓓ Ⓔ
15. Ⓐ Ⓑ Ⓒ Ⓓ Ⓔ	40. Ⓐ Ⓑ Ⓒ Ⓓ Ⓔ	65. Ⓐ Ⓑ Ⓒ Ⓓ Ⓔ
16. Ⓐ Ⓑ Ⓒ Ⓓ Ⓔ	41. Ⓐ Ⓑ Ⓒ Ⓓ Ⓔ	66. Ⓐ Ⓑ Ⓒ Ⓓ Ⓔ
17. Ⓐ Ⓑ Ⓒ Ⓓ Ⓔ	42. Ⓐ Ⓑ Ⓒ Ⓓ Ⓔ	67. Ⓐ Ⓑ Ⓒ Ⓓ Ⓔ
18. Ⓐ Ⓑ Ⓒ Ⓓ Ⓔ	43. Ⓐ Ⓑ Ⓒ Ⓓ Ⓔ	68. Ⓐ Ⓑ Ⓒ Ⓓ Ⓔ
19. Ⓐ Ⓑ Ⓒ Ⓓ Ⓔ	44. Ⓐ Ⓑ Ⓒ Ⓓ Ⓔ	69. Ⓐ Ⓑ Ⓒ Ⓓ Ⓔ
20. Ⓐ Ⓑ Ⓒ Ⓓ Ⓔ	45. Ⓐ Ⓑ Ⓒ Ⓓ Ⓔ	70. Ⓐ Ⓑ Ⓒ Ⓓ Ⓔ
21. Ⓐ Ⓑ Ⓒ Ⓓ Ⓔ	46. Ⓐ Ⓑ Ⓒ Ⓓ Ⓔ	71. Ⓐ Ⓑ Ⓒ Ⓓ Ⓔ
22. Ⓐ Ⓑ Ⓒ Ⓓ Ⓔ	47. Ⓐ Ⓑ Ⓒ Ⓓ Ⓔ	72. Ⓐ Ⓑ Ⓒ Ⓓ Ⓔ
23. Ⓐ Ⓑ Ⓒ Ⓓ Ⓔ	48. Ⓐ Ⓑ Ⓒ Ⓓ Ⓔ	73. Ⓐ Ⓑ Ⓒ Ⓓ Ⓔ
24. Ⓐ Ⓑ Ⓒ Ⓓ Ⓔ	49. Ⓐ Ⓑ Ⓒ Ⓓ Ⓔ	74. Ⓐ Ⓑ Ⓒ Ⓓ Ⓔ
25. Ⓐ Ⓑ Ⓒ Ⓓ Ⓔ	50. Ⓐ Ⓑ Ⓒ Ⓓ Ⓔ	75. Ⓐ Ⓑ Ⓒ Ⓓ Ⓔ

PRACTICE TEST 4

Answer Sheet

1. (A) (B) (C) (D) (E)
2. (A) (B) (C) (D) (E)
3. (A) (B) (C) (D) (E)
4. (A) (B) (C) (D) (E)
5. (A) (B) (C) (D) (E)
6. (A) (B) (C) (D) (E)
7. (A) (B) (C) (D) (E)
8. (A) (B) (C) (D) (E)
9. (A) (B) (C) (D) (E)
10. (A) (B) (C) (D) (E)
11. (A) (B) (C) (D) (E)
12. (A) (B) (C) (D) (E)
13. (A) (B) (C) (D) (E)
14. (A) (B) (C) (D) (E)
15. (A) (B) (C) (D) (E)
16. (A) (B) (C) (D) (E)
17. (A) (B) (C) (D) (E)
18. (A) (B) (C) (D) (E)
19. (A) (B) (C) (D) (E)
20. (A) (B) (C) (D) (E)
21. (A) (B) (C) (D) (E)
22. (A) (B) (C) (D) (E)
23. (A) (B) (C) (D) (E)
24. (A) (B) (C) (D) (E)
25. (A) (B) (C) (D) (E)

26. (A) (B) (C) (D) (E)
27. (A) (B) (C) (D) (E)
28. (A) (B) (C) (D) (E)
29. (A) (B) (C) (D) (E)
30. (A) (B) (C) (D) (E)
31. (A) (B) (C) (D) (E)
32. (A) (B) (C) (D) (E)
33. (A) (B) (C) (D) (E)
34. (A) (B) (C) (D) (E)
35. (A) (B) (C) (D) (E)
36. (A) (B) (C) (D) (E)
37. (A) (B) (C) (D) (E)
38. (A) (B) (C) (D) (E)
39. (A) (B) (C) (D) (E)
40. (A) (B) (C) (D) (E)
41. (A) (B) (C) (D) (E)
42. (A) (B) (C) (D) (E)
43. (A) (B) (C) (D) (E)
44. (A) (B) (C) (D) (E)
45. (A) (B) (C) (D) (E)
46. (A) (B) (C) (D) (E)
47. (A) (B) (C) (D) (E)
48. (A) (B) (C) (D) (E)
49. (A) (B) (C) (D) (E)
50. (A) (B) (C) (D) (E)

51. (A) (B) (C) (D) (E)
52. (A) (B) (C) (D) (E)
53. (A) (B) (C) (D) (E)
54. (A) (B) (C) (D) (E)
55. (A) (B) (C) (D) (E)
56. (A) (B) (C) (D) (E)
57. (A) (B) (C) (D) (E)
58. (A) (B) (C) (D) (E)
59. (A) (B) (C) (D) (E)
60. (A) (B) (C) (D) (E)
61. (A) (B) (C) (D) (E)
62. (A) (B) (C) (D) (E)
63. (A) (B) (C) (D) (E)
64. (A) (B) (C) (D) (E)
65. (A) (B) (C) (D) (E)
66. (A) (B) (C) (D) (E)
67. (A) (B) (C) (D) (E)
68. (A) (B) (C) (D) (E)
69. (A) (B) (C) (D) (E)
70. (A) (B) (C) (D) (E)
71. (A) (B) (C) (D) (E)
72. (A) (B) (C) (D) (E)
73. (A) (B) (C) (D) (E)
74. (A) (B) (C) (D) (E)
75. (A) (B) (C) (D) (E)

16

Practice Tests

PRACTICE TEST 1

Part A

INSTRUCTIONS—*Read the section in the Introduction entitled* HOW TO TAKE THE TESTS.

DIRECTIONS: *For each group of questions below, there is a set of five lettered choices, followed by numbered questions. For each question select the one choice in the set that best answers the question. You may use a lettered choice once, more than once, or not at all in each set.*

QUESTIONS 1-3 refer to the graph which represents the speed of an object moving along a straight line. The time of observation is represented by *t*.

(A) KL **(B)** LM **(C)** NO **(C)** OP **(E)** PR

1. Which choice represents the interval during which the object moves with constant speed?

2. Which choice represents the interval during which the object's speed is increasing?

3. Which choice represents the interval during which the acceleration is constant but not zero?

QUESTIONS 4-8 refer to the following concepts:

(A) Energy **(B)** Power **(C)** Momentum **(D)** Acceleration **(E)** Torque

To which choice is each of the following formulas most closely related? Use the key to the right of the formulas.

4. mgh

5. ms/t

6. $\dfrac{Q^2 R}{t^2}$

7. $\frac{1}{2} ms^2/t^2$

8. $\dfrac{Q^2 R}{t}$

m = mass
g = acceleration due to gravity
h = vertical height
s = displacement
t = time
Q = electric charge
R = electric resistance

QUESTIONS 9-13 may express a relationship to speed or velocity given in these choices:

(A) is proportional to its velocity **(B)** is proportional to the square of its speed **(C)** is proportional to the square root of its speed **(D)** is inversely proportional to its velocity **(E)** is not described by any of the above

158

For each question select the choice which best completes it:

9. The kinetic energy of a given body

10. The acceleration toward the center of an object moving with constant speed around a given circle

11. The momentum of a given body

12. The displacement per second of an object in equilibrium

13. The displacement of an object starting from rest and moving with constant acceleration

QUESTIONS 14 AND 15 deal with the characteristics of a parallel circuit in the following situation:

The following five lengths of thin wire, all of which have the same diameter, are connected in parallel to a battery:

(A) 3 ft of nichrome wire   (B) 3 ft of copper wire   (C) 3 ft of silver wire   (D) 2 ft of nichrome wire   (E) 2 ft of silver wire

14. In which length of wire is the current greatest?

15. Which length of wire dissipates the greatest power?

Part B

DIRECTIONS: *Each of the questions or incomplete statements is followed by five suggested answers or completions. Select the choice that best answers the question or completes the statement.*

16. The resultant of a 3-N and a 4-N force which act on an object in opposite direction to each other is, in newtons,   (A) 0   (B) 1   (C) 5   (D) 7   (E) 12

17. Two forces, one of 6 N and the other of 8 N, act on a point at right angles to each other. The resultant of these forces is, in newtons,   (A) 0   (B) 2   (C) 5   (D) 10   (E) 14

For 18-20. As shown in the diagram, two weights, one of 10 lb and the other of 6 lb, are tied to the ends of a flexible string. The string is placed over a pulley which is attached to the ceiling. Frictional losses and the weight of the pulley may be neglected as the weights and the string are allowed to move.

18. At the instant shown in the diagram, the potential energy of the 10-lb object with respect to the floor is, in foot-pounds,   (A) 0   (B) 2   (C) 20   (D) 50   (E) 70

19. At the instant shown, the acceleration of the moving 10-lb object is (A) 0   (B) less than g (C) g (D) $5g$ (E) $10g$

20. At the instant shown, the tension in rope A is   (A) less than 3 lb   (B) 3 lb   (C) 6 lb   (D) more than 6 but less than 10 lb   (E) 10 lb

21. How many meters will a 2.00-kg ball starting from rest fall freely in 1.00 second?   (A) 4.90   (B) 2.00   (C) 9.81   (D) 19.6   (E) 32

22. The concept or principle which is most important in the explanation of the fact that a steel wire can float on the top of water is   (A) surface tension   (B) adhesion   (C) kinetic theory of matter (D) Archimedes' principle   (E) Pascal's principle

23. A beam of parallel rays is reflected from a smooth plane surface. After reflection the rays will be   (A) converging   (B) diverging   (C) parallel   (D) diffused   (E) focused

For 24-27. In the following table you will find information you need for this set of questions.

	Aluminum	Lead
melting point	660°C	327°C
heat of fusion (cal/g)	77	6.0
specific heat (cal/g•°C)	0.220	0.031
coeff. of linear expansion (per °C)	0.000025	0.000029

24. The number of calories required to melt 10 g of aluminum without change of temperature is **(A)** 2.20 **(B)** 7.7 **(C)** 10 **(D)** 77 **(E)** 770

25. Ten grams of lead are to be vaporized without change of temperature. The number of calories required is **(A)** 0.31 **(B)** 2.2 **(C)** 60 **(D)** 1900 **(E)** not to be calculated with the above information

26. A 100-cm rod of aluminum is heated from 40° F to 50° F. The change, in centimeters, in the length of the rod is **(A)** 0.0025 **(B)** 0.014 **(C)** 0.025 **(D)** 0.045 **(E)** 0.125

27. A block of aluminum is transferred from boiling water to a beaker containing 200 g of water at 10° C. The final temperature of the water is 30° C. The mass of the block is, in grams, **(A)** 200 **(B)** 230 **(C)** 260 **(D)** 290 **(E)** 320

28. Which of the following cannot be plane polarized? **(A)** sound **(B)** FM signals **(C)** RF signals **(D)** infra red light **(E)** yellow light from sodium

29. Light passes through two parallel slits and falls on a screen. The pattern produced is due to interference and **(A)** reflection **(B)** refraction **(C)** polarization **(D)** diffraction **(E)** absorption

30. A tuning fork vibrating gently produces the note C. Another tuning fork produces the note C', an octave higher in pitch than C, and slightly louder than C. The speed of the wave produced by the second fork, as compared with that produced by the first fork, is **(A)** 8 times as great **(B)** 4 times as great **(C)** 2 times as great **(D)** the same **(E)** ½ as great

For 31-34. A ship 4000 ft distant from a large cliff sounds a short note of 222 vib/sec on its foghorn. The speed of the sound is 1110 ft/sec. (Assume a speed of 1090 ft/sec at 0° C.)

31. The time required for the sound to reach the cliff is, approximately, **(A)** less than 0.1 sec **(B)** 0.3 sec **(C)** 1.8 sec **(D)** 3.6 sec **(E)** 7.2 sec

32. The wavelength of the sound in air is, approximately, **(A)** 0.5 ft **(B)** 1 ft **(C)** 2 ft **(D)** 5 ft **(E)** 4×10^6 ft

33. The time between the sounding of the foghorn and the time the echo is heard on the ship is, approximately, **(A)** less than 0.1 sec **(B)** 0.3 sec **(C)** 1.8 sec **(D)** 3.6 sec **(E)** 7.2 sec

34. In question 33, it was necessary to assume **(A)** nothing **(B)** that the amplitude of the sound did not change **(C)** that the frequency of the sound produced by the foghorn remained constant **(D)** that all the sound was beamed towards the cliff **(E)** that the ship was stationary

35. A tank has a volume of 10 m³ and contains air at atmospheric pressure of 10 N/cm². In order to raise the gauge pressure to 90 N/cm², the number of cubic centimeters of air at atmospheric pressure that must be pumped into the tank (assuming temp. to remain constant and an atmospheric pressure of 10 N/cm²) is **(A)** 70 **(B)** 80 **(C)** 90 **(D)** 100 **(E)** 110

36. In the circuit represented, the voltage across R_1 and R_2 is 20 V each. R_1 has a resistance of 40 ohms. S_1 is a switch which can be moved to positions 1, 2, 3, and 4. It is shown in position 1.

With the switch in position 1, the current in R_1 is **(A)** 0 **(B)** $1/3$ A **(C)** $1/2$ A **(D)** 2 A **(E)** 1.5 A

For 37-38 A 5-ohm coil of tungsten wire (M.P. is 3370° C) is immersed in a non-conducting liquid (B.P. is 78° C). The coil is connected to a battery which supplies it with a constant 40 V. When the experiment starts, the liquid is at room temperature; during the experiment the liquid covers the coil.

37. During the experiment the temperature of the liquid **(A)** drops somewhat below room temperature because evaporation is a cooling process **(B)** drops somewhat below room temp. because the wire has to be heated **(C)** rises until a temperature of 78° C is reached **(D)** rises until a temperature of 3370° C is reached **(E)** remains constant because the liquid short-circuits the wire

38. After the circuit has been completed, the current **(A)** remains constant **(B)** decreases somewhat until a temperature of 78° C is reached **(C)** decreases somewhat until a temperature of 3370° C is reached **(D)** increases sharply at 78° C **(E)** increases gradually until a temperature of 78° C is reached

For 39-40 X is a coil of copper wire with many turns wound on a soft iron core. Another coil wound on an iron core is near it, as shown.

39. If switch S' is closed and kept closed, the end of the core which is marked W **(A)** becomes an N-pole momentarily **(B)** becomes and stays an N-pole **(C)** becomes an S-pole momentarily **(D)** becomes and stays an S-pole **(E)** exhibits no effect because of the current

40. The instant after switch S' is closed **(A)** there will be no current in wire YZ **(B)** electron flow in wire YZ will be from Y to Z **(C)** electron flow in wire YZ will be from Z to Y **(D)** electron flow in wire YZ will be from Z to Y and then from Y to Z **(E)** electron flow in wire YZ will be from Y to Z and then from Z to Y

41. The diagram represents two equal negative point charges, Y and Z,

that are a distance d apart. Where would the electric field intensity due to these two charges be zero? **(A)** on Y **(B)** on Z **(C)** on both Y and Z **(D)** midway between Y and Z **(E)** none of the above

42. A positive charge is moving with constant speed at right angles to a uniform magnetic field. If the speed of the particle were doubled, the force exerted on the particle by the magnetic field would be **(A)** unaffected **(B)** quadrupled **(C)** doubled **(D)** halved **(E)** reduced to one-fourth of the original value

43. Of the following, the particle whose mass is closest to that of the neutron is **(A)** meson **(B)** deuteron **(C)** neutrino **(D)** proton **(E)** positron

44. The time of one vibration of a simple pendulum may be decreased by   **(A)** increasing the length of the pendulum   **(B)** decreasing the length of the pendulum   **(C)** using a heavier bob   **(D)** using a lighter bob   **(E)** taking the pendulum up to the top of the Empire State Building

45. In rising from the bottom of a lake to the top, the volume of a bubble triples. The approximate depth of the lake, in meters, is   **(A)** 3   **(B)** 5   **(C)** 10   **(D)** 21   **(E)** 40

46. A certain substance contracts when it melts. If pressure is applied to this substance,   **(A)** its boiling point is not changed   **(B)** its boiling point is lowered   **(C)** its melting point is raised   **(D)** its melting point is lowered   **(E)** its melting point is not changed

47. One can be sure that a rod is electrically charged if it   **(A)** repels a pith ball   **(B)** attracts a pith ball   **(C)** attracts the N-pole of a compass needle   **(D)** repels the N-pole of a compass needle   **(E)** points north

48. The rate of heat production of a wire immersed in ice water and carrying an electric current is proportional to   **(A)** the current   **(B)** the reciprocal of the current   **(C)** the reciprocal of the square of the current   **(D)** the square of the current   **(E)** the square root of the current

49. Fraunhofer lines are chiefly due to   **(A)** absorption in the earth's atmosphere   **(B)** absorption in the sun's atmosphere   **(C)** reflection by meteors   **(D)** absence of certain elements in the sun   **(E)** radioactive francium and hafnium

50. When water cools from 7° C to 1° C,   **(A)** it contracts only   **(B)** it expands only   **(C)** it first contracts and then expands   **(D)** it first expands and then contracts   **(E)** it first expands, then contracts, and then expands again

51. Boyle's law describes the behavior of a gas when   **(A)** its pressure is kept constant   **(B)** its volume is kept constant   **(C)** its density is kept constant   **(D)** its mass is kept constant   **(E)** nothing is kept constant

52. A satellite in circular orbit around the earth at a distance of about 300 miles from the earth completes each orbit in about 1½ hr. The average speed of the satellite is, in miles per hour, approximately   **(A)** 200   **(B)** 400π **(C)** 3000   **(D)** 16,000   **(E)** 25,000

53. The force acting on a satellite in circular orbit around the earth is chiefly   **(A)** the satellite's inertia   **(B)** the satellite's mass   **(C)** the earth's mass   **(D)** the earth's gravitational pull   **(E)** the sun's gravitational pull

54. An object which is black   **(A)** absorbs black light   **(B)** reflects black light   **(C)** absorbs all light   **(D)** reflects all light   **(E)** refracts all light

55. A string's lowest natural frequency is 400 vibrations/sec. Its fundamental frequency is, in vibrations per second,   **(A)** 100   **(B)** 200   **(C)** 400   **(D)** 800   **(E)** 1200

56. A 60-watt, 110-V tungsten filament lamp is operated on 120 V. Which of the following statements regarding the lamp is (are) true?

    I. It will consume more than 60 watts while operating.
    II. It will have a lower resistance than at 110 V.
    III. It will be brighter than at 110 V.
    IV. It will burn out after operation of ½ hour or less.

(A) I, II, and III only
(B) I and III only
(C) II and IV only
(D) IV only
(E) none of the above

57. A person standing in an elevator is taken up by the elevator at constant speed. Which of the following is (are) true of the push which he exerts on the floor of the elevator?

    I. It is equal to his weight.
    II. It is equal to less than his weight.
    III. It is equal to more than his weight.
    IV. It is dependent on the value of this constant speed.

    (A) I, II, and III only
    (B) I and III only
    (C) II and IV only
    (D) IV only
    (E) none of the above

58. An object with a constant mass rests on a smooth and perfectly horizontal table. If a horizontal force F is applied, acceleration a results. If F is doubled without changing the direction, what will be the effect(s) on the acceleration?

    I. The acceleration will remain the same.
    II. The acceleration will be doubled.
    III. The acceleration will decrease.
    IV. The acceleration will increase but not double.

    (A) I, II, and III only
    (B) I and III only
    (C) II and IV only
    (D) IV only
    (E) none of the above

59. An object with constant mass rests on a horizontal surface whose coefficient of friction is 0.2. If a horizontal force F is applied to the object, what will be the effect(s) on the object?

    I. It may move with constant speed in the direction of F once it has been set in motion.
    II. It may remain at rest.
    III. It may accelerate.
    IV. It may move with constant speed in a direction opposite to F.

    (A) I, II, and III only
    (B) I and III only
    (C) II and IV only
    (D) IV only
    (E) none of the above

60. A man pulls an object up an inclined plane with a force F and notes that the object's acceleration is 5 ft/sec^2. He then doubles the force without changing its direction. Which of the following will then be true of the acceleration?

    I. It decreases.
    II. It increases.
    III. It remains the same.
    IV. It is doubled.

    (A) I, II, and III only
    (B) I and III only
    (C) II and IV only
    (D) IV only
    (E) none of the above

61. Which of the following statements is (are) true in regard to the Celsius (centigrade) scale?

    I. 0° occurs where it does because it was intended to coincide with the melting point of ice.

    II. 4° occurs where it does because it was intended to coincide with the temperature of the greatest density of water.

    III. 100° occurs where it does because it was intended to coincide with the boiling point of water at standard pressure.

    IV. 37° occurs where it does because it was intended to coincide with normal body temperature.

    (A) I, II, and III only
    (B) I and III only
    (C) II and IV only
    (D) IV only
    (E) none of the above

62. Assume that you have two balls of identical volume, one weighing 2 N and the other 10 N. Both are falling freely after being released from the same point simultaneously. Which of the following will then be true?

    I. The 10-N ball falling freely from rest will be accelerated at a greater rate than the 2-N ball.

    II. At the end of 4 s of free fall, the 10-N ball will have 5 times the momentum of the 2-N ball.

    III. At the end of 4 s of free fall, the 10-N ball will have the same kinetic energy as the 2-N ball.

    IV. The 10-N ball possesses greater inertia than the 2-N ball.

    (A) I, II, and III only
    (B) I and III only
    (C) II and IV only
    (D) IV only
    (E) none of the above

63. A lighted candle X is placed 20 cm from Y. An observer places her eye 45 cm on the other side of Y and, looking toward X, sees an image of X. Which of the following may object Y be?

    I. A new convex mirror of 10-cm focal length of the type often used in the laboratory.

    II. A new convex lens of 10-cm focal length of the type often used in the laboratory.

    III. A new concave mirror of 10-cm focal length of the type often used in the laboratory.

    IV. A new concave lens of 10-cm focal length of the type often used in the laboratory.

    (A) I, II, and III only
    (B) I and III only
    (C) II and IV only
    (D) IV only
    (E) none of the above

64. A lens is used to produce a sharp image on a screen. When the right half of the lens is covered with an opaque material, how will the image be affected?

    I. The right half of the image will disappear.

    II. The left half of the image will disappear.

    III. The image size will become approximately ½ of the original size.

    IV. The image brightness will become approximately ½ of the original brightness.

    (A) I, II, and III only
    (B) I and III only
    (C) II and IV only
    (D) IV only
    (E) none of the above

65. When a beam of light goes from a rarer to a denser medium like glass and has an angle of incidence equal to zero, which of the following properties of the beam of light does (do) NOT change?

      I. Amplitude
      II. Speed
      III. Wavelength
      IV. Direction

    (A) I, II, and III only
    (B) I and III only
    (C) II and IV only
    (D) IV only
    (E) none of the above

66. Capacitor P is connected to a battery through switch S and wires Y and Z. The capacitor's dielectric is marked X. For a short time after the switch is closed, electrons will move through which of the following?

      I. Y
      II. X
      III. Z
      IV. S

    (A) I, II, and III only
    (B) I and III only
    (C) II and IV only
    (D) IV only
    (E) none of the above

67. A point source of light is placed at the principal focus of a concave lens. Which of the following will be true of the refracted light?

      I. It will diverge.
      II. It will be parallel to the principal axis.
      III. It will seem to come from a point ½ of the radius of curvature from the lens.
      IV. It will converge.

    (A) I, II, and III only
    (B) I and III only
    (C) II and IV only
    (D) IV only
    (E) none of the above

68. In an experiment, ice is wedged in at the bottom of a test tube by means of a bright wire mesh. Water is poured in and then heated near the top. Although the water boils, the ice does not melt. Which of the following explain(s) this phenomenon?

      I. Glass is a good insulator.
      II. Heated water is less dense than cold water.
      III. Water is a good insulator.
      IV. The wire is a good radiator.

    (A) I, II, and III only
    (B) I and III only
    (C) II and IV only
    (D) IV only
    (E) none of the above

69. Which of the following is (are) true of an object starting from rest and accelerating uniformly?

    I. Its kinetic energy is proportional to its displacement.
    II. Its displacement is proportional to the square root of its velocity.
    III. Its kinetic energy is proportional to the square of its speed.
    IV. Its velocity is proportional to the square of elapsed time.

    (A) I, II, and III only
    (B) I and III only
    (C) II and IV only
    (D) IV only
    (E) none of the above

70. All air is removed from the device shown after it is partly filled with a volatile liquid such as ether. The device is then sealed and kept in the position shown. As ice water is allowed to drip on top of bulb Y, but not on X, what will be the effect(s) on the liquid?

    I. The level of the liquid in bulb Y will rise.
    II. The liquid will reach the same level in X as in Y.
    III. The level of the liquid in bulb X will drop.
    IV. The level of the liquid in bulb X will rise.

    (A) I, II, and III only
    (B) I and III only
    (C) II and IV only
    (D) IV only
    (E) none of the above

For 71-73. Monochromatic light falls on a metal surface that has a work function of 6.7×10^{-19} joule. Each photon has an energy of 8.0×10^{-19} joule. (Planck's constant $= 6.63 \times 10^{-34}$ joule-second. One electron-volt $= 1.60 \times 10^{-19}$ joule.)

71. What is the maximum kinetic energy, in joules, of the photoelectrons emitted by the substance?
(A) 1.3×10^{-19} **(B)** 1.6×10^{-19} **(C)** 2.6×10^{-19} **(D)** 6.7×10^{-19} **(E)** 8.0×10^{-19}

72. What is the energy of each photon, expressed in electron volts?   **(A)** 1.6   **(B)** 1.6×10^{-19} **(C)** 5.0   **(D)** 6.7   **(E)** 8.0

73. What is the frequency of the photon, in hertz?   **(A)** 3.7×10^{14} **(B)** 4.2×10^{14} **(C)** 1.2×10^{15} **(D)** 3.7×10^{15} **(E)** 7.0×10^{15}

74. What is the relationship between the atomic number, Z, the mass number, A, and the number of neutrons, N, in a nucleus? **(A)** $Z = AN$ **(B)** $Z = \dfrac{A}{N}$ **(C)** $Z = \dfrac{N}{A}$ **(D)** $Z = A - N$ **(E)** $Z = N - A$

75. When lead, $^{214}_{82}Pb$, emits a beta particle, the resultant nucleus will be **(A)** $^{214}_{83}Bi$ **(B)** $^{214}_{84}Po$ **(C)** $^{213}_{82}Pb$ **(D)** $^{214}_{81}Tl$ **(E)** $^{213}_{81}Tl$

ANSWERS FOR PRACTICE TEST 1

Answer Key for Test 1

1. A	16. B	31. D	46. D	61. B
2. D	17. D	32. D	47. A	62. C
3. B	18. D	33. E	48. D	63. C
4. A	19. B	34. E	49. B	64. D
5. C	20. D	35. C	50. C	65. D
6. B	21. A	36. C	51. D	66. E
7. A	22. A	37. C	52. D	67. E
8. A	23. C	38. B	53. D	68. A
9. B	24. E	39. B	54. C	69. B
10. B	25. E	40. C	55. C	70. B
11. A	26. B	41. D	56. B	71. A
12. A	27. C	42. C	57. E	72. C
13. B	28. A	43. D	58. C	73. C
14. E	29. D	44. B	59. A	74. D
15. E	30. D	45. D	60. E	75. A

Explained Answers for Test 1

1. (A) If the graph is drawn well, *KL* should appear to be a straight line, and *K* and *L* should be at the same distance from the *t*-axis. A visual examination should be adequate; don't look for minute differences. If you don't realize then that *KL* represents motion with constant speed, you need to review the subject of graphs; also see the explanation of the next question.

2. (D) Remember that, except in special cases which are clearly marked, it is customary to have increasing positive values on the axes going to the right (*X*-axis) from the point of intersection of the axes, and up (*Y*-axis). On the graph line *LM* slopes down, and therefore represents decreasing speed. The next interval, *MN*, curves up representing increasing speed, but it is not one of the given choices. The next interval which curves up is *OP*; it represents increasing speed and is choice (D).

3. (B) The straight line *LM* shows that the speed is changing the same amount during each second. This means that the acceleration is constant. In this case the speed is decreasing, and therefore the acceleration is negative. During interval *KL* the speed and direction do not change; the acceleration is zero. For the curved portions of the graph, the speed does not change the same amount during each second; the acceleration is not constant.

4. (A) The potential energy of an object lifted through a vertical height $h = wh = mgh$.

5. (C) Displacement over time (s/t) is the velocity of an object moving with constant velocity. Mass times velocity is momentum.

6. (B) Electric charge over time, Q/t, or the rate with which electric charge moves past a point, is electric current, I. I^2R represents the power used by a resistor.

7. (A) As mentioned in explanation 5, s/t represents velocity, v. Thus s^2/t^2 represents v^2. Then $\frac{1}{2} mv^2$ gives the kinetic energy of an object with mass m moving with speed v.

8. (A) A little difficult. Multiply numerator and denominator by t; this gives Q^2Rt/t^2, which equals I^2Rt, since $Q/t = I$ (see explanation 6). I^2Rt represents power multiplied by time, or energy.

9. (B) The kinetic energy of a body is given by the expression $\frac{1}{2} mv^2$. Since the mass of the body is constant, its kinetic energy is proportional to v^2, the square of its speed.

10. (B) This acceleration equals v^2/r, where v is its speed and r is the radius of its circular path. Since r is constant, the acceleration is proportional to v^2, the square of its speed.

11. (A) The momentum of a body is equal to the product of its mass and its velocity. Since its mass remains constant, its momentum is proportional to its velocity.

12. (A) The acceleration of an object in equilibrium is zero. Its velocity is constant (and may be zero). Its displacement $s = vt$. In this question, $t = 1$ s, a constant. Hence, the displacement is proportional to the velocity.

13. (B) Such motion is described by the relationship $v^2 = 2as$. Since $2a$ is constant, v^2 is proportional to s, and the displacement, s, is proportional to the square of the speed, v.

14. (E) Since the five wires are connected in parallel, they each have the same potential difference—that of the source of voltage. The current in each wire then depends on its resistance. You should remember that silver is the best conductor of electricity; copper is one of the best; nichrome is used as the heating elements in many products, including toasters and soldering irons, and is a much poorer conductor. Apply Ohm's law: $I = V/R$; since the potential difference V is the same for each wire, the current I is inversely proportional to the resistance. For a wire of given material, the resistance is proportional to the length and inversely proportional to the cross section area. Since all the wires have the same diameter, we look for the shortest wire of the best conductor. This is given by choice (E), two feet of silver wire.

15. (E) A useful formula here for the power used by an electric device is that it is the product of its potential difference and its current ($P = VI$). In a parallel circuit each branch has the same potential difference. We already saw in question 14 that the two feet of silver wire has the greatest current; therefore it also uses the greatest power.

16. (B) Two forces which act on an object in opposite directions tend to nullify each other. The resultant of such forces is their difference, and the direction of the resultant is the direction of the larger force.

17. (D) If two forces, acting on the same point, are at right angles to each other, their resultant may be found by applying the Pythagorean theorem. $R^2 = 6^2 + 8^2$; $R = 10$ N. You should have recognized the 3-4-5 right triangle; the two sides, 6 and 8, are twice 3 and 4 respectively, and therefore the hypotenuse, giving the value of the resultant, is twice 5.

18. (D) Potential energy = weight $\times$ height
$$= 10 \text{ lb} \times 5 \text{ ft} = 50 \text{ ft-lb}$$

19. (B) For explanations see next question.

20. (D) To keep the weights from moving, one can apply an additional 4-lb downward force to the 6-lb object. Then the tension at A must be 10 lb to keep the 10-lb object in equilibrium. (The tension in the other parts of the rope around the pulley is also 10 lb.) When the 4-lb force is removed, the 10-lb object starts to move down; that is, it is accelerated. Therefore, the upward pull due to the tension in the rope is less than 10 lb, the downward pull due to gravity. Similarly for the 6-lb object: the upward pull due to the tension in the rope is greater than 6 lb, the downward pull due to gravity. (But the tension is the same throughout the rope.) Therefore the tension in the rope is between 6 and 10 lb. Since the net force on each object is less than its weight, the acceleration is less than g ($F/W = a/g$).

21. (A) For a freely falling object, the distance covered is equal to the product of one-half its acceleration and the square of the time of fall:
$$\text{distance} = \tfrac{1}{2}gt^2$$
$$= \tfrac{1}{2}(9.8 \text{ m/s}^2)(1 \text{ s})^2$$
$$= 4.9 \text{ m}$$

22. (A) Steel is denser than water. The fact that it can float is not explained by Archimedes' principle. The concept of surface tension, however, suggests that the surface of the water acts like a stretched membrane. Unless this membrane is broken, the steel wire is supported by it.

23. (C) This follows from the fact that all the angles of reflection will be equal to each other.

24. (E) Since there is no change in temperature, the heat is required only for change of phase: melting.
$$\text{heat required} = \text{mass} \times \text{heat of fusion}$$
$$= 10 \text{ g} \times 77 \text{ cal/g} = 770 \text{ cal}$$

25. (E) Heat required for vaporization equals mass times heat of vaporization. The heat of vaporization of lead is not given.

26. (B) The coefficient of expansion per F deg $= \frac{5}{9}$ (coefficient of expansion per C deg) $=$
$5 \times \frac{0.000025}{9} = 0.000014$.

$$\begin{aligned} \text{change in length} &= \text{length} \times \text{coeff.} \times \text{temp. change} \\ &= 100 \text{ cm} \times 0.000014 \times 10 \text{ F deg} \\ &= 0.014 \text{ cm} \end{aligned}$$

27. (C) Heat lost $=$ heat gained.

heat lost (or gained) $=$ mass $\times$ sp. ht $\times$ temp. change
heat lost by block $= m \times 0.220$ (cal/g•C°) $\times (100° - 30°)$;
heat gained by water $= 200$ g $\times 1$ (cal/g•C°) $\times (30° - 10°)$.
$m = 0.220 \times 70° = 200 \times 20°$
$m = 260$ g

Note that in problems like this one we assume that the temperature of boiling water is 100° C.

28. (A) Sound is a longitudinal wave and cannot be polarized. All the others are electromagnetic waves; these can be polarized.

29. (D) In the double slit arrangement the light going through each slit is *diffracted:* it bends around behind the barrier; then it spreads out on the screen; the light from the two slits overlaps, and interference occurs.

30. (D) The speed of sound in air is the same for all audible frequencies.

31. (D) For motion with constant speed,

distance $=$ speed $\times$ time.
$$t = \frac{s}{v} = \frac{4000 \text{ ft}}{1110 \text{ ft/sec}} = 3.6 \text{ sec}$$

Noting that this is between 3 and 4 sec would have been enough.

32. (D) $v = f\lambda$; $\quad \lambda = \frac{v}{f} = \frac{1110 \text{ ft/sec}}{222 \text{ vib/sec}} = 5 \text{ ft}$

33. (E) In question 31 we found that it took 3.6 sec for the sound to reach the cliff. It takes another 3.6 sec for the sound to get back to the ship.

34. (E) In the calculations it was assumed that the distance remained 4000 ft and that therefore the time required for the sound to come back is 3.6 sec. Actually, if the ship moved slowly, or moved in such a way that the distance between it and the cliff remained practically constant, the measured time would still be 7.2 sec. (E) is the best choice.

35. (C) Absolute pressure $=$ gauge pressure $+$ atm. pressure. Abs. pressure $= (90 \text{ N/cm}^2) + (10 \text{ N/cm}^2) = 100 \text{ N/cm}^2$. We end up with a gas whose volume $\doteq 10 \text{ m}^3$ and whose pressure $= 100 \text{ N/cm}^2$. At atmospheric pressure (one-tenth of 100 N/cm²) the volume would be $10 \times 10 \text{ m}^3 = 100 \text{ m}^3$. But the tank already had 10 m³ of gas in it. So only 90 m³ had to be added to the tank. (On a test leave such a problem for last.)

36. (C) Don't let a complex circuit scare you away from an easy question. For R_1 you know: $V_1 = 20$ V; $R_1 = 40$ ohms. $I_1 = \frac{V_1}{R_1} = \frac{20 \text{ V}}{40 \text{ }\Omega} = 0.5 \text{ A}$.

37. (C) The electric current heats the wire ($P = I^2 R$); the wire heats the liquid. The temperature of the liquid rises until it starts to boil. With further heating more and more liquid will evaporate, but the temperature of the boiling liquid remains constant.

38. (B) The resistance of tungsten (as for most metals) goes up with temperature. The tungsten is heated by the current and cooled by the liquid. When the liquid reaches its highest temperature (78° C), the wire reaches its highest temperature and therefore its highest resistance.

39. (B) The coil on the left becomes an electromagnet. Electron flow is from minus to plus outside the battery. Grasp the coil with the left hand so that the fingers point in the direction of electron flow; the outstretched thumb points in the direction of the N-pole: in this case, *W.*

40. (C) A changing current in coil X induces a current in the other coil. Current in coil X builds up slowly to its maximum value because of the large self-induced emf in coil X. Until this maximum value is reached, current is induced in the second coil in a direction opposing the current build-up in coil X. For this, the left end of the second coil should be an S-pole, because it will then tend to weaken the left magnet. Then apply the left-hand rule, as in explanation 39.

41. (D) The electric field intensity due to a point charge is proportional to the charge and inversely proportional to the square of the distance from the charge. In this question, charges Y and Z are equal. Therefore at the point midway between them the field intensity due to each charge is the same in magnitude and directed oppositely. (Recall that the direction of the field intensity is the direction of the force on an imagined positive charge.) Therefore the two field intensities cancel each other completely at the point midway between the charges.

42. (C) The force acting on a charge moving perpendicularly through a magnetic field is proportional to the speed with which the charge moves (recall, $F = qvB$). Therefore the force on the charge doubles if the speed doubles.

43. (D) The proton is slightly smaller in mass than the neutron. They differ by about 1 part in 2000.

44. (B) The time of one complete vibration of a simple pendulum or its period is equal to $2\pi\sqrt{L/g}$. If the length is decreased, the period is decreased. If g is decreased, by going up to the top of the Empire State Building, the period is increased. In the simple pendulum, the period is independent of the mass of the bob.

45. (D) The bubble is a gas. If we assume that the temperature is constant, we may apply Boyle's law: the volume of the gas varies inversely as the pressure. The volume of the gas at the bottom of the lake is 1/3 of its volume at the top; the pressure at the bottom must be 3 times as great as at the top. The pressure at the top is approx. 1 atmosphere, produced by the atmosphere, equivalent to that produced by a column of water 10.3 m (see p. 38) high. At a depth of 20.6 m in the lake, we have the pressure due to the water (equal to 2 atmospheres), plus the pressure of the atmosphere which is transmitted without loss by the water (Pascal's principle).

46. (D) The description fits water-ice; think of regelation. If enough pressure is applied to ice it will melt. In order to have it freeze under this pressure, we must lower the temperature. The freezing point is the same as the melting point.

47. (A) The test to see if an object is electrically charged is to see if it will repel an electrically charged object. An uncharged rod will attract, and be attracted by, a charged pith ball.

48. (D) The rate of heat production of a wire $= I^2R$. The resistance of the wire is practically constant. Therefore, the rate of heat production is proportional to the square of the current.

49. (B) This is consistent with various observations on the earth. Choices (C), (D), and (E) are completely irrelevant. Observations during a solar eclipse, as well as observations from high-flying balloons, eliminate choice (A). Satellites may be used for this observation.

50. (C) Water is densest at 4° C. It expands steadily when heated above, or cooled below, this temperature. On being cooled from 7° C to 4° C water contracts; on further cooling it expands again.

51. (D) Boyle's law applies to a definite mass of gas at constant temperature. Pressure and volume, and also density ($=$ mass/vol), change.

52. (D) Assume that the radius of the circular orbit is approximately 4000 miles (not 300). The length of orbit equals $2\pi r = 2\pi \times 4000$ mi.

$$v = s/t = \frac{2\pi \times 4000 \text{ mi}}{1.5 \text{ hr}} \doteq 16{,}000 \text{ mi/hr}.$$

53. (D) If it were not for the earth's pull, the satellite would tend to go off along a straight line tangent to its orbit—until affected by the gravitational pull of some other object.

54. (C) A perfectly black object absorbs all light. There is no visible black light, but the term is sometimes applied to ultraviolet light.

55. (C) By definition, the fundamental frequency of a vibrating object is the lowest frequency at which it can vibrate freely. A string has many such free or natural vibrations.

56. (B) The rating of the lamp is 60 watt at 110 volts. This means that the lamp uses 60 watts when used on 110 V. The lamp may be used on a lower voltage: it will not be as bright—at 60 V it will be quite dim. It may be used on somewhat higher voltages. Higher voltage results in higher current and greater power consumption. Of course, if a much higher than rated voltage is used, the bulb will burn out quickly. However, a 10-volt rise will not shorten the lamp's life drastically; such a rise is not uncommon in the outlet voltage.

57. (E) The person is moving with constant velocity; therefore there is no unbalanced force acting on him. The earth's pull on him (his weight) is balanced by an equal upward push on him by the floor of the elevator. In accordance with Newton's third law, his push on the floor of the elevator equals the floor's push on him: his weight.

58. (C) According to Newton's second law, the acceleration is proportional to the unbalanced force. If the unbalanced force is doubled, the acceleration is doubled. The term *smooth table* implies that friction is negligible. F is then the only horizontal force and is the net force.

59. (A) The maximum force of friction equals the coefficient of friction times the weight of the object. If F is less than this, the object will remain at rest; if F is greater than this, the object will accelerate. How do we get the object to move at constant speed? Once set in motion, the object will move with constant speed if F equals the force of friction. A slightly larger force is needed to start the motion because starting friction is greater than sliding friction.

60. (E) The acceleration will be increased, but not doubled. This can be seen readily with a numerical example. Assume that F is parallel to the plane and equal to 6 lb. Opposed to F is a component of the weight of the object, and there may also be friction; assume this adds up to 2 lb. This leaves an unbalanced force of 4 lb. Doubling F increases it to 12 lb. Opposed to it will be the same 2 lb. The unbalanced force now is 10 lb, more than twice the 4 lb which produced the acceleration in the first case. The new acceleration will be more than twice the first one.

61. (B) The melting point of ice and the boiling point of water were selected to give two fixed points on the Celsius scale: 0° and 100°. The other numbers on the scale between 0 and 100 are obtained by subdividing the intervening space.

62. (C) If air resistance is negligible, freely falling objects have the same acceleration. Then, after 4 s of free fall, both will have the same speed. Their momentums ($= mv$) will then be in the same ratio as their mass; this is also true of their kinetic energy ($\frac{1}{2} mv^2$). The 10-N ball will have 5 times the momentum and 5 times the kinetic energy of the 2-N ball. Mass is a measure of an object's inertia; the greater the mass, the greater the inertia.

63. (C) May be too tricky. The conventional mirrors do not transmit light and nothing can be seen through them. If Y is a concave lens, then a virtual image of X is seen when the eye is placed on the other side of the lens; this is the conventional case. This is not obvious for the case when Y is a convex lens. Here, X is at twice the focal length from the lens. A real image is brought to a focus on the other side of the lens, 20 cm from the lens. But there is no screen there, and the light keeps traveling on, and will diverge from there as though an object were there. To the eye it will be the same as though an object were 25 cm away from it. The normal eye will see an image of X.

64. (D) In the formation of a real image with a lens, all the rays starting from one point on the object go, after refraction by the lens, to the same point of the image. All parts of the lens are usually used for this purpose. If half of the lens is covered, the other half of the lens will still function to produce each point of the image, but only half as much light will get to each point; the image will, consequently, be half as bright.

65. (D) If the angle of incidence is zero, the ray is normal to the surface. Such a ray is not deviated;

in going from air to water it would not be bent at all. The frequency does not change either, but the wave is slowed up. Hence the wavelength must change: $v = f \lambda$. There is some reflection of the wave at the new surface. Less energy means a lower amplitude of the wave.

66. (E) All parts are conductors except the dielectric X. Electrons will move through the metallic conductors until the capacitor is charged.

67. (E) Light from the point source is diverging when it gets to the concave lens; the lens makes it more diverging. Do not confuse lenses with mirrors. For lenses the relationship between position of image and radius of curvature is not as simple as suggested by choice III.

68. (A) The water near the top is very hot; the water near the ice stays cold for a long time. Why? Heat is not conducted down by the water or the glass because they are good insulators. Convection currents do not start readily because the hot water at the top, being less dense than the cold water, does not sink.

69. (B) The object's kinetic energy is proportional to the square of its speed ($E_k = \frac{1}{2} mv^2$). The square of its speed is proportional to its displacement ($v^2 = 2\ as$). Hence, the kinetic energy is proportional to the displacement.

70. (B) A volatile liquid vaporizes readily at ordinary room temperatures. The space above the liquid in X and Y is saturated with the vapor. Ice water dripped on Y causes some of the vapor in Y to condense; the pressure of the vapor in Y is reduced. The vapor pressure in X remains relatively high because of the higher temperature. This higher pressure pushes some of the liquid from X into Y.

71. (A) In the *photoelectric effect* the energy of the incident photon is used to pull the electron away from the metal; if the photon has more energy than is needed to just overcome the attractive force of the metal, the remaining energy gives the freed electron its kinetic energy:

$$\text{energy of photon} = \text{work function} + \text{kinetic energy}$$
$$8.0 \times 10^{-19} \text{ joule} = 6.7 \times 10^{-19} \text{ joule} + \text{kinetic energy}$$
$$\text{kinetic energy} = 1.3 \times 10^{-19} \text{ joule}$$

72. (C) We are told that each photon has an energy of 8.0×10^{-19} joule and that one electron volt = 1.60×10^{-19} joule. By inspection we note that the energy of the photon is 5 times as great, or 5 electron-volts.

73. (C) The energy of a photon is equal to the product of Planck's constant and its frequency:

$$E = hf$$
$$8.0 \times 10^{-19} \text{ joule} = (6.63 \times 10^{-34} \text{ joule-second}) f$$
$$f = 1.2 \times 10^{15} \text{ hertz}$$

74. (D) The *mass number* of a nucleus, or of the atom of which it is a part, is equal to the number of protons (its atomic number) and the number of neutrons:

$$\text{mass number} = \text{atomic number} + \text{number of neutrons}$$
$$A = Z + N$$
$$Z = A - N$$

If you have any trouble with this, think of the mass number as approximately the total mass of the nucleus, where the unit of mass is taken as the mass of the proton. The mass of a neutron is approximately the same as the mass of a proton.

75. (A) The beta particle is an electron, which has a charge of -1. When a nucleus with a charge of $+82$ loses a -1 charge, it must become more positive by one more unit; that is, the charge must become $+83$. This charge is its atomic number. Of the given choices, only one has a subscript of 83, which is the atomic number. Actually we don't have to do anything further. But at this point, just for review, we should note that the loss of an electron does not change the mass number of the nucleus. Choice (A) has not only the correct subscript, 83, but also the expected unchanged superscript, 214.

PRACTICE TEST 2

Part A

DIRECTIONS: *For each group of questions below, there is a set of five lettered choices, followed by numbered questions. For each question select the one choice in the set that best answers the question. You may use a lettered choice once, more than once, or not at all in each set.*

QUESTIONS 1-6 refer to the following laws and principles:

(A) Conservation of momentum   (B) Conservation of kinetic energy   (C) Boyle's law   (D) Charles' law   (E) None of these

KEY for questions 1-6

m = mass
v = velocity
p = pressure
V = volume
T = absolute temperature
h = vertical height
g = acceleration due to gravity

To which choice is each of the following equations most closely related?

1. $m_1 v_1^2 = m_2 v_2^2$
2. $m_1 v_1 = m_2 v_2$
3. $V_1 T_1 = V_2 T_2$
4. $V_1 T_2 = V_2 T_1$
5. $p_1 V_1 = p_2 V_2$
6. $mgh = mv^2$

QUESTIONS 7-13 refer to the following concepts:

(A) Work   (B) Power   (C) Series circuit   (D) Parallel circuit   (E) Hydrogen spectrum

KEY for questions 7-13

F = force
s = distance
p = pressure
A = area
e = electron
I = electric current
V = potential difference
R = electric resistance
v = speed

To which choice is each of the following expressions most closely related?

7. Fs
8. pAs
9. Fv
10. $V_1 = V_2$
11. $I_1 = I_2$
12. $I^2 R$
13. eV

QUESTIONS 14 and 15 refer to the following laboratory experiment. Two small, identical metal spheres are projected at the same time from the same height by two identical spring guns. Each gun provides the same push on its sphere except that one sphere is projected vertically upward while the other one is projected horizontally. Frictional losses are negligible.

(A) It is the same **(B)** It is twice as great **(C)** It is greater but not necessarily twice as great **(D)** It is one-half as great **(E)** It is less but not necessarily one-half as great.

14. How does the time required for the vertically projected sphere to hit the level floor compare with that for the horizontally projected one?

15. How does the kinetic energy with which the vertically projected sphere hits the floor compare with that for the horizontally projected one?

Part B

DIRECTIONS: *Each of the following questions or incomplete statements is followed by five choices. Select the choice that best answers the question or completes the statement.*

16. Of the following, the smallest quantity is **(A)** 0.635 km **(B)** 0.635×10^4 cm **(C)** 6.35×10^4 m **(D)** 0.635×10^6 mm **(E)** 0.635×10^3 m

17. 55 mm is approx. equivalent to **(A)** 2.3 in. **(B)** 6 in. **(C)** 11 in. **(D)** 18 in. **(E)** 23 in.

18. Two forces of 10 N and 7 N, respectively, are applied simultaneously to an object. The maximum value of their resultant is, in newtons, **(A)** 7 **(B)** 10 **(C)** 17 **(D)** $17\sqrt{3}$ **(E)** 70

For 19-20. In the graphs, *v* stands for speed, *s* stands for distance, *t* for time. The acceleration of a

certain object starting from rest and moving with constant acceleration along a straight line is represented by graph *X*.

19. The speed of the object is represented by **(A)** graph *A* **(B)** graph *B* **(C)** graph *C* **(D)** graph *D* **(E)** none of these

20. The distance covered by the object is represented by **(A)** graph *K* **(B)** graph *L* **(C)** graph *M* **(D)** graph *N* **(E)** none of these

For 21-22. A man weighs 150 lb and exerts a force of 30 N parallel to a rough inclined plane as he pushes a 90-N object 6 meters up along the plane at constant speed.

21. The force of friction is **(A)** less than 30 N **(B)** 30 N **(C)** more than 30 N but less than 90 N **(D)** 90 N **(E)** more than 90 N

22. The potential energy gained by the object is, in joules, **(A)** less than 180 **(B)** 180 **(C)** 540 **(D)** 900 **(E)** more than 900

For 23-24. An object is made of material whose specific gravity is 4. Its volume is 30 cm³. It is suspended from a string while submerged in water; it does not touch the bottom or sides of the container.

23. The tension in the string is, in dynes, **(A)** 3000 **(B)** 30,000 **(C)** 60,000 **(D)** 90,000 **(E)** 120,000

24. The weight of the displaced water is, in dynes, **(A)** 3000 **(B)** 30,000 **(C)** 60,000 **(D)** 90,000 **(E)** 120,000

For 25- 26. Two small masses, X and Y, are d centimeters apart. The mass of X is 4 times as great as that of Y. Then X attracts Y with a force of 16 dynes.

25. Y attracts X with a force of **(A)** 1 dyne **(B)** 4 dynes **(C)** 16 dynes **(D)** 32 dynes **(E)** 64 dynes

26. If the distance between X and Y is changed to 2d centimeters, X will attract Y with a force of **(A)** 1 dyne **(B)** 4 dynes **(C)** 8 dynes **(D)** 16 dynes **(E)** 32 dynes

27. The period of a simple pendulum in a laboratory does not depend on **(A)** the altitude of the laboratory **(B)** the acceleration due to gravity in the laboratory **(C)** the length of the string **(D)** the vibration in the laboratory **(E)** the mass of the bob

28. A car is traveling on a level highway at a speed of 15 meters per second. A braking force of 3,000 newtons brings the car to a stop in 10 seconds. The mass of the car is **(A)** 1,500 kg **(B)** 2,000 kg **(C)** 2,500 kg **(D)** 3,000 kg **(E)** 45,000 kg

29. An elevator weighing 2.5×10^4 newtons is raised to a height of 10 meters. Neglecting friction, the work done is **(A)** 2.5×10^4 joules **(B)** 2.5×10^5 joules **(C)** 2.5×10^3 joules **(D)** 7.5×10^4 joules **(E)** 98 joules

30. A 10-kg rocket fragment falling toward the earth has a net downward acceleration of 5 meters per second^2. The net downward force acting on the fragment is **(A)** 5 newtons **(B)** 10 newtons **(C)** 50 newtons **(D)** 98 newtons **(E)** 320 newtons

31. A racing car is speeding around a flat, unbanked circular track whose radius is 250 meters. The car's speed is a constant 50.0 meters per second. The mass of the car is 2.00×10^3 kilograms. The centripetal force necessary to keep the car in its circular path is provided by **(A)** the engine **(B)** the brakes **(C)** friction **(D)** the steering wheel **(E)** the stability of the car

32. The magnitude of the centripetal force on the car in question 31 is, in newtons, **(A)** 1.00×10^1 **(B)** 4.00×10^2 **(C)** 4.00×10^3 **(D)** 2.00×10^4 **(E)** 4.00×10^4

For 33- 34. Three wires of the same length and cross-sectional area are connected in series to a battery. The wires are made of copper, silver, and nichrome, respectively.

33. The current through the copper is **(A)** the same as through the silver and nichrome **(B)** greater than that through the silver or the nichrome **(C)** less than that through the silver or the nichrome **(D)** greater than that through the silver but less than that through the nichrome **(E)** greater than that through the nichrome but less than that through the silver

34. The potential difference across the copper is **(A)** the same as across the silver and nichrome **(B)** greater than that across the silver or the nichrome **(C)** less than that across the silver or the nichrome **(D)** greater than that across the silver but less than that across the nichrome **(E)** greater than that across the nichrome but less than that across the silver.

35. X is a coil of wire with a hollow core. The permanent magnet is pushed at constant speed from the right into the core and out again at the left. During this motion **(A)** there will be no current in wire YZ **(B)** electron flow in wire YZ will be from Y to Z **(C)** electron flow in wire YZ will be from Z to Y **(D)** electron flow in wire YZ will be from Z to Y and then from Y to Z **(E)** electron flow in wire YZ will be from Y to Z and then from Z to Y

36. A compass is placed to the east of a vertical conductor. When electrons go through the wire, the N-pole of the compass needle is deflected to point towards south. The direction of electron flow in the wire is **(A)** east **(B)** south **(C)** west **(D)** up **(E)** down

For 37-38. In the following circuit, *V* stands for a good voltmeter and *A* for a good ammeter.

37. The voltmeter should measure the potential difference across **(A)** the ammeter **(B)** R_1 **(C)** R_3 **(D)** the generator **(E)** the switch

38. The ammeter should measure the current through **(A)** the voltmeter **(B)** R_1 **(C)** R_2 **(D)** R_3 **(E)** the generator

39. One way in which a transistor differs from a semiconductor diode is that the transistor, but not the diode, **(A)** has a heated cathode **(B)** has a metal grid **(C)** can amplify signals **(D)** uses a crystal with added impurities **(E)** can be made very small

40. Two hundred calories of heat are added to a mixture of 5 g of ice and 40 g of water at 0° C. The resulting temperature will be **(A)** 0° C **(B)** 0.5° C **(C)** 3° C **(D)** 5° C **(E)** 4.5° C

41. The sound of a siren to the west of you is transmitted to your ear by air **(A)** vibrating in a north-south direction **(B)** vibrating in a west-east direction **(C)** vibrating in a vertical direction **(D)** moving continuously westward **(E)** moving continuously eastward

42. A man hears a musical sound produced by a tuning fork. The frequency of the sound may be, in vibrations per second, **(A)** 4 **(B)** 400 **(C)** 40,000 **(D)** 100,000 **(E)** 400,000

43. The volume of a gas at constant pressure is directly proportional to the temperature as measured on the **(A)** Celsius scale **(B)** Fahrenheit scane **(C)** Reamur scale **(D)** Baume scale **(E)** Kelvin scale

For 44-45. The coefficient of thermal expansion of a metal is 0.000045 per Celsius degree.

44. Its coefficient per Fahrenheit degree is **(A)** negative **(B)** 0.000025 **(C)** 0.000045 **(D)** 0.000081 **(E)** 32.00003

45. If a 100-cm rod of this material is heated from 30° C to 50° C, its change in length will be, in centimeters, **(A)** 0.00050 **(B)** 0.00090 **(C)** 0.00180 **(D)** 0.090 **(E)** 0.180

For 46-47. Two heating coils, *X* and *Y*, are each connected to 120-volt direct current. The resistance of *X* is twice that of *Y*.

46. The current through *X* is **(A)** twice that through *Y* **(B)** equal to that through *Y* **(C)** one-half that through *Y* **(D)** one-fourth that through *Y* **(E)** one-eighth that through *Y*

47. The rate at which *X* produces heat is **(A)** 4 times that produced by *Y* **(B)** 2 times that produced by *Y* **(C)** the same as that produced by *Y* **(D)** one-half that produced by *Y* **(E)** one-fourth that produced by *Y*

48. An atom of an element differs from an atom of one of its isotopes in the number of **(A)** neutrons in the nucleus **(B)** protons in the nucleus **(C)** valence electrons **(D)** electrons outside the nucleus **(E)** protons outside the nucleus

49. A woman is 10 m away from a plane mirror. Her distance from her image is **(A)** 5 m **(B)** 10 m **(C)** 15 m **(D)** 20 m **(E)** 25 m

50. When a person uses a convex lens as a magnifying glass, the distance that the object must be from the lens is **(A)** less than one focal length **(B)** more than one but less than two focal lengths **(C)** two focal lengths **(D)** more than two but less than four focal lengths **(E)** at least four focal lengths

51. In sound frequency determines pitch. In light frequency determines **(A)** speed **(B)** velocity **(C)** distance **(D)** the kind of polarization **(E)** color

52. The image of an erect object on the retina of the eye is **(A)** real and erect **(B)** real and inverted **(C)** virtual, erect, and enlarged **(D)** virtual, inverted, and enlarged **(E)** virtual, inverted, and reduced in size

53. The pages of this book are visible because they **(A)** absorb light **(B)** emit light **(C)** reflect light **(D)** refract light **(E)** polarize light

54. In monochromatic red light, a blue book will probably appear to be **(A)** blue **(B)** black **(C)** purple **(D)** yellow **(E)** green

55. When light emerges from water and enters air **(A)** the light will be refracted **(B)** the frequency of the light will go up **(C)** the frequency of the light will go down **(D)** the speed of the light will go down **(E)** the speed of the light will go up

56. A girl holds a nickel in a space ship flying at a speed close to the speed of light. To a fixed observer viewing the face of the coin as it passed by, the nickel might appear the width of a **(A)** dime **(B)** nickel **(C)** quarter **(D)** half-dollar **(E)** silver dollar

57. The force restraining an object's motion on an inclined plane **(A)** is directed into the plane **(B)** is directed sideways **(C)** may be friction **(D)** is always friction **(E)** is measured in joules

58. The diagram below shows a conducting loop rotating clockwise in a uniform magnetic field.

As the loop rotates, the induced voltage will be a maximum **(A)** at 0° and 90° **(B)** at 0° and 180° **(C)** at 90° and 270° **(D)** at 180° and 270° **(E)** and constant throughout the rotation

59. In question 58, the induced voltage won't be decreased by doing each of the following EXCEPT **(A)** increasing the speed of rotation **(B)** using stronger magnets **(C)** using a rotating loop with an iron core **(D)** using a commutator **(E)** moving the north and south poles further apart

60. Which of the following is (are) present at the red end of the visible spectrum?

     I. Slower waves than at the violet
    II. Lower energy quanta than at the violet
    III. Longitudinal waves
    IV. Longer wavelengths than at the violet

(A) I, II, and III only
(B) I and III only
(C) II and IV only
(D) IV only
(E) none of the above

61. The principle of interference is necessary to explain adequately which of the following?

    I. The production of beats
    II. The production of green color of leaves
    III. The appearance of colors in thin oil films
    IV. The appearance of a virtual image, rather than a real image, in a plane mirror

(A) I, II, and III only
(B) I and III only
(C) II and IV only
(D) IV only
(E) none of the above

62. Which of the following represents the same quantity as 6.50×10^{-3} ampere?

    I. 6.50 mA
    II. 65.0×10^{-4} A
    III. 0.00650 A
    IV. 65.0×10^{-2} A

(A) I, II, and III only
(B) I and III only
(C) II and IV only
(D) IV only
(E) none of the above

63. Which of the following properties of the light is (are) NOT changed when a beam of light goes obliquely from a rarer to a denser medium?

    I. Amplitude
    II. Direction
    III. Wavelength
    IV. Frequency

(A) I, II, and III only
(B) I and III only
(C) II and IV only
(D) IV only
(E) none of the above

64. Which of the following is (are) true of an object starting from rest and accelerating uniformly?

    I. Its kinetic energy is proportional to its displacement.
    II. Its speed is proportional to the square root of its displacement.
    III. Its kinetic energy is proportional to the square of its speed.
    IV. Its velocity is proportional to the square of the elapsed time.

(A) I, II, and III only
(B) I and III only
(C) II and IV only
(D) IV only
(E) none of the above

65. A man pulls an object up an inclined plane with a force *F* and notes that the object's acceleration is 3 m/s^2. When he triples the force without changing its direction, what will be the effect(s) on the acceleration?

     I. It decreases.
     II. It increases.
     III. It remains the same.
     IV. It triples.

(A) I, II, and III only
(B) I and III only
(C) II and IV only
(D) IV only
(E) none of the above

66. A woman is standing in an elevator that goes up with constant positive acceleration. Which of the following is (are) true of the push she exerts on the floor of the elevator?

     I. It is equal to her weight.
     II. Its value depends on the elevator's acceleration.
     III. It is equal to less than her weight.
     IV. It is equal to more than her weight.

(A) I, II, and III only
(B) I and III only
(C) II and IV only
(D) IV only
(E) none of the above

67. The lowest note which can be produced by a vibrating object is known as which of the following?

     I. Fundamental frequency
     II. First overtone
     III. First harmonic
     IV. First basso

(A) I, II, and III only
(B) I and III only
(C) II and IV only
(D) IV only
(E) none of the above

68. Assume that you have a coil of copper wire whose resistance is 100 ohms. To obtain a coil of copper wire with less resistance, which of the following may you use?

     I. Copper wire that has the same length but is thicker.
     II. Copper wire that has the same thickness but is shorter.
     III. Copper wire that is thicker and shorter.
     IV. Copper wire that is thinner and longer.

(A) I, II, and III only
(B) I and III only
(C) II and IV only
(D) IV only
(E) none of the above

69. Small pieces of iron may be attracted by which of the following?

    I. The N-pole of a magnet
    II. A negatively charged rubber rod
    III. The S-pole of a magnet
    IV. A positively charged glass rod

    (A) I, II, and III only
    (B) I and III only
    (C) II and IV only
    (D) IV only
    (E) none of the above

70. Monochromatic light with a wavelength of 6.0×10^{-7} meter is incident upon two slits that are 2.0×10^{-5} meter apart. As a result an interference pattern appears on a screen 2.0 meters away from the slits and parallel to the slits. What is the expected distance between the central maximum and the next bright line on the screen? **(A)** 1.0×10^{-2} m **(B)** 3.0×10^{-2} m **(C)** 1.7×10^{-2} m **(D)** 6.0×10^{-2} m **(E)** 1.2×10^{-1} m

71. A metal is illuminated by light above its threshold frequency. Which determines the number of electrons emitted by the metal? **(A)** color **(B)** frequency **(C)** intensity **(D)** speed **(E)** wavelength

72. Some of the energy levels of hydrogen are shown below (not to scale).

Energy Levels for Hydrogen

Which transition will result in the emission of the photon with the greatest energy? **(A)** $n = 5$ to $n = 4$ **(B)** $n = 5$ to $n = 3$ **(C)** $n = 5$ to $n = 2$ **(D)** $n = 3$ to $n = 2$ **(E)** $n = 2$ to $n = 1$

73. What is the frequency, in hertz, of the photon for the transition from $n = 3$ to $n = 2$? **(A)** 6.0×10^{-19} **(B)** 2.0×10^{14} **(C)** 4.6×10^{14} **(D)** 6.8×10^{14} **(E)** 6.8×10^{15}

74. If the half-life of $^{234}_{90}$Th is 24 days, the amount of a 12-gram sample remaining after 96 days is **(A)** 1 gram **(B)** 0.75 gram **(C)** 6 grams **(D)** 1.6 grams **(E)** 3 grams

75. Given the equation $^{27}_{13}\text{Al} + ^{4}_{2}\text{He} \rightarrow ^{30}_{15}\text{P} + X$; the correct symbol for X is **(A)** $+^{0}_{1}e$ **(B)** $-^{0}_{1}e$ **(C)** $^{4}_{2}\text{He}$ **(D)** $^{1}_{0}n$ **(E)** $+^{1}_{1}p$

ANSWERS FOR PRACTICE TEST 2

Answer Key for Test 2

1. B	16. B	31. C	46. C	61. B
2. A	17. A	32. D	47. D	62. A
3. E	18. C	33. A	48. A	63. D
4. D	19. B	34. D	49. D	64. A
5. C	20. C	35. E	50. A	65. E
6. E	21. A	36. D	51. E	66. C
7. A	22. A	37. B	52. B	67. B
8. A	23. D	38. C	53. C	68. A
9. B	24. B	39. C	54. B	69. E
10. D	25. C	40. A	55. E	70. D
11. C	26. B	41. B	56. A	71. C
12. B	27. E	42. B	57. C	72. E
13. E	28. B	43. E	58. C	73. C
14. C	29. B	44. B	59. E	74. B
15. A	30. C	45. D	60. C	75. D

Explained Answers for Test 2

1. (B) The kinetic energy of an object with mass m equals $\frac{1}{2} mv^2$. If, as in an elastic collision, kinetic energy is conserved, the kinetic energy before collision is equal to the kinetic energy of the masses after collision: $\frac{1}{2} m_1 v_1^2 = \frac{1}{2} m_2 v_2^2$. If we divide both sides by $\frac{1}{2}$, we get the equality of question 1: $m_1 v_1^2 = m_2 v_2^2$.

2. (A) The momentum of an object is the product of its mass and velocity: mv. In the collision of two objects or in an explosion, momentum is conserved; the momentum of the masses before the event equals the momentum of the masses after the event.

3. (E) Also see explanation 4.

4. (D) Write the relationship as a proportion:

$$\frac{V_1}{V_2} = \frac{T_1}{T_2}$$ (check by cross-multiplying).

This expresses Charles' law; the volume of a gas is proportional to its absolute temperature, if the pressure is constant.

5. (C) This is one way of expressing Boyle's law: If the temperature remains constant, the product of the pressure and volume of a gas remains constant.

6. (E) The formula mgh gives the potential energy of an object; mv^2 is *not* the kinetic energy of the object. (Kinetic energy, of course, is $\frac{1}{2} mv^2$.)

7. (A) Work done by a force is equal to the product of the force and the distance moved in the direction of the force.

8. (A) Pressure equals force per unit area; $p = F/A$; $pA = F$; $pAs = Fs$. This represents work, as stated in explanation 7. This could represent the work done in pushing the piston of a cylinder containing gas under pressure p.

9. (B) You may recognize this expression for power directly. If not, substitute for v its equivalent: s/t. Then $Fv = Fs/t$, which shows that we are talking about the rate of doing work, that is, power.

10. (D) This is always true in a parallel circuit: the voltage across one branch equals the voltage across another branch.

11. (C) This is always true in a series circuit: the current in one part of the circuit equals the current in any other part of the circuit.

12. (B) Perhaps too easy. The expression I^2R gives the electrical power used by a resistor.

13. (E) The electron-volt is a unit of energy and is used, for example, in describing the energy levels and spectrum of the hydrogen atom.

14. (C) The time required for the horizontally projected sphere to hit the floor depends only on the vertical height from which it starts. The horizontal velocity does not affect the vertical velocity; the initial vertical velocity of this sphere is zero. The initial vertical velocity of the vertically projected sphere is not zero. It is gradually slowed by gravity as it rises. At some greater height its velocity will be momentarily zero, and its time of fall from that greater height is greater than the time of fall for the other sphere. In addition, of course, some time was required to reach that greater height. Not enough information is provided to calculate actual times.

15. (A) Since the guns are identical, the springs do the same work on the spheres. This results in the two spheres leaving the guns with the same kinetic energy. In addition, the spheres initially have the same gravitational potential energy because they leave the guns from the same height. As the spheres fall, this potential energy is converted to kinetic energy. In the case of the vertically projected sphere another conversion occurs first. While it rises during the first part of its motion, its initial kinetic energy is converted to gravitational potential energy. This adds to the initial potential energy.

16. (B) One way to find the smallest quantity is to first write each quantity in standard scientific notation using the same unit, such as the meter. This converts the choices to: **(A)** 6.35×10^2 m **(B)** 6.35×10 m **(C)** 6.35×10^4 m **(D)** 6.35×10^2 m **(E)** 6.35×10^2 m. Of these, 6.35×10 m is the smallest.

17. (A) An approximate calculation is satisfactory. 1 in. = 2.54 cm = 25.4 mm. Therefore, 55 mm is a little more than 2 in., and much less than 3 in.

18. (C) The resultant of two forces is greatest when they act in the same direction. Their resultant is then equal to their sum.

19. (B) For an object starting from rest and moving with constant acceleration, the speed is given by $v = at$. The graph of v vs. t for this relationship is a straight line going through the origin.

20. (C) For such an object the distance covered is given by $s = \frac{1}{2}at^2$. The graph of s vs. t is a parabola symmetrical about the s-axis.

21. (A) The 30-N force is required to overcome two forces: the force of friction and the component of the weight parallel to the plane. The latter is not negligible for a rough plane.

22. (A) In this case we don't know the vertical height through which the object has been lifted. However, we do know that the man did 180 joules of work. This work was done for two purposes: one to overcome friction, the other to lift the object to a higher level. Since friction is not zero in this problem, only part of the 180 joules is left to raise the object. This part, of course, is the potential energy gained by the object.

23. (D) The tension in the string is the pull at either end of the string. The downward pull of the mass of the object is counteracted by the buoyant force of the water. The mass of the object = vol. $\times$ density; $m = (30 \text{ cm}^3)(4 \text{ g/cm}^3) = 120$ g. Its weight in air = $mg = (120 \text{ g})(980 \text{ cm/s}^2) \doteq 120{,}000$ dynes.

The *buoyant force* of the water equals the weight of the displaced water (Archimedes' principle). The object sinks, since its specific gravity is greater than that of water, and displaces 30 cm^3 of water. This water weighs $(30 \text{ g})(980 \text{ cm/s}^2) = 30{,}000$ dynes, and therefore the *tension* = $(120{,}000 - 30{,}000)$ dynes = 90,000 dynes (= 0.9 newton).

24. (B) See explanation 23.

25. (C) In accordance with Newton's third law: If X exerts a force on Y, then Y exerts an equal and opposite force on X.

26. (B) Gravitational, magnetic, and electrostatic forces vary inversely as the square of the distance between the small objects. Since the distance is doubled, the force must become one-fourth as great.

27. (E) Recall the formula for the period of a simple pendulum: $T = 2\pi\sqrt{L/g}$. This should remind you that the period depends on the length and on the acceleration due to gravity. The greater the altitude, the less the acceleration due to gravity. Vibration in the laboratory may interfere with the point of suspension and affect the period. Changing the mass of the bob of a simple pendulum does not change its period.

28. (B) The car is decelerated by an unbalanced force of 3,000 newtons. We apply Newton's second law of motion, which can be stated as: the unbalanced force acting on an object is equal to the product of the object's mass and the resulting acceleration:
$$F = ma.$$
First we calculate the acceleration. Acceleration is defined as the ratio of the change in velocity divided by the time in which the change takes place:
$$a = \Delta v/t$$
$$= (15 \text{ m/s})/(10 \text{ s})$$
$$= 1.5 \text{ m/s}^2$$
Substituting in $F = ma$,
$$3,000 \text{ N} = m\,(1.5 \text{ m/s}^2)$$
$$m = 2,000 \text{ kg}$$
Another method is to use a different form of the second law: The impulse acting on an object is equal to the resulting change in momentum. The *impulse* is equal to the product of the unbalanced force and the time during which it acts. Therefore,
$$Ft = mv$$
$$(3,000 \text{ N})(10 \text{ s}) = m\,(15 \text{ m/s})$$
$$m = 2,000 \text{ kg}$$
Note that the object started with a velocity of 15 m/s and then came to rest; therefore the change in velocity is 15 m/s.

29. (B) The work done in lifting an object is equal to the product of the object's weight and the vertical height through which it is lifted:
$$\text{Work} = \text{weight} \times \text{height}$$
$$\text{work} = (2.5 \times 10^4 \text{ N})(10 \text{ m})$$
$$= 2.5 \times 10^5 \text{ joules}$$

30. (C) According to Newton's second law of motion, the net or unbalanced force acting on an object is equal to the product of the object's mass and the resulting acceleration:
$$F = ma$$
$$= (10 \text{ kg})(5 \text{ m/s}^2)$$
$$= 50 \text{ newtons}$$

31. (C) When an object moves at constant speed around a circle, the centripetal acceleration is always directed towards the center of the circle. An unbalanced force acting on the object from the outside is needed to provide this acceleration. Here it is the friction between the wheels and the road that provides the centripetal force acting on the car. The engine turns the wheels to make the motion possible; the steering wheel turns the wheels in the desired direction of motion, but unless there is friction the car would merely continue sliding in a straight line.

32. (D) The centripetal force is equal to the product of the mass of the car and its centripetal acceleration:
$$F = mv^2/r$$
$$= (2 \times 10^3 \text{ kg})(50 \text{ m/s})^2/(250 \text{ m})$$
$$= 2 \times 10^4 \text{ N}$$

33. (A) In a series circuit the current is the same in every part.

34. (D) The potential difference across each wire is equal to the IR-product. Since the current I is the same in each of the wires, the potential difference is proportional to the resistance. You should know that, of all metals, silver has the highest conductivity (or lowest resistivity); copper and aluminum are close behind. Therefore, the resistance R of the silver wire is the least, that of the copper next, and that of the nichrome highest. The potential differences follow in the same sequence.

35. (E) Because the magnet moves with respect to the coil, an emf is induced in the coil. In accordance with Lenz's law, the direction of the induced current has to be such as to oppose the motion of the magnet. When the magnet approaches the coil, the right end of X has to become an S-pole, and the left end an N-pole. The left-hand rule indicates that the direction of electron flow is from Y to Z. When the magnet emerges and moves away to the left, the polarity of, and electron flow in, X must reverse, if the motion of the magnet is to be opposed.

36. (D) You may use your pencil as a prop. Hold it so that it is vertical. Apply the left-hand rule; the fingers point in the direction that the N-pole of the compass needle points. The thumb will point up, in the direction of the electron flow.

37. (B) The voltmeter measures the potential difference between its terminals. The voltmeter is in parallel with R_1; therefore the voltage across them is the same. Remember, in such a diagram the straight line implies zero resistance. The fact that the voltmeter is drawn along a diagonal means nothing special.

38. (C) The ammeter is in series with R_2; the current through these two is the same.

39. (C) The basic function of a diode is to change alternating current to direct current. The transistor is similar to the vacuum tube triode in that they are both capable of amplifying a signal if the common circuits are used. Neither semiconductor device uses a heated cathode. Both are made from crystals to which a small, precise amount of impurities has been added, and both can be made very small. The vacuum tube triode has a metal grid.

40. (A) All the ice has to be melted before the temperature can go above 0° C. 80 calories are needed to melt 1 g of ice at 0° C; 400 calories would be required to melt all 5 g. Since only 200 cal are supplied, half of the ice will melt. The resulting ice-water mixture will remain at 0° C.

41. (B) The energy must travel from west to east; it is transmitted by a sound wave. Sound waves are longitudinal waves: waves in which the medium vibrates back and forth in a direction parallel to the direction in which the energy travels.

42. (B) The range of audible frequencies depends on the individual, but is roughly 16-16,000 vib/sec or 16-20,000 vib/sec.

43. (E) The volume of a gas is directly proportional to the absolute temperature. The Kelvin scale and the Rankine scale are absolute scales of temperature.

44. (B) A Fahrenheit degree is 5/9 of a Celsius degree. Therefore the coefficient per Fahrenheit degree is 5/9 of the coefficient per Celsius degree; this equals 5/9 × 0.000045 = 0.000025.

45. (D) Change in length = length × coefficient × temp. change = 100 cm × 0.000045/C° × (50° − 30°) C = 0.090 cm.

46. (C) Apply Ohm's law. $I = V/R$. Since the voltage V is the same for X and Y, the currents through them compare inversely as the resistance. Then X has a resistance which is twice as large; therefore it has a current half as large as Y.

47. (D) Since the voltage is the same for X and Y, it is convenient to compare their rates of heat production (or power consumption) by $P = V^2/R$. This shows that their rate of heat production varies inversely as their resistance. (You may recall that, in a parallel circuit, the device with the lesser resistance consumes the greater power.) Then X has twice as much resistance as Y; therefore it consumes ½ the power.

48. (A) This is a simple fact. Of course, in ordinary neutral atoms all the protons are in the nucleus and the number of electrons outside the nucleus equals the number of protons in the nucleus.

49. (D) The woman is 10 m in front of the mirror. In a plane mirror her image is 10 m behind the mirror. The distance between her and her image is 20 m.

50. (A) This is almost pure recall of a fact. You should also think of the fact that, when you use a magnifying glass, you are using a convex lens to get a virtual, enlarged, erect image. A virtual image is obtained with a convex lens only if the object is less than one focal length away from the lens.

51. (E) In light, frequency determines color. In vacuum the speed of light is independent of frequency: in vacuum all electromagnetic waves travel at the same speed. (A) would therefore be a poor choice.

52. (B) The eye has a convex lens of fairly short focal length. In general, the objects we see are more than one focal length away from our eye; objects more than one focal length away from a convex lens always produce real, inverted images.

53. (C) Nonluminous opaque objects are seen by the light they reflect. Luminous objects are seen by the light they emit.

54. (B) Monochromatic red light contains only red light. An ideal blue object will reflect only blue light; when illuminated by monochromatic red light, there is no blue light for the object to reflect. When no light enters our eye we "see" blackness. (An actual book may reflect other colors, such as green, in addition to the blue. However, such colors will not be present in monochromatic red light.)

55. (E) You should know as a fact that light travels faster in air than in water or glass. In addition, the light will be refracted if it reaches the surface obliquely; it will not be refracted if it is normal to the surface.

56. (A) Einstein's special theory of relativity tells us that at speeds near the speed of light, lengths are shortened according to $l_{relativistic} = l_{rest} \sqrt{1-(v^2/c^2)}$, where v = speed of space ship and c = speed of light.

57. (C) The restraining force on an inclined plane is often friction. However, an object could be held in place by a rope or a magnetic force, for example.

58. (C) At the instant shown in the diagram, the magnetic flux from the N-pole to the S-pole is perpendicular to the face of the loop. At this instant, the voltage induced in the loop is zero. One way to look at this is to think of the top and bottom wires of the loop. At the instant shown they are moving parallel to the magnetic flux and therefore are not cutting any lines of force; thus no voltage is induced. One-quarter of a rotation later, the top wire is at 90° and the bottom wire is at 270°. At that instant a maximum voltage is induced in them since they are moving perpendicularly across the lines of force. Another half of a rotation later, the top wire is at 270° and the bottom wire is at 90°. Again a maximum voltage is induced, but this time in the opposite direction around the loop because the wire that moved down across the field before is now moving up, and vice versa.

59. (E) The voltage induced in the coil is proportional to the flux density provided by the external magnets and the speed of rotation of the loop. The flux density decreases between the two poles when the poles are moved further apart. This decreases the induced voltage. When the loop is wound around an iron core, the flux density is increased. Using a commutator (see page 123) merely changes the current in the external circuit to direct current.

60. (C) In vacuum all electromagnetic waves travel at the same speed. In materials like glass and water, violet light travels more slowly than red light. The wavelengths of red light are greater than those of violet light. Therefore, the frequencies of red light are lower than those of violet light $(c = f\lambda)$. The energy of a quantum equals Planck's constant times the frequency $(E = hf)$. Hence each quantum of red light has less energy than a quantum of violet light.

61. (B) Beats are produced by the constructive and destructive interference of two different frequencies. Where the waves are in phase, they reinforce each other; where they are out of phase, they tend to annul each other. Reinforcement leads to comparative loudness; annulment to comparative quiet.

A color spectrum is produced with thin oil films and soap bubbles because light is reflected by both surfaces of the film; the beams from the two surfaces interfere with each other. At different angles of vision different colors are annulled.

Green leaves appear green in ordinary light because the leaves absorb most of the light. Green predominates in the reflected light.

62. (A) $1 \text{ mA} = 10^{-3} \text{ A}$. Therefore, $6.50 \text{ mA} = 6.50 \times 10^{-3} \text{ A} = 65.0 \times 10^{-4} \text{ A} = 0.00650 \text{ A}$. But, choice IV, $65.0 \times 10^{-2} \text{ A} = 6.50 \times 10^{-1} \text{ A}$.

63. (D) The amplitude changes because there is always some reflection when a wave goes from one medium to another with a different index of refraction. When the energy of a given wave decreases, the amplitude of the wave decreases.

The direction changes: when a ray goes obliquely from a rarer to a denser medium, it is bent toward the normal. The frequency of the wave is the same in the two media, but the speed is lower in the denser medium. Therefore the wavelength is smaller in the denser medium ($v = f\lambda$).

64. (A) The kinetic energy of the object equals $\frac{1}{2} mv^2$ (proportional to the square of its speed). For an object starting from rest, $v^2 = 2as$. Therefore, kinetic energy $= \frac{1}{2} m \times 2as = mas$ (kinetic energy is proportional to its displacement s). Since $v^2 = 2as$, $v = \sqrt{2as}$ (speed proportional to the square root of its displacement).

Its velocity is proportional to time; $v = at$, and a is constant.

65. (E) If the net force were tripled, the acceleration would be tripled. However, the force the man exerts is not the net force. Suppose the force he exerts is 5 N. Part of this is needed to overcome friction and another part is needed to overcome a component of the weight. Suppose these two parts add up to 1 N. The net force is only 4 N. Tripling the original force results in an applied force of 15 N, the net force will be 14 N. In this example, the net force, and therefore the acceleration, are more than tripled ($14/4 = 3.5$).

66. (C) The woman's push on the floor of the elevator equals the floor's push on her. This push moves her up with the same acceleration as the elevator. The push that would be required merely to keep the woman in equilibrium is equal to her weight. An additional force is required to accelerate her. According to Newton's second law, this force is proportional to the acceleration.

67. (B) First harmonic is another name for fundamental frequency. In addition to the fundamental frequency, many vibrating objects produce higher frequencies called overtones. ("First basso" is not a physics term.)

68. (A) The resistance of a wire $= kL/A$. If we make the length smaller, the resistance becomes less. If we make the cross-section area A larger, the resistance becomes less. Doing the opposite will increase the resistance.

69. (E) A charged rod will attract small pieces of anything, including iron. Magnetic material, which has not been magnetized, will be attracted by north and south poles.

70. (D) In the interference pattern produced by two slits, the distance between two adjacent bright lines is given by a fairly simple relationship. If x is this distance,

$$x = \lambda L/d$$

where λ = the wavelength of the light
L = the distance between the double slit and the screen
d = the distance between the two slits

Substituting, we get $x = (6.0 \times 10^{-7} \text{ m})(2.0 \text{ m})/2.0 \times 10^{-5} \text{ m})$
$= 6.0 \times 10^{-2} \text{ m}$

71. (C) The intensity of the arriving light determines how many photons arrive each second. If the frequency of the light is above the threshold frequency, the greater the number of the arriving photons, the greater the number of emitted electrons.

72. (E) This question requires only rough mental calculation. On a test it would be a big waste of time to do anything other than that. Quick inspection shows that a transition from $n = 2$ to $n = 1$ results in a release of a photon with an energy of about 10 eV. Any drop to a level other than the ground state will involved at most a release of 3.4 eV.

73. (C) The frequency of a photon is proportional to its energy: $E = hf$. The energy is determined by subtracting the energy of the second state from the energy of the first state:

$$n = 3: \quad -1.5 \text{ ev}$$
$$n = 2: \quad \underline{-(-3.4 \text{ ev})}$$
$$1.9 \text{ ev}$$

Changing the energy to joules and substituting, we get

$$1.9 \cancel{ev} \times \frac{1.6 \times 10^{-19} \text{ J}}{1 \cancel{ev}} = (6.6 \times 10^{-34} \text{ J} \cdot \text{s}) f$$

$$f = 4.6 \times 10^{14} \text{ Hz}$$

74. (B) The *half-life* of an isotope of an element is the time required for one-half of the nuclei of a sample of the isotope to break up. In this example we start with 12 grams of thorium (Th). In 24 days only 6 grams are left. In another 24 days (a total of 48 days) one-half of the 6 grams disintegrates, and only 3 grams of thorium are left. After still another 24 days (a total of 72 days) one-half of the remaining 3 grams breaks up, leaving 1.5 grams of thorium. Finally, after another 24 days (a total of 96 days) one-half of the 1.5 grams has broken up, leaving 0.75 gram of thorium.

75. (D) When the symbol of an element is written with a superscript and a subscript, the superscript is the mass number and the subscript is the atomic number. In the case of the given isotope of aluminum, Al, the mass number is 27, and the atomic number is 13. The equation describes a nuclear change. In all nuclear changes mass number and atomic number are conserved. This means that the sum of the mass numbers on the left side of the equation must equal the sum of the mass numbers on the right. The sum of the mass numbers on the left is 27 + 4, or 31. On the right side the mass number of P is 30. Therefore the mass number of X must be 1, because 30 + 1 = 31. Since atomic number is also conserved, the algebraic sum of the subscripts on the left side must equal the algebraic sum on the right. The sum on the left is 13 + 2, or 15. The subscript for X must be zero, because 15 + 0 = 15. The neutron is the particle that has a mass number of 1 and an atomic number (or charge) of zero.

PRACTICE TEST 3

Part A

DIRECTIONS: *For each group of questions below, there is a set of five lettered choices, followed by numbered questions. For each question select the one choice in the set that best answers the question. You may use a lettered choice once, more than once, or not at all in each set.*

QUESTIONS 1–7 refer to the following units:
(A) hertz   **(B)** watt   **(C)** joule   **(D)** volt   **(E)** half-life

1. What unit is used to express a quantity of energy?
2. To express a measure of emf, which unit would be used?
3. In which unit would you express a measure of radioactivity?
4. What is the unit for power?
5. If you want to express a quantity of heat, what unit would you use?
6. What unit is used for the same property as cycle/second?
7. What unit expresses work per unit charge?

QUESTIONS 8-13 refer to the following laws and principles:

(A) Newton's first law of motion   **(B)** Newton's second law of motion   **(C)** Archimedes' principle
(D) Hooke's law   **(E)** Bernoulli's principle

Which choice is most closely associated with each of the following?

8. Circular motion with constant speed
9. Rectilinear motion with constant speed
10. A freely falling object
11. An object projected vertically up
12. The fact that a hydrometer floats higher in salt water than in freshwater
13. The stretching of a rubber band

QUESTIONS 14-15 refer to the formation of images using an object, a screen, and one or more of these:

     I. a plane mirror
     II. a concave lens (diverging)
     III. a convex lens (converging)

   (A) I only
   (B) II only
   (C) III only
   (D) I and II only
   (E) none of these

14. Which of items I–III can be used to produce a virtual image larger than the object?
15. Which of items I–III can be used to produce a real image the same size as the object?

Part B

DIRECTIONS: *Each of the following questions or incomplete statements is followed by five choices. Select the choice that best answers the question or completes the statement.*

16. Of the following, the one that is most like a gamma ray in its properties is   **(A)** alpha ray   **(B)** beta ray   **(C)** X ray   **(D)** electron   **(E)** proton

17. The sun's energy is believed to be a result of   **(A)** oxidation of carbon   **(B)** oxidation of hydrogen   **(C)** oxidation of helium   **(D)** nuclear fission   **(E)** nuclear fusion

18. The emission of one alpha particle from the nucleus of an atom produces a change of   **(A)** -1 in atomic number   **(B)** -1 in atomic mass   **(C)** -2 in atomic number   **(D)** -2 in atomic mass   **(E)** $+2$ in atomic mass

19. Two forces of 10 N and 7 N, respectively, are applied simultaneously to an object. The minimum value of their resultant is, in newtons,   **(A)** 0   **(B)** 3   **(C)** 7   **(D)** $7\sqrt{3}$ **(E)** 10

20. Two forces act together on an object. The magnitude of their resultant is greatest when the angle between the forces is   **(A)** $0°$ **(B)** $45°$ **(C)** $60°$ **(D)** $90°$ **(E)** $180°$

21. Of the following, the largest quantity is   **(A)** 0.047 cm   **(B)** 47×10^{-4} cm   **(C)** 4.7×10^{-2} cm   **(D)** 0.00047×10^{2} cm   **(E)** 0.000047×10^{4} cm

22. The Celsius temperature of an object is increased 90°. Its increase on the Kelvin scale will be   **(A)** 50 K   **(B)** 90 K   **(C)** 162 K   **(D)** 180 K   **(E)** 273 K

23. The work done in holding a weight of 40 N at a height of 3 m above the floor for 2 s is, in joules,   **(A)** 0   **(B)** 40   **(C)** 80   **(D)** 120   **(E)** 240

24. When alpha particles are directed at a thin metallic foil, it can be observed that most of the particles   **(A)** pass through with virtually no deflection   **(B)** bounce backward   **(C)** are absorbed **(D)** are widely scattered   **(E)** change to hydrogen

25. A lithium nucleus contains 3 protons and 4 neutrons. What is its atomic number?   **(A)** 1   **(B)** 7   **(C)** 3   **(D)** 4   **(E)** 12

26. A string 80 cm long has a fundamental frequency of 300 vib/sec. If the length of the string is changed to 40 cm without changing the tension, the fundamental frequency will be, in vibrations per second,   **(A)** 150   **(B)** $150\sqrt{2}$ **(C)** 300   **(D)** $300\sqrt{2}$ **(E)** 600

For 27–28. A sonar depth finder uses sound signals to determine the depth of water. Four seconds after the sound leaves the boat it returns to the boat because of reflection from the bottom. Assume the speed of the sound in water is 4800 ft/sec.

27. The speed of the sound in water, expressed in meters/second, is   **(A)** 330   **(B)** 1090   **(C)** 1460   **(D)** 14,400   **(E)** 186,000

28. The depth of the water is, in feet,   **(A)** 2200   **(B)** 4400   **(C)** 4800   **(D)** 9600   **(E)** 19,200

29. A pendulum, consisting of a string of length L and a small metal ball of mass m at the free end, is allowed to swing freely after being released from point A. The highest point it reaches on the other side is C and the lowest point of swing is B. At B the mass m has   **(A)** zero potential energy and zero kinetic energy   **(B)** maximum potential and maximum kinetic energy   **(C)** minimum potential and maximum kinetic energy   **(D)** maximum potential and zero kinetic energy   **(E)** zero potential and the same kinetic energy as at C.

30. In question 29, if we want the period of the pendulum to be doubled, we should change the length of the string to   **(A)** ¼L **(B)** ½L **(C)** 2L **(D)** 4L **(E)** 2L and the mass to 2m

31. A horizontal force of 15 newtons accelerates a 4.0-kilogram object from rest along a horizontal surface at a rate of 3 m/s^2. At the end of 2 seconds the object's momentum will be, in kilogram•meters per second,   **(A)** 12   **(B)** 24   **(C)** 30   **(D)** 45   **(E)** 60

32. In question 31 what is the frictional force, in newtons, that is retarding the forward motion of the object?   **(A)** 3   **(B)** 4   **(C)** 12   **(D)** 40   **(E)** 60

For 33–34. A 40-N object is lifted 10 m above the ground and then released.

33. After the object has fallen 4 m and is 6 m above the ground, its kinetic energy will be, in joules   **(A)** 5   **(B)** 160   **(C)** 240   **(D)** 400   **(E)** 5120

34. Just before it hits the ground, the object's kinetic energy will be, in joules   **(A)** 12   **(B)** 160   **(C)** 240   **(D)** 400   **(E)** 12,800

35. Ball X is projected horizontally at the same time as ball Y is released and allowed to fall. If air resistance is negligible and both start from the same height,   **(A)** X and Y will reach the level ground at the same time   **(B)** X will reach the level ground first   **(C)** Y will reach the ground first   **(D)** we must know the mass of X and Y to tell which will hit the ground first   **(E)** we must know the density to tell which will hit the ground first

36. Ball X is projected vertically up at the same time as ball Y is projected horizontally. If air resistance is negligible and both start from the same height,   **(A)** X and Y will reach the level ground at the same time   **(B)** X will reach the level ground first   **(C)** Y will reach the level ground first   **(D)** we must know the mass of X and Y to tell which will hit the ground first   **(E)** we must know the density to tell which will hit the ground first

37. Object X is dropped at the same time as object Y is projected vertically upward and object Z is projected horizontally. Air resistance is negligible.   **(A)** objects X and Y have the same downward acceleration and this is greater than Y's   **(B)** objects X and Z have the same downward acceleration and this is less than Y's   **(C)** objects Y and Z have the same downward acceleration and this is greater than X's   **(D)** objects Y and Z have the same downward acceleration and this is less than X's   **(E)** objects X, Y, and Z have the same downward acceleration

38. A metal cube, 2 cm on edge, is suspended in air so that the top and bottom faces are horizontal. The force exerted on the bottom face by the atmosphere is **(A)** 2 N **(B)** 4 N **(C)** 20 N **(D)** 30 N **(E)** 40 N

For 39-41. This set of graphs applies to the next three questions.

39. The graph which shows most nearly the variation of the pressure of a gas against its volume, at constant temperature, is **(A)** A **(B)** B **(C)** C **(D)** D **(E)** E

40. The graph which most nearly shows the variation of current through a given resistor against the voltage applied to it is **(A)** A **(B)** B **(C)** C **(D)** D **(E)** E

41. The graph which most nearly shows the variation of current supplied by a given dry cell as the external resistance is increased (axes: current against resistance) is **(A)** A **(B)** B **(C)** C **(D)** D **(E)** E

42. The diagram shows the path of a ray of light through 4 media separated from each other by horizontal surfaces. The medium in which the speed of the light is greatest is **(A)** I **(B)** II **(C)** III **(D)** IV **(E)** indeterminate on the basis of the given information

43. A bright-line spectrum may be obtained by using light from **(A)** the sun **(B)** a sodium vapor lamp **(C)** a tungsten filament bulb **(D)** a clean glowing platinum wire **(E)** a clean glowing nichrome wire

44. Colors in a soap bubble are caused **(A)** solely by pigments **(B)** solely by reflection **(C)** solely by absorption **(D)** by polarization **(E)** by interference

45. A compass is placed to the west of a vertical conductor. When electrons go through the conductor, the N-pole of the compass needle is deflected to point towards the south. The direction of electron flow in the conductor is **(A)** down **(B)** up **(C)** east **(D)** west **(E)** south

For 46-47. In the circuit shown, each of the three resistors has a resistance of 40 ohms. The fuse F is rated at 10 amperes and has negligible resistance. The battery supplies 120 volts and has negligible internal resistance.

46. When the switch S is open as shown, the current through R_1 is, in amperes, **(A)** 0 **(B)** 1 **(C)** 2 **(D)** 6 **(E)** 9

47. When switch S is closed, the current through R_2 is **(A)** 3 amperes **(B)** 6 amperes **(C)** 10 amperes **(D)** 12 amperes **(E)** zero because the fuse will blow

48. If pith ball X attracts pith ball Y but repels pith ball Z, **(A)** Y must be positively charged **(B)** Y must be negatively charged **(C)** Y may be positive or negative but not neutral **(D)** Y may be neutral or charged **(E)** Y must be neutral

49. The sp. ht. of ice is 0.5 cal/g•C°. The heat required to change 20 g of ice at −5° C to water at 0° C is, in calories, **(A)** 10 **(B)** 50 **(C)** 130 **(D)** 450 **(E)** 1650

For 50-53. *Base your answers on the information below.*

Two parallel slits 2.0×10^{-6} meter apart are illuminated by parallel rays of monochromatic light of wavelength 6.0×10^{-7} meter, as shown. The interference pattern is formed on a screen 2.0 meters from the slits.

50. The distance X is **(A)** 6.0×10^{-1} m **(B)** 6.0×10^{-7} m **(C)** 3.0×10^{-1} m **(D)** 3.3 m **(E)** 330 m

51. The difference in path length for the light from the two slits to the first maximum is **(A)** λ **(B)** 2λ **(C)** $\dfrac{\lambda}{2}$ **(D)** 0 **(E)** 3λ

52. If the wavelength of the light passing through the slits is doubled, the distance from the central maximum to the first maximum **(A)** is halved **(B)** is doubled **(C)** remains the same **(D)** is quadrupled **(E)** is tripled

53. If the screen is moved to 1.0 meter from the slits, the distance between the central maximum and the first maximum **(A)** is halved **(B)** is doubled **(C)** remains the same **(D)** is quadrupled **(E)** is tripled

54. Two hundred cm³ of a gas are heated from 30° C to 60° C without letting the pressure change. The volume of the gas will **(A)** be halved **(B)** be decreased by about 10% **(C)** remain the same **(D)** be doubled **(E)** be increased by about 10%.

55. X is a coil of wire with a hollow core. Brass rod R is pushed at constant speed from the right into the core (and out again at the left). During this complete motion, **(A)** there will be no current in wire YZ **(B)** electron flow will be from Y to Z **(C)** electron flow will be from Z to Y **(D)** electron flow will be from Z to Y and then from Y to Z **(E)** electron flow will be from Y to Z and then from Z to Y.

56. If yellow light emerges from a box, which of the following will be true in regard to the light?

    I. It may contain red light.
    II. It must contain a wavelength shorter than 8000 Å (1 Å = 10^{-10} m).
    III. It may be of a single wavelength.
    IV. It must contain a wavelength which by itself would appear yellow.

    (A) I, II, and III only
    (B) I and III only
    (C) II and IV only
    (D) IV only
    (E) none of the above

57. All air is removed from the device shown after a volatile liquid, such as ether, is poured in at *Y*. Then the device is sealed and portion *X* is surrounded by ice. What will be the result(s)?

    I. Some of the liquid will appear at *X* because the vapor is condensed at *X*.
    II. The volume of the liquid in *Y* will increase because it is at a higher temperature than X.
    III. The level of the liquid in *Y* will decrease.
    IV. No change will take place.

(A) I, II, and III only
(B) I and III only
(C) II and IV only
(D) IV only
(E) none of the above

58. A gas is allowed to expand isothermally from a volume of 100 cm³ to a volume of 400 cm³. The original pressure of the gas was 4 atmospheres. What will the new pressure be?

    I. 1 atmosphere
    II. 16 atmospheres
    III. 76 cm of mercury
    IV. It cannot be calculated without knowing the temperature.

(A) I, II, and III only
(B) I and III only
(C) II and IV only
(D) IV only
(E) none of the above

59. If air is kept saturated with water vapor, which of the following will be true of its relative humidity?

    I. It will be high at high temperatures.
    II. It will be high at low temperatures.
    III. It will depend on the mass of water vapor in it.
    IV. It will be 100%.

(A) I, II, and III only
(B) I and III only
(C) II and IV only
(D) IV only
(E) none of the above

60. Two halves of an iron washer are placed between two magnets as shown in the diagram. What will be the result(s)?

    I. *X* will be an S-pole and *Y* an N-pole.
    II. *Y* will be an N-pole and *Z* an S-pole.
    III. *Y* and *W* will be S-poles.
    IV. *X* and *Z* will be S-poles.

(A) I, II, and III only
(B) I and III only
(C) II and IV only
(D) IV only
(E) none of the above

For 61-62. Select the choice which fits the question best.

61. An emf of 0.003 volt is induced in a wire when it moves at right angles to a uniform magnetic field with a speed of 4.0 m/s. If the length of wire in the field is 15 cm, what is the flux density, in teslas?
(A) 0.003   **(B)** 0.005   **(C)** 6   **(D)** 12   **(E)** 2000

62. In question 61 if the wire were to move at an angle of 30° to the field instead of at right angles, the value of the induced emf would be **(A)** unchanged **(B)** two times as great **(C)** three times as great **(D)** four times as great **(E)** one-half as great

63. What is the weight of a 5.0-kilogram object at the surface of the Earth? **(A)** 5.0 kg **(B)** 25 N **(C)** 49 N **(D)** 49 kg **(E)** 98 N

64. A wool cloth becomes positively charged as it **(A)** gains protons **(B)** gains electrons **(C)** loses protons **(D)** loses electrons **(E)** gains neutrons

65. If the frequency of a sound wave in air at STP remains constant, its energy can be varied by changing its **(A)** amplitude **(B)** speed **(C)** wavelength **(D)** period **(E)** direction

66. A magnetic field will be produced by **(A)** moving electrons **(B)** moving neutrons **(C)** stationary protons **(D)** stationary ions **(E)** stationary electrons

67. A charged particle is placed in an electric field E. If the charge on the particle is doubled, the force exerted on the particle by the field E is **(A)** unchanged **(B)** doubled **(C)** halved **(D)** quadrupled **(E)** quartered

68. At which temperature is water densest? **(A)** 0° C **(B)** 4° C **(C)** 0° F **(D)** 4° F **(E)** 100° C

For 69-70. In the following graph, the velocity of an object as it moves along a horizontal straight line is plotted against time.

69. The distance traveled by the object during the first 2 seconds is **(A)** 2 m **(B)** 4 m **(C)** 8 m **(D)** 16 m **(E)** 24 m

70. The average speed of the object during the first 4 seconds is, in meters per second, **(A)** zero **(B)** 1.2 **(C)** 2.5 **(D)** 4 **(E)** 8

71. Which point in the wave shown in the diagram is in phase with point A? **(A)** F **(B)** B **(C)** C **(D)** D **(E)** E

72. The diagram represents a wave pattern produced by a vibrating source moving at constant speed. Towards which point is the source moving? **(A)** 1 **(B)** 2 **(C)** 3 **(D)** 4 **(E)** perpendicularly into the page

73. If the source were to accelerate, the wavelength immediately in front of the source would **(A)** increase only **(B)** decrease only **(C)** first increase and then decrease **(D)** first decrease and then increase **(E)** remain the same

74. The graph below shows the maximum kinetic energy of the photoelectrons ejected when

photons of different frequencies strike a metal surface. The slope of the graph is Planck's constant, h. The work function of this metal is, in joules, **(A)** $h \times 10^{14}$ **(B)** $2h \times 10^{14}$ **(C)** $3h \times 10^{14}$ **(D)** $4h \times 10^{14}$ **(E)** $8h \times 10^{14}$

75. An electron moves with constant speed at right angles to a uniform magnetic flux. If the flux density were doubled, the force on the electron would be **(A)** unaffected **(B)** reduced to one-fourth **(C)** halved **(D)** doubled **(E)** quadrupled

ANSWERS FOR PRACTICE TEST 3

Answer Key for Test 3

1. C	16. C	31. B	46. C	61. B
2. D	17. E	32. A	47. A	62. E
3. E	18. C	33. B	48. D	63. C
4. B	19. B	34. D	49. E	64. D
5. C	20. A	35. A	50. A	65. A
6. A	21. E	36. C	51. A	66. A
7. D	22. B	37. E	52. B	67. B
8. B	23. A	38. E	53. A	68. B
9. A	24. A	39. C	54. E	69. B
10. B	25. C	40. A	55. A	70. C
11. B	26. E	41. B	56. A	71. D
12. C	27. C	42. A	57. B	72. A
13. D	28. D	43. B	58. B	73. B
14. C	29. C	44. E	59. E	74. B
15. C	30. D	45. A	60. E	75. D

Explained Answers for Test 3

1. (C) Some units of energy are the joule, erg, watt-hour, foot-pound, calorie, Btu.

2. (D) emf is the difference of potential produced by devices like batteries and generators. It is the voltage between the terminals when the current is zero.

3. (E) The half-life of a radioactive substance is the length of time it takes for one-half of its mass to decay into something else.

4. (B) Power is energy per unit of time. In *SI* units, 1 Joule/1 second = 1 watt.

5. (C) Heat is a form of energy. See explanation 1.

6. (A) The hertz or cycle per second is the unit of frequency.

7. (D) The volt is work per unit charge: $V = W/q$.

8. (B) Although the speed is constant, the velocity is not constant because the direction is constantly changing: at one instant the object may be going north; half a revolution later it will be going south. Since the object's velocity is changing, the object is accelerated. Newton's second law is associated with accelerated motion: acceleration takes place in the direction of the net force.

9. (A) Motion with constant speed along a straight line is motion with constant velocity, motion without acceleration. This is the subject of Newton's first law: if an object moves with constant (or zero) velocity, the net force acting on the object is zero.

10. (B) A freely falling object is accelerated because of the earth's pull on it. Newton's second law is associated with accelerated motion.

11. (B) The velocity of a vertically projected object is constantly changing. Change in velocity, or acceleration, is the subject of Newton's second law.

12. (C) Archimedes' principle tells that the weight in air of a floating object is equal to the weight of the displaced liquid in which it floats. Salt water is denser than fresh water. A smaller volume of salt water than of fresh water will equal the weight of the hydrometer. When a hydrometer floats higher (as it does in salt water), it displaces a smaller volume. Bernoulli's principle deals with the flowing of a liquid or a gas. The greater the speed, the lower the pressure.

13. (D) This is a case where "most closely associated with" must be taken seriously. The stretching of a rubber band illustrates the behavior of elastic substances. Hooke's law says the change in length of an elastic substance is proportional to the stretching force. However, rubber is a non-linear material. It does not follow Hooke's law exactly.

14. (C) A *plane mirror* always produces a virtual image which is the same size as the object. (If we look at our image in a plane mirror as we walk backwards away from it, our image will *appear* to get smaller for the same reason that a real person will look smaller to us as the distance between us and the person increases: it is a visual effect.) A *concave lens* produces a virtual image whose size is smaller than the object and decreases as the distance between the object and lens increases.

A *convex lens* produces a virtual image larger than the object when the object's distance from the lens is less than one focal length. A magnifying glass is an application of this characteristic.

15. (C) A convex lens produces a real image the same size as the object when the object's distance from the lens is two focal lengths. (Also read the explanation for question 14.)

16. (C) Both X rays and gamma rays are usually classified as electromagnetic waves. Their wavelength is of the order of 10^{-8} cm. The others are classified as part of ordinary matter. Alpha rays are streams of helium nuclei; beta rays are streams of electrons.

17. (E) Oxidation reactions yield very little energy compared with nuclear fission or fusion. The sun's vast energy is believed to be the result of a cycle of reactions involving the fusion of hydrogen nuclei.

18. (C) Alpha particles are helium nuclei. They have a mass number of 4 and charge of +2 (they consist of 2 protons and 2 neutrons). Therefore, when an alpha particle emerges from a nucleus, the positive charge of the remaining portion has decreased by 2; that is, its atomic number, which is the charge of the nucleus, is reduced by 2.

19. (B) The resultant of two forces applied to an object at the same time depends on their direction with respect to each other. The resultant is largest when the two forces act in the same direction—at an angle of 0°. Then the resultant is equal to the sum of the two forces. As the angle between the two forces increases, the value of the resultant decreases until the angle between the forces is 180°. The resultant then has a minimum value and is equal to the difference between the two forces.

20. (A) See explanation 19.

21. (E) You may be able to get the answer quickly by eliminating some of the choices after a quick inspection. Systematic comparison can be made by writing all the choices in standard form (scientific notation) or as decimal fractions. We'll use the former method. The choices then become: **(A)** 4.7×10^{-2} **(B)** 4.7×10^{-5} **(C)** 4.7×10^{-2} **(D)** 4.7×10^{-2} **(E)** 4.7×10^{-1}

22. (B) Each Kelvin unit represents the same *change* in temperature as the Celsius degree. Therefore a change of 90° on the Celsius scale is also a change of 90 kelvins on the Kelvin scale.

23. (A) Considering the choices, it is clear that you are asked to find the work done on the object. Although a force is exerted, the force doesn't move and the object doesn't move. Hence no work is done; work equals force times distance moved in the direction of the force.

24. (A) When Rutherford directed a stream of alpha particles at a thin metallic foil, he noticed that most of the alpha particles went right through without being deflected. This convinced him that most of the atom is empty space.

A very small fraction of the alpha particles bounce backward. They are reflected from the nucleus by the strong electrostatic repulsion between the positive nucleus and the positive alpha particle. Other alpha particles are scattered through various angles as they approach the nucleus.

25. (C) The *atomic number* of an atom is the number of protons in its nucleus.

26. (E) The frequency of a vibrating string is inversely proportional to its length. If the length is decreased, the frequency is increased. If the length is halved, the frequency is doubled.

27. (C) One way to get the answer for this question is to make the actual conversion: 4800 ft/sec = (12×4800) in./sec = $\dfrac{12 \times 4800}{39.37}$ m/s. You can round off a little ($39.37 \doteq 40$) and get 1440 m/s as the answer.

Another way is easier, if you remember that the speed of sound in air is approx. 1100 ft/sec or 330 m/s. The speed in water is given as a little more than 4 times 1100 ft/sec. Hence it should be a little more than 4 times 330 m/s. More exact calculation gives 1460 m/s.

28. (D) If it takes 4 sec for the sound to go down and up again, it takes only 2 sec just to go to the bottom.
$$\text{Distance} = \text{speed} \times \text{time.}$$
$$\text{Distance} = 4800 \text{ ft/sec} \times 2 \text{ sec} = 9600 \text{ ft.}$$

29. (C) As the pendulum bob swings back and forth, at the highest point of its swing, at *A* and *C*, all of its energy is potential. At those points it is momentarily at rest. As it swings through its arc from its highest point, the potential energy is converted to kinetic. At the lowest point of the swing, at *B*, the potential energy has been converted to kinetic. Then as it swings up towards *C* the kinetic energy is converted to potential. If air friction is negligible, *C* is at the same height as *A*, and the bob has the same potential energy there as at *A*. Also, in that case, throughout the swing the sum of the potential and kinetic energy remains constant.

30. (D) The period of a simple pendulum is proportional to the square root of its length. If the length is multiplied by 4, the period is multiplied by the square root of 4, which is 2. The complete formula for the period of the pendulum is: $T = 2\pi\sqrt{L/g}$, where g is the acceleration due to gravity at that location.

31. (B) The momentum of an object is equal to the product of its mass and its velocity:
$$\text{momentum} = \text{mass} \times \text{velocity}$$
$$= (4.0 \text{ kg}) (3 \text{ m/s}^2) (2 \text{ s})$$
$$= 24 \text{ kg} \cdot \text{m/s}$$

We calculated the final velocity at the end of 2 seconds by multiplying the constant acceleration by the time. Note also that the question did not say that the 15-N force is a net force. Therefore the quick use of the relationship that the impulse is equal to the change in momentum would not be well-advised. (Unfortunately, in some questions the absence of friction has to be assumed.) This will be more apparent from question 32.

32. (A) The horizontal force of 15 N was used to give the object acceleration and also to overcome friction. According to Newton's second law of motion, the force which gives an object acceleration is equal to the product of the object's mass and its acceleration:

$$F = ma$$
$$= (4 \text{ kg}) (3 \text{ m/s}^2) = 12 \text{ N}$$

The force of friction is equal to the difference between the total force and the net force: $(15 \text{ N}) - (12 \text{ N}) = 3 \text{ N}$

33. (B) Potential energy = Wt $\times$ height.
At the top, 10 m above the ground, the object's potential energy = 40 N $\times$ 10 m = 400 joules.
When it is 6 m above the ground, the object's potential energy = 40 N $\times$ 6 m = 240 joules.
The difference in potential energy is the kinetic energy which the object acquired. Kinetic energy = $(400 - 240)$ joules = 160 joules.

34. (D) Just before it hits the ground, all the object's potential energy has been converted to kinetic energy.

35. (A) This is one of the classic experiments. It shows that horizontal motion does not affect vertical motion (that is, vertical motion is affected only by a vertical force or by a force having a vertical component).

36. (C) This follows from the result of the experiment described in question 35. Ball X must first rise to a greater height than ball Y; we can think of it as then falling freely from the highest point it reaches. In the meantime ball Y has already started on its downward trip. Of course, mass and density have nothing to do with the time it will take to reach ground, if air resistance is negligible.

37. (E) The change in velocity of the three objects is due to gravity only; the acceleration due to gravity is the same for all objects near the surface of the earth.

38. (E) The pressure due to the atmosphere is approximately 10 N/cm². The force due to the atmosphere is equal to the pressure times the area on which it acts (since $p = F/A$):
The area of the face of the cube = 2 cm $\times$ 2 cm = 4 cm².
$F = pA = (10 \text{ N/cm}^2) (4 \text{ cm}^2) = 40 \text{ N}$. (Of course this is balanced by the almost equal downward force of the atmosphere on the upper surface.)

39. (C) This refers to Boyle's law: the pressure of a gas varies inversely as its volume. The graph is a hyperbola. Choice B is not satisfactory, since graph B would indicate that the volume of the gas could be reduced to zero.

40. (A) This refers to Ohm's law.
$V = IR$. As the applied voltage increases, the current increases. The only graph which shows such a variation is graph A.

41. (B) When the external resistance is zero (a short circuit across the dry cell), the current supplied by the dry cell is large, but not infinite. (In a 6-in. dry cell this current may be about 30 amperes.) This value is represented by point K on graph B. As the external resistance becomes larger and larger, the current becomes less and less, approaching zero as the external resistance becomes that of an insulator. This cannot be the graph of a straight line, such as graph E.
$I = \dfrac{E}{r + R}$, where E is the emf of the cell, r its internal resistance, and R the external resistance.

42. (A) An oblique ray is bent towards the normal when it enters a medium in which the wave is slowed up. In the diagram, the ray is shown bent more and more towards the normal as it goes from medium I towards medium IV. The light travels more slowly in each of the successive media.

43. (B) A bright-line spectrum is usually obtained from a glowing gas or vapor. In the laboratory, sodium vapor is often used as the source of such a spectrum. A special sodium vapor lamp may be used; frequently ordinary salt (sodium chloride) is sprinkled into the gas flame, giving the necessary light. Glowing tungsten, platinum, or nichrome provide a continuous spectrum. The sun's spectrum contains the dark absorption lines, known as *Fraunhofer lines*.

44. (E) The rainbow colors of soap bubbles and oil films are produced by interference of light.

45. (A) Hold a pencil in a vertical position in front of you. Imagine that you are facing north. Then to the left of the pencil is west. Imagine the compass placed to the left of the pencil. According to the question, the compass needle points south. Apply the left hand rule: grasp the wire with your left hand so that your fingers, when on the left side of the wire, will point south. To do this, your thumb will have to point down; this gives the direction of electron flow.

46. (C) When switch S is open, it has no effect on the circuit. R_1 is then in series with the parallel combination of R_2 and R_3. The combined resistance of R_2 and R_3, two equal resistors in parallel, is $R/n = 40\ \Omega/2 = 20\ \Omega$. The total resistance of the circuit then is $R_1 + 20\ \Omega = 40\ \Omega + 20\ \Omega = 60\ \Omega$. $I_1 = I_T = V_T/R_T = 120\ \text{V}/60\ \Omega = 2\ \text{A}$.

47. (A) The effect of closing the switch is to eliminate the effect of R_1 from the circuit. The circuit is the same as though we had only the parallel combination of R_2 and R_3 connected to the 120-volt source through a fuse. (If you wish, you can think of the zero-resistance switch in parallel with R_1; the resistance of this parallel combination is zero ohms.)
The full 120 V is then applied to R_2 (and also to R_3). $I_2 = V_2/R_2 = 120\ \text{V}/40\ \Omega = 3\ \text{A}$

48. (D) If two nonmagnetic objects repel each other, both objects must be electrified, and the charge on the two must be of the same kind; both positive or both negative. Hence, since X repels Z, X must be charged, but it may be positive or negative. A charged object will attract neutral objects and objects oppositely charged. Since charged object X attracts Y, Y may be neutral or charged.

49. (E) Heat required = heat to raise temp. of ice to 0° C + heat to melt ice at 0° C.
Heat required = mass $\times$ sp. ht. $\times$ temp. change + mass $\times$ heat of fusion
$\quad\quad\quad\quad = 20\ \text{g} \times 0.5\ \text{cal/g} \times 5°\ \text{C} + 20\ \text{g} \times 80\ \text{cal/g}$
$\quad\quad\quad\quad = 50\ \text{cal} + 1600\ \text{cal}$
$\quad\quad\quad\quad = 1650\ \text{cal}$

50. (A) This question refers to Young's double slit experiment. When monochromatic light passes through two small slits, a series of bright lines is seen on a distant screen. The distance x of the first maximum or bright line away from the central maximum can be calculated from the following relationship:

$$\frac{x}{L} = \frac{\lambda}{d}$$

where L is the distance from the slits to the screen
$\quad \lambda$ is the wavelength of the light
$\quad d$ is the distance between the slits.
Substituting, we get:

$$\frac{x}{2.0\ \text{m}} = \frac{6 \times 10^{-7}\ \text{m}}{2 \times 10^{-6}\ \text{m}}$$
$$x = 6 \times 10^{-1}\ \text{meter}.$$

51. (A) In the interference pattern, wherever there is a bright region or maximum, the waves from the two slits must arrive in phase. This means that they must arrive a whole number of wavelengths apart, which means that the path length from the two slits to the bright regions must differ by a whole number of wavelengths. The path difference to the first maximum is one wavelength.

52. (B) From the above formula, we see that x and λ are proportional to each other. (If we increase the numerator on the left, we must also increase the one on the right to keep the two fractions equal.) Therefore, if the wavelength is increased, the distance x between the two maxima also increases.

53. (A) From the above formula, we see that x is proportional to L, the distance between the slits and the screen. (If the numerator of the fraction increases, the denominator must also increase if the value of the fraction doesn't change.) Therefore, when the screen is moved closer to the slits, the distance between the two maxima also decreases.

54. (E) At constant pressure, the volume of a gas is proportional to the absolute temperature. The absolute temperature increases from $(273 + 30)$ K to $(273 + 60)$ K. An increase from 303 to 333 is an increase of about 10%. The volume should also increase by about 10%.

55. (A) Brass is nonmagnetic and cannot be magnetized. Therefore its motion with respect to a conductor will not induce a current in the conductor.

56. (A) Yellow light may be light of a single wavelength, or it may be the result of a mixture of two or more wavelengths. For example, you should know that, if red and green light are mixed, yellow light is produced. The visible range of light is approximately 3900 — 7800 angstrom units.

57. (B) By definition, since the liquid is volatile, it will vaporize readily at room temperature. The space at X will be quickly saturated with the vapor, as will the space in Y. Since the space at X is kept cold by use of the ice, the saturated vapor coming to X from Y contains more vapor than it can hold at the lower temperature. Some of the vapor condenses, producing liquid at X. Since the pressure of the vapor in X becomes less than the pressure of the vapor near Y, more vapor keeps being pushed over to X, where it condenses. More and more of the liquid has to disappear from Y.

58. (B) Boyle's law applies. Since the volume is quadrupled, the pressure is reduced to one-fourth of its original value: from 4 atmospheres to 1 atmosphere. The pressure of 1 atmosphere is the same as the pressure of a column of mercury 76 cm high.

59. (E) Answer choices (A), (B), (C), and (D) are not correct because I, II, III, and IV are all true. If air is saturated, its relative humidity is 100% whether the temperature is high or low. The mass of the water vapor that gives 100% relative humidity will vary with the temperature.

60. (E) We may use the molecular theory of magnetism and the law of magnets to determine what will happen. The molecular magnets in the washer-pieces will orient themselves so that, near the poles of the permanent magnet, opposite poles will predominate: at X mostly S-poles. The opposite poles of the molecular magnets have to point in the opposite direction from X. Hence, at Y and W, N-poles will predominate. The reverse happens in the other half of the washer, which is nearer to the S-pole. Therefore Z will be an S-pole.

61. (B) An emf is induced in a wire when it cuts across magnetic flux lines. This emf is maximum when the wire cuts across at right angles to the flux, and it is then equal to the product of the magnetic flux density, the length of wire in the field, and the speed of cutting:

$$\text{emf} = BLv$$
$$0.003 \text{ V} = B\,(0.15 \text{ m})\,(4 \text{ m/s})$$
$$B = 0.005 \text{ tesla}$$

62. (E) As stated in question 61, the emf is maximum when the angle of cutting is 90°. It is less for any other angle. Only choice (E) satisfies this. (Actually the emf is proportional to the sine of the angle. The sine of 30° is 0.5.)

63. (C) The weight of an object on the Earth is equal to the product of the object's mass and the free-fall acceleration at that place on the Earth:

$$w = mg$$
$$= (5.0 \text{ kg})\,(9.8 \text{ m/s}^2)$$
$$= 49 \text{ N}$$

Note that 1 newton = 1 kg•m/s².

64. (D) Usually objects become electrically charged by gaining or losing electrons. Since electrons are negatively charged, the wool cloth had to lose electrons to become positively charged.

65. (A) When the amplitude of a wave is increased, the energy of the wave increases. Since temperature and pressure of the air are constant at standard conditions, the speed of sound would remain constant. Since frequency is being kept constant, the wavelength must also remain constant because the speed of a wave equals the product of frequency and wavelength. The period is the reciprocal of frequency, so it is also constant. Direction is not involved.

66. (A) A magnetic field is produced by an electric current; an electric current in a wire consists of moving electrons. Neutrons are electrically neutral; magnetic fields are not produced by a stream of neutral particles. Stationary particles do not produce a magnetic field.

67. (B) The electric field is defined as the force exerted on a unit charge placed in that field:

$$E = \frac{F}{q}$$

This shows that the force on any charge placed in the field is proportional to the field and the magnitude of the charge:

$$F = Eq$$

If the charge is doubled. the force is also doubled.

68. (B) The temperature at which water is densest is 4° C. This is approximately 39° F. The temperatures 0° C and 100° C are fixed points on the thermometer, but are not the temperatures where water is densest.

69. (B) On a graph of velocity against time, the distance traveled (actually the displacement) is given by the area under the graph. Another method, which we shall use here, is to multiply the average speed by the time traveled. The graph for the first two seconds is an oblique straight line. This represents motion with constant acceleration. For such motion the average speed is the sum of the initial and final speeds divided by two. The initial speed is zero. The average speed is (final speed/2) = (4 m/s)/2 = 2m/s.

$$\text{distance} = \text{(average speed) (time)}$$
$$= \text{(2 m/s) (2 s)}$$
$$= 4\ m$$

70. (C) We shall first find the total distance traveled during the first 4 seconds. We already know the distance traveled during the first 2 s. During the 3rd second, the speed remains constant at 4 m/s.

$$\text{distance} = \text{(4 m/s) (1 s)}$$
$$= 4\ m$$

During the 4th second the average speed is again equal to (4 m/s)/2, or 2 m/s.

$$\text{distance} = \text{(2 m/s) (1 s)}$$
$$= 2\ m$$

Total distance = (4 m + 4 m + 2 m) = 10 m.

$$\text{Average speed} = \text{(total distance)/time}$$
$$= \text{(10 m)/4 s}$$
$$= 2.5\ m/s$$

71. (D) Two points in a wave are in phase if they are going through the same part of the vibration at the same time. We can think of the diagram as

representing a periodic wave which is continuously transmitting energy to the right. *Two points in phase are then a whole number of wavelengths apart.* In the above diagram one wavelength is the distance between *K* and *L*, two adjacent peaks on the curve. This is equal to the distance from *A* to *Y*. We can think of the curve *ABKCY* as completing one cycle; then the same wave pattern is shown again by the curve *YLD*. The distance between *Y* and *D* is another wavelength. *D* is 2 wavelengths from *A*. Points *A*, *Y*, and *D* are going through the same part of the vibration at the same time.

72. (A) The *Doppler effect* deals with the apparent change in the frequency of a wave when there is relative motion between the source of the wave and an observer. Here we are told that the vibrating source is moving. The circles represent the spherical wave fronts produced by the source. The wavelength is the distance between two adjacent wave fronts—in this diagram, the distance between two adjacent circles. If the source were stationary, the distance between wave fronts would be the same in all directions. We notice in the diagram that the circles are much closer to each other near point 1 than anywhere else.

This shows that the source keeps moving closer to point 1 as it sends out compressions. At the same time it keeps moving away from point 2. As the wave reaches an observer at point 1, he would get a wave whose length, and therefore whose frequency, is different from what it would be if the source were stationary. Its frequency would be greater than the actual frequency of the source.

73. (B) Students are often confused about this part of the Doppler effect. In the above question the source was moving with constant velocity towards point 1. An observer at point 1 would get a wave of constant frequency and wavelength, but different from what it would be if the source were stationary. If the source now starts to move faster, it would tend to catch up with the wave front it has just sent out towards point 1. The new wave front would therefore be closer to the preceding wave front than if the source were moving with constant velocity. The wavelength therefore would decrease.

74. (B) As we lower the frequency of the radiation incident on a photoemissive material, the maximum kinetic energy of the photoelectrons becomes less and less. The energy of the photon which would just give it zero kinetic energy is the work function of this material. Its frequency would be the threshold frequency, f_0. On the graph this is the point where the graph intersects the axis, 2×10^{14} Hz. The value of the work function is equal to the product of Planck's constant and the threshold frequency:

$$\text{work function} = hf_0$$
$$= h\,(2 \times 10^{14}\,\text{Hz})$$

75. (D) The force on an electron moving at right angles to a uniform magnetic flux is equal to the product of the flux density, the charge of the electron, and the speed of the electron ($F = qvB$). If the flux density is doubled, the force is doubled.

PRACTICE TEST 4
Part A

DIRECTIONS: *For each group of questions below, there is a set of five lettered choices, followed by numbered questions. For each question select the one choice in the set that best answers the question. You may use a lettered choice once, more than once, or not at all in each set.*

QUESTIONS 1-3 refer to the following situation. A 70-newton object rests on the middle of a rough horizontal board. Then one end of the board is raised slowly, rotating the board through an angle of 50° without causing the object to slide.

(A) It remains zero. **(B)** It remains 70 newtons. **(C)** It first increases and then decreases. **(D)** It steadily decreases. **(E)** It steadily increases.

 1. While one end of the board is being raised, what is the effect on the force of friction between the board and the object?
 2. What is the effect on the normal force between the board and the object?
 3. What is the effect on the gravitational pull on the object?

QUESTIONS 4-5 refer to the graph, which shows how the lengths of certain materials change as they are heated.

 4. Which material has the largest coefficient of expansion?

 5. Which material is shown as being heated to the highest temperature?

QUESTIONS 6-7 deal with the following subatomic particles:

(A) Photon   **(B)** Electron   **(C)** Meson   **(D)** Alpha particle   **(E)** Proton

 6. Which particle always has the same charge as the positron?
 7. The mass of which particle is the same as that of the positron?

QUESTIONS 8-10 refer to an experiment in which a ball is projected vertically upward from the surface of the earth and reaches its maximum height in 4.0 seconds.

(A) Zero   **(B)** 20   **(C)** 40   **(D)** 80   **(E)** 100

 8. Approximately what was the ball's initial speed, in meters per second?
 9. Approximately what was the maximum height, in meters, reached by the ball?
10. What is the total displacement, in meters, of the ball from the time it is thrown until it returns to the point from which it was thrown?

 QUESTIONS 11–13 refer to the diagram, which represents a 6.0 kilogram object being moved at constant speed along a straight line on a level surface by a force of 10.0 newtons.

(A) Zero   **(B)** Less than 2, but not zero   **(C)** 2   **(D)** 10   **(E)** 20

11. What is the change in kinetic energy, in joules, of the object as it moves from point *X* to point *Y*?
12. If energy is supplied at the rate of 10 watts, how much energy, in joules, is supplied in 2 seconds?
13. If the object's momentum is 12 kilogram•meters per second, what is its velocity, in meters per second?

QUESTIONS 14-15 refer to the concept of conductivity.

(A) Free electrons, only   **(B)** Positive ions, only   **(C)** Negative ions, only   **(D)** Positive and negative ions, only   **(E)** Positive ions, negative ions, and electrons

14. On which does the conductivity in metallic wires depend?

15. On which does the conductivity of salt solutions depend?

Part B

DIRECTIONS: *Each of the following questions or incomplete statements is followed by five choices. Select the choice that best answers the question or completes the statement.*

16. Three forces are acting on a particle in equilibrium. The three forces are 6, 8, and 10 newtons, respectively. The resultant of the 8-newton and 10-newton forces has a magnitude of   **(A)** 2 N   **(B)** 6 N   **(C)** 9 N   **(D)** 13 N   **(E)** 18 N

17. Two rectangular tanks stand next to each other on a horizontal table. The area of the bottom of the first tank is 40 square centimeters; that of the second tank is 80 square centimeters. Both tanks are filled with water to the same height. The ratio of the liquid pressure on the bottom of the second tank to that on the bottom of the first tank is   **(A)** 1   **(B)** 2   **(C)** 4   **(D)** 8   **(E)** 16

For 18–21. Base your answers on the graph below, which represents the motion of cars *A* and *B* on straight parallel tracks. Car *B* passes car *A* at the same instant that car *A* starts from rest at *t* = 0 second.

18. What is the acceleration, in meters per second squared, of car *A* during the interval between *t* = 0 and *t* = 60 seconds?   **(A)** 0   **(B)** 1   **(C)** 20   **(D)** 30   **(E)** 40

19. How far did car *A* travel in the interval between *t* = 0 and *t* = 60?   **(A)** 15 m   **(B)** 30 m   **(C)** 360 m   **(D)** 1800 m   **(E)** 3600 m

20. How long, in seconds, after *t* = 0 did it take car *A* to catch up to car *B*?   **(A)** 0   **(B)** 10   **(C)** 20   **(D)** 30   **(E)** 60

21. During the time intervals given below, which car traveled the greatest distance?   **(A)** car *B* from *t* = 0 to *t* = 30   **(B)** car *B* from *t* = 30 to *t* = 60   **(C)** car *A* from *t* = 0 to *t* = 20   **(D)** car *A* from *t* = 20 to *t* = 40   **(E)** car *A* from *t* = 40 to *t* = 60

22. Two freely falling objects, one 10 pounds and one 20 pounds, are dropped from the same height at the same time. Air resistance is negligible. Which of the following statements is (are) true?

    I. Both objects have the same potential energy at the top.
    II. Both objects fall with the same acceleration.
    III. Both objects have the same speed just before hitting the ground.

  (A) I only
  (B) III only
  (C) I and II only
  (D) II and III only
  (E) I, II, and III

23. Which of the following units may be used to express the amount of heat absorbed by a body?

    I. Calories
    II. Joules
    III. Ergs

  (A) I only
  (B) III only
  (C) I and II only
  (D) II and III only
  (E) I, II, and III

24. A steel ball is projected horizontally from a certain height. It hits the ground in 10 seconds. If air resistance is negligible, and the initial speed of the object is 30 meters per second, its acceleration during the third second is   **(A)** 980 cm/s^2 **(B)** 32 cm/s^2 **(C)** 96 cm/s^2 **(D)** 327 cm/s^2 **(E)** greater than during the first second

25. The horizontal distance traveled by the steel ball in question 24 during the first 5 seconds is   **(A)** 150 m   **(B)** 160 m   **(C)** 80 m   **(D)** 20.5 m   **(E)** 4900 m

26. If a stone at the end of a string is whirled in a circle, the inward pull of the string on the stone   **(A)** is known as the centrifugal force   **(B)** is inversely proportional to the speed of the object   **(C)** is inversely proportional to the square of the speed   **(D)** is proportional to the speed   **(E)** is proportional to the square of the speed

27. Momentum is a quantity whose unit might be the   **(A)** foot-pound   **(B)** erg   **(C)** newton   **(D)** gram•centimeter per second   **(E)** calorie per second

28. A man weighing 600 newtons pushes against a box with a force of 20 newtons, but the box does not move. The box weighs 3000 newtons. The force which the box exerts on the man is   **(A)** zero   **(B)** 20 N   **(C)** 100 N   **(D)** 150 N   **(E)** 3000 N

29. A change in temperature of 45° C corresponds to a change in Fahrenheit degrees of   **(A)** 25   **(B)** 45   **(C)** 81   **(D)** 113   **(E)** 7

30. A temperature of 300° C corresponds to an absolute temperature in kelvin units of   **(A)** 27   **(B)** −27   **(C)** 523   **(D)** 573   **(E)** 572

31. A rod is made of a certain metal which has a coefficient of linear expansion of 0.000020 per Celsius degree. The rod is 100 centimeters long, has a diameter of 2.0 centimeters, and is heated from 30° C to 60° C. The change in length of the rod is   **(A)** negligible   **(B)** 0.00060 cm   **(C)** 0.0060 cm   **(D)** 0.060 cm   **(E)** 0.12 cm

32. The diameter of the rod in question 31, after heating, will be   **(A)** still 2.0 cm   **(B)** slightly more than 2.0 cm   **(C)** more than 3.0 cm   **(D)** slightly less than 2.0 cm   **(E)** less than 1.5 cm

33. The bending of a bimetallic strip when heated is due primarily   **(A)** to the good conductivity of the two metals   **(B)** the large coefficient of expansion of both metals   **(C)** the unequal expansion of the two metals   **(D)** the unequal specific gravity of the two metals   **(E)** the effect of gravity

34. An object weighing 40 newtons is dragged a distance of 20 meters by a force of 5 newtons in the direction of motion. The work done by the 5-newton force   **(A)** is 5 J   **(B)** is 100 J   **(C)** is 200 J   **(D)** is 800 J   **(E)** cannot be calculated without knowing the force of friction

35. A man holds two solid steel objects above the ground; one weighs 10 newtons and the other 20 newtons. As compared with the potential energy of the 10-newton object, the potential energy of the 20-newton object is   **(A)** greater even if air is present   **(B)** greater only in vacuum   **(C)** the same even if air is present   **(D)** the same only in absence of air   **(E)** less

36. If a gas is heated at constant pressure, which of the following descriptions will apply?

     I. Its volume increase is proportional to the temperature.
     II. The kinetic energy of the molecules decreases.
     III. The kinetic energy of the molecules increases.

  (A) I only
  (B) III only
  (C) I and II only
  (D) I and III only
  (E) II and III only

37. A certain mass of water is cooled from 3° C to 2° C. Which of the following statements is (are) true?

     I. Its density increases.
     II. Its density decreases.
     III. More H_2O molecules form bonds with each other.

  (A) I only
  (B) III only
  (C) I and II only
  (D) I and III only
  (E) II and III only

38. An electric transformer intended to be used with 220-volt alternating current is accidentally connected to low-voltage direct current. Which of the following statements is (are) true?

     I. Eddy currents will be practically zero.
     II. The emf induced in the secondary winding will be practically zero.
     III. Hysteresis losses will be practically zero.

  (A) I only
  (B) III only
  (C) I and II only
  (D) II and III only
  (E) I, II, and III only

39. A 20-ohm and a 60-ohm resistor are connected in series to a DC generator. The voltage across the 20-ohm resistor is 80 volts. The current through the 60-ohm resistor   **(A)** cannot be calculated with the given information   **(B)** is about 1.3 A   **(C)** is 4.0 A   **(D)** is 1.0 A   **(E)** is 5.0 A

40. A stone is thrown vertically upward from sea level to a height of 20 meters. Assume that air resistance is negligible. After the stone leaves the hand, its acceleration is **(A)** downward at a decreasing value until it reaches its highest point   **(B)** upward at a decreasing value until it reaches its highest point   **(C)** upward at 9.8 m/s^2 **(D)** not known   **(E)** none of the above

41. An object is placed 10 centimeters from a concave spherical mirror whose radius of curvature is 12 centimeters. What is the distance of the image from the mirror?   **(A)** 5 cm   **(B)** 10 cm   **(C)** 15 cm   **(D)** 20 cm   **(E)** 24 cm

42. If two sounds have the same wavelength in air at the same temperature, what other property must they also have in common?

  I. Intensity
  II. Amplitude
  III. Frequency

  (A) I only
  (B) III only
  (C) I and II only
  (D) II and III only
  (E) I, II, and III

43. Two frequencies sounded together produce 3 beats per second. If one of the frequencies is 400 vibrations per second, what may the other frequency be?

  I. 1200 vib/sec
  II. 403 vib/sec
  III. 397 vib/sec

  (A) I only
  (B) III only
  (C) I and II only
  (D) II and III only
  (E) I, II, and III

44. Two conducting spheres are negatively charged. The distance between them is 20 cm. The force that these two spheres exert on each other is 4.0×10^{-4} newton. If the distance between them is increased to 40 cm, the electrostatic force between them becomes, in newtons, **(A)** 1.0×10^{-4} **(B)** 2.0 **(C)** 2.0×10^{-4} **(D)** 8.0×10^{-4} **(E)** 1.6

45. A 3.0-centimeter length of wire is moved at right angles across a magnetic field with a speed of 2.0 meters per second. If the flux density is 10 teslas, what is the magnitude of the induced emf? **(A)** 0.06 V **(B)** 0.6 V **(C)** 1.2 V **(D)** 10 V **(E)** 20 V

46. With which of the following may a virtual image be obtained?

  I. Plane mirror
  II. Convex lens
  III. Concave lens

  (A) I only
  (B) III only
  (C) I and II only
  (D) II and III only
  (E) I, II, and III

47. An electric toaster-oven is rated 120 volts, 1500 watts. What is the resistance of the heater coil when it operates under these conditions, and what is the current going through it? **(A)** 12.5 Ω, 9.6 A **(B)** 1190 Ω, 8.0 A **(C)** 8.0 Ω, 15.0 A **(D)** 18.7 Ω, 8.0 A **(E)** 9.6 Ω, 12.5 A

48. A ^{238}U nucleus differs from a ^{235}U nucleus in that it contains three more **(A)** neutrons **(B)** alpha particles **(C)** protons **(D)** electrons **(E)** positrons

49. The mass of a $_2^4He$ nucleus is **(A)** 2 g **(B)** 4 g **(C)** equal to the mass of two protons plus two electrons **(D)** equal to the mass of two protons plus two neutrons **(E)** slightly less than the mass of two protons plus two neutrons

50. If graphite is used in a nuclear reactor, its function is to **(A)** absorb alpha particles **(B)** absorb neutrons **(C)** slow down neutrons **(D)** absorb electrons **(E)** slow down electrons

51. A gamma ray photon makes a collision with an electron at rest. During the interaction the change in the photon will be **(A)** a decrease in momentum only **(B)** a decrease in kinetic energy only **(C)** an increase in momentum only **(D)** an increase in kinetic energy only **(E)** a decrease in momentum and kinetic energy

52. X rays consist of **(A)** a stream of neutrons **(B)** a stream of Compton particles **(C)** a stream of electrons **(D)** radiation similar to radon **(E)** radiation similar to gamma rays

53. If a lens produces an image the same size as the object when the object is 20 centimeters from the lens, then the largest real image of this object can be obtained when the distance of the object from the lens is approximately **(A)** 5 cm **(B)** 10 cm **(C)** 15 cm **(D)** 30 cm **(E)** 40 cm

54. If two sounds have the same pitch but different loudness, the louder sound has **(A)** the higher frequency **(B)** the lower frequency **(C)** the greater amplitude **(D)** the smaller amplitude **(E)** the greater repetition rate

55. For a given sound wave traveling through air at constant temperature, the speed of a compression **(A)** is unrelated to the speed of the rarefaction **(B)** is the same as the speed of the rarefaction **(C)** is always less than the speed of the rarefaction **(D)** is always greater than the speed of the rarefaction **(E)** is greater than the speed of the rarefaction only when the temperature is greater than the critical temperature

56. During the time that sound travels 1100 feet in air, light can travel in vacuum a distance of about **(A)** 1100 mi **(B)** 200,000 ft **(C)** 200,000 m **(D)** 200,000 mi **(E)** 200,000 km

57. Maximum destructive interference of two waves occurs at points where the phase difference between the two waves is **(A)** 0° **(B)** 45° **(C)** 90° **(D)** 180° **(E)** 270°

58. In the diagram below, a metal sphere M, whose mass is 2.0 kilograms, is suspended by a string from point P, as in a pendulum. The sphere is released from a vertical height h and passes through its

lowest position (sometimes referred to as its *rest position*) with a speed of 10 meters per second. The height h from which the object was released is approximately   **(A)** 2.5 m **(B)** 5.0 m **(C)** 7 m **(D)** 8 m **(E)** 9 m

59. In question 58, the centripetal force on object M as it passes through the rest position is approximately **(A)** 10 N **(B)** 20 N **(C)** 50 N **(D)** 200 N **(E)** 2000 N

60. It is desired to reduce the resistance of a coil of wire to one-half of its value. Which of the following methods will accomplish this?

   I. Cut off one-half of the wire.
   II. Reduce the coil's temperature to one-half of its value.
   III. Double the current.

(A) I only
(B) III only
(C) I and II only
(D) II and III only
(E) I, II, and III

61. An object with a mass of 4.0 kilograms is kept motionless on an inclined plane by a force parallel to the plane. The angle of the incline is 30°; the object is at a vertical height of 10 meters above the bottom; friction is negligible. What is the value of the force, in newtons? **(A)** 4.0 **(B)** 4.9 **(C)** 9.8 **(D)** 19.6 **(E)** 39.2

62. Since light rays are always diverged by concave lenses, such lenses **(A)** cannot form images **(B)** form only black and white images **(C)** form only inverted images **(D)** form only erect images **(E)** form only magnified images

63. For measuring resistance quickly, the most useful device is the **(A)** resistometer **(B)** voltmeter **(C)** ohmmeter **(D)** potentiometer **(E)** pyknometer

64. All of the following pure elements are good electrical conductors EXCEPT **(A)** copper **(B)** aluminum **(C)** silver **(D)** silicon **(E)** iron

65. All of the following can become good magnets EXCEPT **(A)** iron **(B)** cobalt **(C)** nickel **(D)** a solenoid **(E)** copper

66. The most common isotope of each of the following elements is radioactive EXCEPT **(A)** lead **(B)** polonium **(C)** radium **(D)** radon **(E)** uranium

67. All of the following may be used to express a quantity of energy EXCEPT the **(A)** joule **(B)** kilogram•meter squared per second squared **(C)** newton per second **(D)** watt-hour **(E)** erg

68. All of the following refer to electromagnetic waves EXCEPT **(A)** X rays **(B)** beta rays **(C)** gamma rays **(D)** radio waves **(E)** red light

69. By which of the following can cathode rays be appreciably deflected?

    I. An electric field
    II. A nearby stationary magnet
    III. A magnetic field

  (A) I only
  (B) III only
  (C) I and II only
  (D) II and III only
  (E) I, II, and III

70. A neutral body is rubbed and its charge becomes positive. It must have **(A)** gained positrons **(B)** gained protons **(C)** gained neutrons **(D)** lost protons **(E)** lost electrons

For 71–73. Two parallel slits are 1.0×10^{-3} meter apart. The light passing through them has a wavelength of 5.4×10^{-7} meter. It falls on a viewing screen 2.0 meters away from the slits.

71. What is the wavelength of the light, in millimeters? **(A)** 5.4×10^{-3} **(B)** 5.4×10^{-4} **(C)** 5.4×10^{-6} **(D)** 5.4×10^{-10} **(E)** 5.4×10^{4}

72. Approximately what is the distance, in meters, between the central bright band and the first band next to it? **(A)** 1.1×10^{-3} **(B)** 2.1×10^{-3} **(C)** 2.6×10^{-3} **(D)** 3.0×10^{-3} **(E)** 3.6×10^{-3}

73. Approximately what is the distance between the first and second bright bands compared with the correct answer for question 72? **(A)** the same **(B)** half as much **(C)** twice as much **(D)** 2½ times as much **(E)** three times as much

74. The approximate speed of light in water is, in meters per second, **(A)** 5.8×10^{8} **(B)** 1.0×10^{8} **(C)** 2.3×10^{8} **(D)** 2.8×10^{8} **(E)** 3.0×10^{8}

75. When switch *S* is open as shown in the diagram, what is the difference of potential between points *A* and *B*?   **(A)** zero   **(B)** 20 V   **(C)** 30 V   **(D)** 40 V   **(E)** 60 V

ANSWERS FOR PRACTICE TEST 4

Answer Key for Test 4

1. E	16. B	31. D	46. E	61. D
2. D	17. A	32. B	47. E	62. D
3. B	18. B	33. C	48. A	63. C
4. A	19. D	34. B	49. E	64. D
5. B	20. E	35. A	50. C	65. E
6. E	21. E	36. B	51. E	66. A
7. B	22. D	37. E	52. E	67. C
8. C	23. E	38. E	53. B	68. B
9. D	24. A	39. C	54. C	69. E
10. A	25. A	40. E	55. B	70. E
11. A	26. E	41. C	56. D	71. B
12. E	27. D	42. B	57. D	72. A
13. C	28. B	43. D	58. B	73. A
14. A	29. C	44. A	59. B	74. C
15. D	30. D	45. B	60. A	75. E

Explained Answers for Test 4

1. (E) As long as there is no sliding, the force of friction is just equal and opposite to the component of the weight parallel to the plane. This component is zero when the plane is horizontal and steadily increases when the angle of incline increases: component parallel to the plane is equal to the weight times the height of the plane divided by the length of the plane.

2. (D) The normal force is the component perpendicular to the board. It is equal to the weight when the plane is horizontal and steadily decreases as the angle of incline increases: component perpendicular to the plane is equal to the weight multiplied by the base divided by the length of the plane.

3. (B) The gravitational pull on the object is practically the Earth's pull on it toward the center of the Earth. It is the weight of the object even when it is supported.

4. (A) Change in length = original length × temp. change × coeff. of linear expansion. Since all materials shown start with the same length, the one that has the greatest change in length after a given temperature change has the greatest coefficient. This is true of choice (A). Another way to think of the problem is to say that the material with the greatest slope has the largest coefficient.

5. (B) The lines have been drawn so that choice (B) goes furthest to the right, the direction of the temperature axis. From the graphs we can't tell what the other materials will do at the higher temperatures. For example, they might melt.

6. (E) The positron has a single positive charge equal to that of the proton. The alpha particle has twice this charge. The charge of the electron is negative. Mesons may be positive, negative, or neutral. Photons have no charge.

7. (B) The *positron* is the antiparticle of the electron. It has the same mass as the electron, but an equal and opposite charge.

8. (C) Throughout its upward motion the ball is slowed down by the acceleration due to gravity. Since the final speed at the top is momentarily zero, the initial speed is equal to the product of the acceleration due to gravity and the time to reach the top:

$$v = gt = (9.8 \text{ m/s}^2)(4.0 \text{ s}) = 39.2 \text{ m/s}$$

9. (D) One method we can use to calculate the distance traveled is to multiply the average speed by the time of travel: distance = ($\frac{1}{2}$ × 39.2 m/s) (4 s) = 78 m.

10. (A) The *displacement* of an object is the change in its position. It is a vector quantity and is the distance from the starting point to the end point (in the direction from the first point to the second one). Here the two points coincide; therefore the displacement is zero.

11. (A) The *kinetic energy* of an object is equal to one-half of the product of its mass and the square of its speed. Here the mass and speed do not change. Therefore the kinetic energy does not change, either.

12. (E) One watt is equivalent to one joule per second. If energy is supplied at the rate of 10 joules per second, then in 2 seconds, 20 joules are supplied.

13. (C) The momentum of an object is equal to the product of its mass and its velocity:

$$\text{momentum} = \text{mass} \times \text{velocity}$$
$$12 \text{ kg} \cdot \text{m/s} = (6.0 \text{ kg})(v)$$
$$v = 2 \text{ m/s}$$

14. (A) In metals some electrons are only loosely held by the atoms. When a difference of potential is applied to the wire, these electrons are free to move in the direction opposite to the electric field. The rest of the atom is fixed in position.

15. (D) The solid salts have a crystalline structure consisting of positive and negative ions. When the salts are dissolved in a liquid such as water, they dissociate and the negative ions are free to move toward a positive electrode, and the positive ions toward a negative electrode.

16. (B) If three forces acting on a particle are in equilibrium, any one force is the equilibrant of the other two. Therefore, the 6-N force is the equilibrant of the 8-N and 10-N forces. But the equilibrant is equal and opposite to the resultant.

17. (A) Liquid pressure = depth × density. Depth and density of the water are the same in both tanks. Liquid pressure is independent of the area of the bottom. Therefore the pressure in both tanks is the same.

18. (B) *Acceleration* is defined as the change in velocity divided by the time in which the change takes place:

$$a = \Delta v / \Delta t$$

Car A starts from rest: its initial speed is zero. At the end of the 60 s, its speed, as read from the graph, is 60 m/s. Therefore its acceleration is
$$a = (60 \text{ m/s})/(60 \text{ s}) = 1 \text{ m/s}^2$$

19. (D) For an object starting from rest and moving with constant acceleration, the distance traveled is equal to one-half the product of its acceleration and the square of the time traveled:
$$\text{distance} = \tfrac{1}{2} \, at^2$$
$$= \tfrac{1}{2} \, (1 \text{ m/s}^2) \, (60 \text{ s})^2 = 1800 \text{ m}$$

20. (E) We see from the graph that car B is traveling with a constant speed of 30 m/s. For objects moving with constant speed, the distance traveled is equal to the product of that speed and the length of time traveled:
$$\text{distance} = \text{speed} \times \text{time} = 30t$$

In this question car A covers the same distance as car B in the same time. We set the two expressions for·distance equal to each other.
$$\tfrac{1}{2} \, at^2 = 30t$$

We recall that $a = 1$ m/s². Making that substitution, and dividing both sides by t, we get $\tfrac{1}{2} \, t = 30$. Therefore $t = 60$ s.

21. (E) Probably the easiest way to do this question is to examine the graph and to make use of the fact that, on a graph of speed against time, the distance traveled is given by the area under the graph. Let us consider the first two choices. Car B travels at a constant speed. In each of the 30-second intervals the area under the graph is 9 squares. For car A we have to examine 20-second intervals. We can notice quickly that for the first two intervals the area is small: two squares for the first one, and 5½ for the second one. For the third interval the area adds up to 10 squares.

22. (D) Acceleration is the same and constant for all falling objects, if air resistance is negligible. The speed of a falling object starting from rest is proportional to the acceleration and the time of fall, $v = at$, and both are independent of the mass of the object. The *potential energy* of the object is proportional to its mass. Only II and III are correct.

23. (E) Since heat is a form of energy, any unit of energy may be used to describe the quantity of heat.

24. (A) Horizontal motion does not affect vertical motion. The acceleration remains constant for the vertical motion and has the value of g, which is 980 cm/s² in the CGS system.

25. (A) Vertical motion does not affect horizontal motion. The speed in the horizontal direction remains constant: $s = vt$; $s = 30 \text{ m/s} \times 5 \text{ s} = 150 \text{ m}$.

26. (E) The pull of the string on the stone is the centripetal force. This force is proportional to the square of the speed of the object moving in the circle.

27. (D) Momentum is the product of mass and velocity. Therefore the unit of momentum is a unit of mass times a unit of velocity.

28. (B) This is an example of Newton's third law of motion: action equals reaction.

29. (C) This question deals not with actual temperatures but with temperature change. A change in Fahrenheit degrees equals ⁹⁄₅ times the change in Celsius degrees = (⁹⁄₅) (45) = 81.

30. (D) Kelvin units = ° C + 273° = 300° + 273° = 573 K.

31. (D) Change in length = original length × change in temperature × coefficient of linear expansion = 100 cm × (60 − 30) × 0.000020 per C deg = 0.060 cm. This is small, but may not be negligible in a given situation.

32. (B) For most substances the coefficient of linear expansion is the same in all directions. When the rod is heated, its diameter will also increase. As in question 31, the change will be small, even less than the 0.060 cm calculated there.

33. (C) The strip will bend in spite of gravity. The coefficients are quite small. The important thing is that the coefficients be different; the greater the difference, the greater the effect.

34. (B) Work done by the effort = effort × distance moved by effort in the direction of the force: 5 N × 20 m = 100 J.

35. (A) Potential energy (with respect to ground) = weight × vertical distance (above ground). The vertical distance is the same for both objects; therefore the heavier object has the greater potential energy. The presence of air has nothing to do with it.

36. (B) As a gas is heated at constant pressure, the kinetic energy of the molecules increases and the temperature rises. Perhaps you were misled by choice A. According to Charles' law, the volume (not the volume change) is proportional to the *absolute* temperature of the gas.

37. (E) Water is densest at 4° C. As the temperature goes in either direction from 4°, up or down, water gets less dense. Water molecules form hydrogen bonds with each other. These are abundant in ice and decrease in relative abundance as the temperature of water rises.

38. (E) Eddy currents, hysteresis, and induced emf depend on varying magnetic fields; they will not be produced by the steady magnetic field associated with a steady direct current.

39. (C) Across the 20-ohm resistor the voltage is 80 volts. Since current is equal to the ratio of voltage to resistance, it can be calculated:

$$I = \frac{80 \text{ V}}{20 \text{ } \Omega}$$
$$= 4 \text{ A}$$

In a series circuit, the current is the same everywhere. The 4 A also go through the 60-Ω resistor.

40. (E) Throughout the stone's motion the only force acting on it is the Earth's gravitational pull *downward*, since air resistance is negligible. According to Newton's second law of motion, the acceleration is in the direction of the unbalanced force.

41. (C) The calculation for a concave spherical mirror is similar to the calculation for a convex lens: the reciprocal of the object distance plus the reciprocal of the image distance is equal to the reciprocal of the focal length:

$$\frac{1}{p} + \frac{1}{q} = \frac{1}{f}$$

The focal length of a spherical mirror is one-half of its radius:

$$f = \frac{r}{2}$$
$$= \frac{12 \text{ cm}}{2}$$
$$= 6 \text{ cm}$$

Substituting in the above equation gives:

$$\frac{1}{10 \text{ cm}} + \frac{1}{q} = \frac{1}{6 \text{ cm}}$$
$$q = 15 \text{ cm}$$

42. (B) Wavelength = speed/frequency. At the same temperature, all sound waves have the same speed. Since the wavelength is the same, the frequency is also the same.

43. (D) The number of beats per second equals the difference between the two frequencies.

44. (A) The force between two point charges, or two charged conducting spheres, varies inversely as the square of the distance between them. When the distance between them increases, the electrostatic force between them decreases. When the distance between them becomes twice as great, the force between them becomes one-fourth as much:

$$(½)^2 (4.0 \times 10^{-4} \text{ N}) = 1.0 \times 10^{-4} \text{ N}$$

45. (B) When a wire is moved at right angles to a magnetic field, the voltage induced in the wire is equal to the product of the flux density, the length of wire in the field, and the speed with which the wire is moved:

$$V = Blv$$
$$= (10. \text{ T}) (0.03 \text{ m}) (2.0 \text{ m/s})$$
$$= 0.6 \text{ V}$$

46. (E) All images produced by plane mirrors, concave lenses, and convex mirrors are virtual. A virtual image may be obtained with a convex lens if the object is placed less than a focal length from the lens.

47. (E) The *power* consumed by an electric device is given by the relationship

$$P = V^2/R$$

where V is the voltage applied to the device, and R is the resistance of the device. Substituting, we get

$$1500 \text{ watts} = (120 \text{ V})^2/R$$
$$R = 9.6 \text{ }\Omega$$

According to Ohm's law, the current is

$$I = V/R$$
$$= (120 \text{ V})/9.6 \text{ }\Omega$$
$$= 12.5 \text{ A}$$

48. (A) Isotopes of the same element differ from each other in the number of neutrons in the nucleus.

49. (E) The $_2^4$He nucleus contains two protons and two neutrons; the total mass is a tiny fraction of a gram. The reason that the mass of the nucleus is slightly less than the sum of the masses of the individual particles is that significant energy (binding energy) would have to be used to break up the nucleus into separate protons and neutrons. The mass equivalent of this energy accounts for the greater mass of the sum of the isolated particles.

50. (C) Graphite is a *moderator* material used in nuclear reactors. Moderators slow down the neutrons during fission.

51. (E) This problem refers to the Compton effect. When a high-energy photon, such as we get from X rays and gamma rays, interacts with an electron, an elastic collision as between two particles results. Momentum and energy are conserved. The photon loses part of its energy and momentum to the electron.

52. (E) Choices (A), (B), (C), and (D) refer to particle emissions. Radon is a radioactive chemical element that emits alpha particles. X rays and gamma rays are both types of electromagnetic wave radiations.

53. (B) To produce an image the same size as the object, the object must be two focal lengths away from a convex lens. Therefore, $2f = 20$ cm; $f = 10$ cm. As the object gets closer and closer to the lens, the image on the screen becomes larger and larger. However, when the object distance is less than one focal length, a real image is no longer obtained.

54. (C) Other things remaining the same, the greater the amplitude of a sound wave the greater is the loudness.

55. (B) A sound wave in air consists of compressions and rarefactions traveling in succession away from the source. They travel with the same speed, the speed of the wave.

56. (D) It takes sound approximately 1 second to travel 1100 feet (330 meters) in air. In 1 second light travels 186,000 miles in air (3.0×10^8 meters or 300,000 kilometers).

57. (D) Two waves are 180° out of phase (or have a phase difference of 180°) when the peak of one coincides with the trough of the other. The two waves then interfere with each other destructively, and the resultant wave has an amplitude equal to the difference in amplitudes of the original waves. In the diagram below, waves IV and V are 180° out of phase. With this phase difference the amplitude of the resultant wave, wave VI, is a minimum. If the amplitudes of IV and V were equal, we would get complete annulment.

Waves IV and V tend to annual each other, producing VI

58. (B) The gain in gravitational potential energy of an object is equal to the product of its weight and the vertical height it is raised above the reference level. The weight of an object is equal to the product of its mass and the value of the acceleration due to gravity: $w = mg$. The reference level here is the lowest point during the swing. Therefore, when the object M is at its highest point, it has a potential energy with respect to the lowest point equal to mgh. At the lowest point, all of this has been converted to kinetic energy:

$$E_p = mgh = \tfrac{1}{2}mv^2$$
$$gh = \tfrac{1}{2}v^2$$
$$(9.8 \text{ m/s}^2)h = \tfrac{1}{2}(10 \text{ m/s})^2$$
$$h = 5.0 \text{ m}$$

59. (B) The centripetal force acting on an object is given by the expression $F_c = mv^2/r$. Making the substitution we obtain

$$F_c = \frac{(2 \text{ kg})(10 \text{ m/s})^2}{10 \text{ m}}$$
$$= 20 \text{ N}$$

60. (A) The resistance of a wire is practically independent of the applied voltage and the current through it (except for the change in temperature which may be produced). The resistance of a wire does depend on its temperature, but is not proportional to it. The resistance of a wire is proportional to its length.

61. (D) A quick sketch is helpful. For an inclined plane, the sine of the angle of incline is equal to the ratio of the component of the object's weight parallel to the plane, to the weight of the object.

$$\text{sine of angle} = \frac{\text{parallel component}}{\text{weight}}$$

When friction is negligible, the object can be kept from sliding by applying to it a force which is equal to this parallel component and directed opposite to it.

$$\text{sine of angle} = \frac{\text{force parallel to plane}}{\text{weight}}$$

The force parallel to the plane then equals (weight $\times$ sine of the angle)
$$= (4.0 \text{ kg}) (9.8 \text{ m/s}^2) (0.5) \overset{\bullet}{=} 20 \text{ N}$$

If the sine of the angle is not given, and you don't remember it, from your sketch you can get the ratio, height of plane/length.

62. (D) Diverging lenses always form erect, *virtual* images. That is, the light rays do not actually travel to the images.

63. (C) The ohmmeter is commonly used for quick measurements of resistance, if high precision is not needed.

64. (D) Among the solids, metals and graphite are good conductors of electricity. Silicon and germanium are semiconductors.

65. (E) Iron, nickel, and cobalt are good magnetic elements. A *solenoid* is a metallic coil wound around a magnetic core; when electric current goes through the coil, it becomes a magnet. The greater the current, the stronger is the magnet. Copper is not a magnetic substance.

66. (A) Radium, radon, and all the isotopes of uranium are radioactive elements. You may not be sure about polonium (it *is* radioactive), but you should know that ordinary or common lead is not radioactive, although lead has some radioactive isotopes.

67. (C) You should recognize the joule, watt-hour, and erg as units of energy. You should be able to figure out that the unit (or dimension) of choice (B) represents the product of a unit of force (1 N = 1 kg•m/s²) and a unit of distance (m); that is, it is a unit of energy. Choice (C) does not represents any special quantity.

68. (B) Beta rays are streams of electrons. The electron is usually thought of as a particle. (Under certain conditions it shows wave properties.)

69. (E) Cathode rays consist of moving electrons. Moving electrons are deflected by a magnetic field (which may be provided by a magnet). Moving or stationary electrons are deflected by an electric field.

70. (E) Ordinary solids are made of neutrons, protons, and electrons. When two different solids are rubbed together, one solid may lose electrons to the other. For example, when a rubber rod is rubbed with a piece of wool, the wool loses electrons to the rod. The rod becomes negatively charged, and the wool becomes positive. The protons and neutrons are tightly held in the nucleus. Positrons are not present in ordinary matter.

71. (B) The wavelength is given as 5.4×10^{-7} meter. One meter equals 10^3 mm.

$$5.4 \times 10^{-7} \text{ m} \times 10^3 \text{ mm/m} = 5.4 \times 10^{-4} \text{ mm}$$

72. (A) This question refers to the interference phenomenon produced when monochromatic light goes through two parallel slits and falls on a screen. On the screen is seen a central bright band with equally spaced bright bands on each side of the central band. The distance from the central bright maximum to the first bright band on either side is given by the following relationship:

$$\frac{\lambda}{d} = \frac{x}{L}$$

where λ is the wavelength of the light, d is the distance between the two slits, x is the distance between the central bright maximum and the first bright band next to it, and L is the distance from the slits to the screen. Substituting, we get:

$$\frac{5.4 \times 10^{-7} \text{ m}}{1.0 \times 10^{-3} \text{ m}} = \frac{x}{2.0 \text{ m}}$$

$$x = 1.1 \times 10^{-3} \text{ m}$$

73. (A) It can be shown that for the above situation the distance between adjacent bright bands is approximately the same as the distance between the central bright band and its adjacent bright band.

74. (C) The absolute index of refraction of water is the smallest of the values for the common liquids and solids that we encounter. It is 1.33, and is worthwhile remembering. The index of refraction of a substance is equal to the ratio of the speed of light in vacuum to the speed of light in the substance:

$$n = \frac{c}{v}$$

$$1.33 = \frac{3.0 \times 10^8 \text{ m/s}}{v}$$

$$v = 2.3 \times 10^8 \text{ m/s}$$

75. (E) When the switch is open, there is no current through the 20-ohm resistor. Therefore there is no voltage drop across the resistor, and the difference of potential between A and B is the same as that across the terminals of the battery.

Values of the Trigonometric Functions

Angle	Sin	Cos	Tan	Angle	Sin	Cos	Tan
1°	.0175	.9998	.0175	46°	.7193	.6947	1.0355
2°	.0349	.9994	.0349	47°	.7314	.6820	1.0724
3°	.0523	.9986	.0524	48°	.7431	.6691	1.1106
4°	.0698	.9976	.0699	49°	.7547	.6561	1.1504
5°	.0872	.9962	.0875	50°	.7660	.6428	1.1918
6°	.1045	.9945	.1051	51°	.7771	.6293	1.2349
7°	.1219	.9925	.1228	52°	.7880	.6157	1.2799
8°	.1392	.9903	.1405	53°	.7986	.6018	1.3270
9°	.1564	.9877	.1584	54°	.8090	.5878	1.3764
10°	.1736	.9848	.1763	55°	.8192	.5736	1.4281
11°	.1908	.9816	.1944	56°	.8290	.5592	1.4826
12°	.2079	.9781	.2126	57°	.8387	.5446	1.5399
13°	.2250	.9744	.2309	58°	.8480	.5299	1.6003
14°	.2419	.9703	.2493	59°	.8572	.5150	1.6643
15°	.2588	.9659	.2679	60°	.8660	.5000	1.7321
16°	.2756	.9613	.2867	61°	.8746	.4848	1.8040
17°	.2924	.9563	.3057	62°	.8829	.4695	1.8807
18°	.3090	.9511	.3249	63°	.8910	.4540	1.9626
19°	.3256	.9455	.3443	64°	.8988	.4384	2.0503
20°	.3420	.9397	.3640	65°	.9063	.4226	2.1445
21°	.3584	.9336	.3839	66°	.9135	.4067	2.2460
22°	.3746	.9272	.4040	67°	.9205	.3907	2.3559
23°	.3907	.9205	.4245	68°	.9272	.3746	2.4751
24°	.4067	.9135	.4452	69°	.9336	.3584	2.6051
25°	.4226	.9063	.4663	70°	.9397	.3420	2.7475
26°	.4384	.8988	.4877	71°	.9455	.3256	2.9042
27°	.4540	.8910	.5095	72°	.9511	.3090	3.0777
28°	.4695	.8829	.5317	73°	.9563	.2924	3.2709
29°	.4848	.8746	.5543	74°	.9613	.2756	3.4874
30°	.5000	.8660	.5774	75°	.9659	.2588	3.7321
31°	.5150	.8572	.6009	76°	.9703	.2419	4.0108
32°	.5299	.8480	.6249	77°	.9744	.2250	4.3315
33°	.5446	.8387	.6494	78°	.9781	.2079	4.7046
34°	.5592	.8290	.6745	79°	.9816	.1908	5.1446
35°	.5736	.8192	.7002	80°	.9848	.1736	5.6713
36°	.5878	.8090	.7265	81°	.9877	.1564	6.3138
37°	.6018	.7986	.7536	82°	.9903	.1392	7.1154
38°	.6157	.7880	.7813	83°	.9925	.1219	8.1443
39°	.6293	.7771	.8098	84°	.9945	.1045	9.5144
40°	.6428	.7660	.8391	85°	.9962	.0872	11.4301
41°	.6561	.7547	.8693	86°	.9976	.0698	14.3007
42°	.6691	.7431	.9004	87°	.9986	.0523	19.0811
43°	.6820	.7314	.9325	88°	.9994	.0349	28.6363
44°	.6947	.7193	.9657	89°	.9998	.0175	57.2900
45°	.7071	.7071	1.0000	90°	1.0000	.0000	

Summary of Formulas

torque = force × length of moment arm   *(p. 10)*

sum of clockwise moments = sum of counterclockwise moments   *(p. 11)*

$s = v_{av}t$ *(p. 17)*

$a = \dfrac{v_f - v_i}{t}$ *(p. 17)*

$v_{av} = v_f/2$ *(p. 18)*

$v_f = at$ *(p. 18)*

$s = \frac{1}{2}at^2$ *(p. 18)*

$v_f^2 = 2as$ *(p. 18)*

$\dfrac{F}{w} = \dfrac{a}{g}$ *(p. 19)*

$F = ma$ *(p. 19)*

$w = mg$ *(p. 20)*

Ft = change in momentum   *(p. 21)*

Momentum = mass × velocity   *(p. 22)*

$F = \dfrac{Gm_1 m_2}{r^2}$ *(p. 24)*

work = force × distance; $W = Fd$ or $W = Fs$ *(p. 28)*

potential energy = wh *(p. 29)*

kinetic energy = $\frac{1}{2}mv^2$ *(p. 29)*

energy produced = mc^2 *(p. 29)*

coefficient of friction = $\dfrac{\text{force of friction during motion}}{\text{normal force}}$ *(p. 30)*

work against friction = friction × distance object moves   *(p. 30)*

$\dfrac{F}{w} = \dfrac{h}{L}$ *(p. 30)*

$F = w \sin \theta$ *(p. 31)*

$F = kx$; $PE_s = \frac{1}{2}kx^2$ *(p. 32)*

power = $\dfrac{\text{work}}{\text{time}}$ *(p. 32)*

$$\text{power} = \frac{\text{force} \times \text{distance}}{\text{time}} \qquad (p.\ 32)$$

$$\text{AMA} = \frac{\text{resistance}}{\text{actual effort}}\ ;\ \text{AMA} = \frac{F_R}{F_E} \qquad (p.\ 33)$$

$$\text{work output} = F_R S_R \qquad (p.\ 33)$$

$$\text{work input} = F_E S_E \qquad (p.\ 33)$$

$$\frac{F_R}{F_E} = \frac{S_E}{S_R} = \text{ideal MA (IMA)} \qquad (p.\ 33)$$

$$\text{efficiency} = \frac{\text{work output}}{\text{work input}} = \frac{\text{AMA}}{\text{IMA}} = \frac{\text{ideal effort}}{\text{actual effort}} \qquad (p.\ 33)$$

$$\frac{\text{length of plane}}{\text{height of plane}} = \text{IMA} = \frac{\text{weight of object}}{\text{ideal effort}} \qquad (p.\ 34)$$

$$\text{density} = \frac{\text{mass}}{\text{volume}} \qquad (p.\ 39)$$

$$\text{sp. gr.} = \frac{\text{density of substance}}{\text{density of water}} = \frac{\text{weight of substance}}{\text{weight of equal volume of water}} = \frac{\text{mass of substance}}{\text{mass of equal volume of water}} \qquad (p.\ 39)$$

$$p = \frac{F}{A} \qquad (p.\ 39)$$

$$p = hdg \qquad (p.\ 40)$$

$$F = hdgA \qquad (p.\ 40)$$

$$\text{IMA} = \frac{F}{f} = \frac{A}{a} = \frac{(\text{diameter of large piston})^2}{(\text{diameter of small piston})^2} \qquad (p.\ 41)$$

$$\text{sp. gr.} = \frac{\text{weight in air}}{\text{apparent loss of weight in water}} \qquad (p.\ 42)$$

$$\text{sp. gr.} = \frac{\text{apparent loss in weight of solid in liquid}}{\text{apparent loss in weight of solid in water}} \qquad (p.\ 42)$$

$$\text{change in Fahrenheit degrees} = \tfrac{9}{5}\ (\text{change in Celsius degrees}) \qquad (p.\ 47)$$

$$F = \tfrac{9}{5}\,C + 32° \qquad \text{or} \qquad C = \tfrac{5}{9}\,(F - 32°) \qquad (p.\ 48)$$

$$\text{change in length} = \text{original length} \times \text{coeff. of expansion} \times \text{temp. change} \qquad (p.\ 48)$$

$$\frac{V_1}{V_2} = \frac{T_1}{T_2} \qquad \text{or} \qquad \frac{V_1}{V_2} = \frac{C_1 + 273°}{C_2 + 273°} \qquad (p.\ 49)$$

$$p_1 V_1 = p_2 V_2 \qquad (p.\ 49)$$

$$\frac{p_1 V_1}{T_1} = \frac{p_2 V_2}{T_2} \qquad (p.\ 49)$$

Heat lost by hot object = heat gained by cold object   *(p. 52)*

Heat lost (or gained) = mass × sp. heat × temp. change   *(p. 53)*

Heat required for melting = mass × H_F *(p. 54)*

Heat required for vaporization = mass $\times H_v$ *(p. 55)*

Heat gained (or lost) = mass $\times$ sp. ht. $\times$ temp. change

$\qquad\qquad\qquad$ + mass melted $\times$ heat of fusion

$\qquad\qquad\qquad$ + mass vaporized $\times$ heat of vaporization   *(p. 55)*

$Q = \Delta U + W$ *(p. 60)*

$T = \dfrac{1}{f}$ *(p. 65)*

$v = f\lambda$ *(p. 65)*

number of beats = difference between two frequencies   *(p. 69)*

$\lambda = 4l_a$ *(p. 70)*

$\lambda = 2l_a$ *(p. 71)*

$\lambda = 2l_s$ *(p. 71)*

decibels $= 10 \log \dfrac{p_1}{p_2}$ *(p. 72)*

$f = \dfrac{R}{2}$ *(p. 77)*

index of refraction $= \dfrac{\text{sine of the angle in the rarer medium}}{\text{sine of the angle in the denser medium}} = \dfrac{\text{speed of light in air (or vacuum)}}{\text{speed of light in the substance}}$ *(p. 78)*

$\dfrac{1}{\text{object distance}} + \dfrac{1}{\text{image distance}} = \dfrac{1}{\text{focal length}} ; \dfrac{1}{p} + \dfrac{1}{q} = \dfrac{1}{f}$ *(p. 81)*

$\dfrac{\text{size of image}}{\text{size of object}} = \dfrac{\text{image distance}}{\text{object distance}} = $ magnification (m) *(p. 81)*

telescope magnification $= \dfrac{\text{focal length of the objective}}{\text{focal length of eyepiece}}$ *(p. 83)*

illumination $= \dfrac{\text{intensity of source}}{(\text{distance})^2}$ *(p. 85)*

$\dfrac{\lambda}{d} = \dfrac{x}{L}$ *(p. 93)*

$F = \dfrac{kq_1q_2}{d^2}$ *(p. 102)*

$E = \dfrac{F}{q}$ *(p. 104)*

$V = \dfrac{\text{work}}{q}$ or   volts $= \dfrac{\text{joules}}{\text{coulomb}}$ *(p. 105)*

$E = \dfrac{V}{d}$ *(p. 106)*

$R = \dfrac{kL}{A}$ *(p. 107)*

SUMMARY OF FORMULAS

(Formulas for Ohm's law and electric circuits are summarized on p. 108)

$V_T = \text{emf} - Ir$ *(p. 108)*

$H = 0.24\,I^2Rt$ (calories) and I^2Rt (joules)   *(p. 109)*

$P = VI = I^2R = V^2/R$ *(p. 110)*

energy = power $\times$ time   *(p. 110)*

$F = ILB$ *(p. 119)*

$F \propto \dfrac{I_1 I_2}{d}$ *(p. 119)*

$F = qvB$ *(p. 119)*

$\text{emf} = lvB$ *(p. 121)*

$\dfrac{\text{secondary emf}}{\text{primary emf}} = \dfrac{\text{number of turns on secondary}}{\text{number of turns on primary}}$ *(p. 122)*

power supplied by secondary = efficiency $\times$ power supplied to primary   *(p. 122)*

$V_s I_s = V_p I_p \times \text{efficiency}$ *(p. 122)*

$Q = CV$ *(p. 129)*

$\text{P.E.} = \tfrac{1}{2}CV^2 = \tfrac{1}{2}QV = \tfrac{1}{2}\dfrac{Q^2}{C}$ *(p. 130)*

$E_k = hf - W$ *(p. 139)*

$W = hf_0$ *(p. 139)*

$p = \dfrac{h}{\lambda}$ or $\lambda = \dfrac{h}{mv}$ *(p. 142)*

$E = mc^2$ *(p. 142)*

$\text{mass}_{\text{relativistic}} = \dfrac{\text{mass}_{\text{rest}}}{\sqrt{1 - \left(\dfrac{v^2}{c^2}\right)}}$ *(p. 145)*

$\text{length}_{\text{relativistic}} = \text{length}_{\text{rest}}\sqrt{1 - \left(\dfrac{v^2}{c^2}\right)}$ *(p. 145)*

APPENDIX I

Physics Reference Tables

List of Physical Constants

Gravitational constant (G)	6.67×10^{-11} newton•meter^2/kilogram^2
Acceleration due to gravity (g) (near Earth's surface)	9.81 meters/second^2
Speed of light (c)	3.00×10^8 meters/second
Speed of sound at STP	3.31×10^2 meters/second
Mass-energy relationship	1 amu = 9.31×10^2 MeV
Electrostatic constant	$k = 9.00 \times 10^9$ newton•meters^2/coulomb^2
Charge of the electron = 1 elementary charge	1.60×10^{-19} coulomb
One coulomb	6.25×10^{18} electrons
	6.25×10^{18} elementary charges
Electron volt (eV)	1.60×10^{-19} joule
Planck's constant (h)	6.63×10^{-34} joule•second
Rest mass of the electron (m_e)	9.11×10^{-31} kilogram = 0.0005486 amu
Rest mass of the proton (m_p)	1.67×10^{-27} kilogram = 1.007277 amu
Rest mass of the neutron (m_n)	1.67×10^{-27} kilogram = 1.008665 amu

Wavelengths of Light in a Vacuum

VIOLET	$4.0 – 4.2 \times 10^{-7}$ meter
BLUE	$4.2 – 4.9 \times 10^{-7}$ meter
GREEN	$4.9 – 5.7 \times 10^{-7}$ meter
YELLOW	$5.7 – 5.9 \times 10^{-7}$ meter
ORANGE	$5.9 – 6.5 \times 10^{-7}$ meter
RED	$6.5 – 7.0 \times 10^{-7}$ meter

HEAT CONSTANTS

	Specific Heat (Average) (kJ/kg•C°)*	Melting Point (° C)	Boiling Point (° C)	Heat of Fusion (kJ/kg)*	Heat of Vaporization (kJ/kg)*
Alcohol (ethyl)	2.43 (liq.)	−117	79	109	855
Aluminum	0.90 (sol.)	660	2467	396	10500
Ammonia	4.71 (liq.)	−78	−33	332	1370
Copper	0.39 (sol.)	1083	2567	205	4790
Iron	0.45 (sol.)	1535	2750	267	6290
Lead	0.13 (sol.)	328	1740	25	866
Mercury	0.14 (liq.)	−39	357	11	295
Platinum	0.13 (sol.)	1772	3827	101	229
Silver	0.24 (sol.)	962	2212	105	2370
Tungsten	0.13 (sol.)	3410	5660	192	4350
Water { ice	2.05 (sol.)	0	—	334	—
Water { water	4.19 (liq.)	—	100	—	2260
Water { steam	2.01 (gas)	—	—	—	—
Zinc	0.39 (sol.)	420	907	113	1770

*Multiply by (1 kilocalorie/4.19 kilojoules) to obtain kilocalories

ABSOLUTE INDICES OF REFRACTION

$(\lambda = 5.9 \times 10^{-7} \text{ m})$

Air	1.00	Carbon Tetrachloride	1.46	Glycerol	1.47
Alcohol	1.36	Diamond	2.42	Lucite	1.50
Benzene	1.50	Glass, Crown	1.52	Quartz, Fused	1.46
Canada Balsam	1.53	Glass, Flint	1.61	Water	1.33

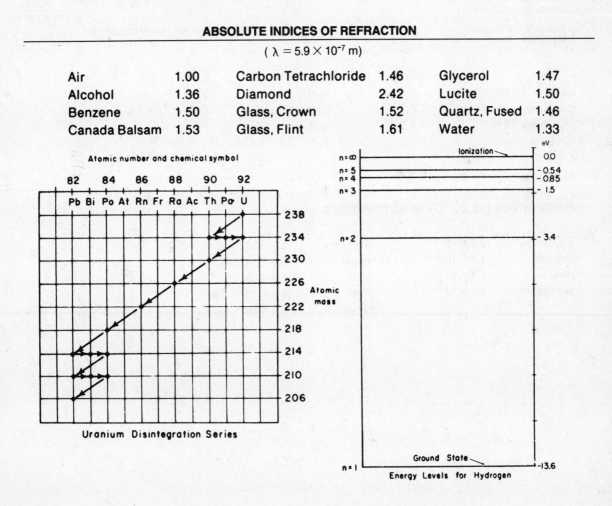

Uranium Disintegration Series

Energy Levels for Hydrogen

APPENDIX II

Densities of Some Substances in grams/cubic centimeter

Solids

aluminum	2.7	iron	7.8
brass	8.5	lead	11.3
copper	8.9	marble	2.6
cork	0.24	paraffin	0.9
glass	2.6	platinum	21.5
gold	19.3	silver	10.5
ice	0.92	steel	7.7
		sulfur	2.0

Liquids

alcohol	0.79	kerosene	0.8
carbon tetrachloride	1.6	mercury	13.6
gasoline	0.7	sulfuric acid	1.84
glycerine	1.3	water	1.0

Resistivities (at 20° C) in ohm-meters

aluminum	2.8×10^{-8}	nichrome	1.1×10^{-6}
copper	1.7×10^{-8}	nickel	6.8×10^{-8}
iron	1.0×10^{-7}	silver	1.6×10^{-8}
manganin	4.4×10^{-7}	steel	1.8×10^{-7}
		tungsten	5.6×10^{-8}

INTERNATIONAL ATOMIC MASSES*
Based on the Atomic Mass of C-12 = 12 atomic mass units (amu or u)

Name	Symbol	Atomic Number*	Atomic Mass*	Name	Symbol	Atomic Number*	Atomic Mass*
Actinium	Ac	89	[227]	Holmium	Ho	67	164.93
Aluminum	Al	13	26.98	Hydrogen	H	1	1.01
Americium	Am	95	[243]	Indium	In	49	114.82
Antimony	Sb	51	121.75	Iodine	I	53	126.90
Argon	Ar	18	39.95	Iridium	Ir	77	192.2
Arsenic	As	33	74.92	Iron	Fe	26	55.85
Astatine	At	85	[210]	Krypton	Kr	36	83.80
Barium	Ba	56	137.34	Lanthanum	La	57	138.91
Berkelium	Bk	97	[247]	Lawrencium	Lr	103	[261]
Beryllium	Be	4	9.01	Lead	Pb	82	207.19
Bismuth	Bi	83	208.98	Lithium	Li	3	6.94
Boron	B	5	10.81	Lutetium	Lu	71	174.97
Bromine	Br	35	79.90	Magnesium	Mg	12	24.31
Cadmium	Cd	48	112.40	Manganese	Mn	25	54.94
Caesium	Cs	55	132.91	Meitnerium**	Mt	109	[266]
Calcium	Ca	20	40.08	Mendelevium	Md	101	[258]
Californium	Cf	98	[251]	Mercury	Hg	80	200.59
Carbon	C	6	12.01	Molybdenum	Mo	42	95.94
Cerium	Ce	58	140.12	Neilsbohrium**	Ns	107	[262]
Chlorine	Cl	17	35.45	Neodymium	Nd	60	144.24
Chromium	Cr	24	52.00	Neon	Ne	10	20.18
Cobalt	Co	27	58.93	Neptunium	Np	93	237.05
Copper	Cu	29	63.55	Nickel	Ni	28	58.71
Curium	Cm	96	[247]	Niobium	Nb	41	92.90
Dysprosium	Dy	66	162.50	Nitrogen	N	7	14.01
Einsteinium	Es	99	[254]	Nobelium	No	102	[259]
Erbium	Er	68	167.26	Osmium	Os	76	190.2
Europium	Eu	63	151.96	Oxygen	O	8	16.00
Fermium	Fm	100	[257]	Palladium	Pd	46	106.4
Fluorine	F	9	19.00	Phosphorus	P	15	31.97
Francium	Fr	87	[223]	Platinum	Pt	78	195.09
Gadolinium	Gd	64	157.25	Plutonium	Pu	94	[244]
Gallium	Ga	31	69.72	Polonium	Po	84	[210]
Germanium	Ge	32	72.59	Potassium	K	19	39.10
Gold	Au	79	196.97	Praseodymium	Pr	59	140.90
Hafnium	Hf	72	178.49	Promethium	Pm	61	[145]
Hahnium**	Ha	105	[262]	Protactinium	Pa	91	231.04
Hassia**	Hs	108	[265]	Radium	Ra	88	[226]
Helium	He	2	4.00	Radon	Rn	86	[222]

Name	Symbol	Atomic Number*	Atomic Mass*	Name	Symbol	Atomic Number*	Atomic Mass*
Rhenium	Re	75	186.2	Terbium	Tb	65	158.92
Rhodium	Rh	45	102.91	Thallium	Tl	81	204.37
Rubidium	Rb	37	85.47	Thorium	Th	90	232.03
Ruthenium	Ru	44	101.07	Thulium	Tm	69	168.93
Rutherfordium**	Rf	104	[261]	Tin	Sn	50	118.69
Samarium	Sm	62	150.35	Titanium	Ti	22	47.90
Scandium	Sc	21	44.95	Tungsten	W	74	183.85
Selenium	Se	34	78.96	Unnihexium**	Unh	106	[263]
Silicon	Si	14	28.09	Uranium	U	92	238.03
Silver	Ag	47	107.87	Vanadium	V	23	50.94
Sodium	Na	11	22.99	Xenon	Xe	54	131.30
Strontium	Sr	38	87.62	Ytterbium	Yb	70	173.04
Sulfur	S	16	32.06	Yttrium	Y	39	88.91
Tantalum	Ta	73	180.95	Zinc	Zn	30	65.37
Technetium	Tc	43	[99]	Zirconium	Zr	40	91.22
Tellurium	Te	52	127.60				

*Most of the listed atomic masses are for naturally occurring mixtures of the isotopes, also known as atomic weights. A value given in brackets is the mass number of the most stable known isotope.

**The names of the elements with atomic numbers 104 and above have not been officially adopted.

Index